D1369970

An Introduction to Multinational Management

AN INTRODUCTION TO MULTINATIONAL MANAGEMENT

S.B. PRASAD

Ohio University

Y. KRISHNA SHETTY

Utah State University

Prentice-Hall, Inc., Englewood Cliffs, New Jersey

Library of Congress Cataloging in Publication Data

Prasad, S Benjamin.
An introduction to multinational management.

Bibliography: p.
Includes index.
1. International business enterprises—Management. I. Shetty, Y. Krishna, joint author.
II. Title.
HD69.I7P7 658.1'8 75-44264
ISBN 0-13-489203-8

Printed in the United States of America

10 9 8 7 6 5 4 3

Prentice-Hall International, Inc., London
Prentice-Hall of Australia Pty. Limited, Sydney
Prentice-Hall of Canada, Ltd., Toronto
Prentice-Hall of India Private Limited, New Delhi
Prentice-Hall of Japan, Inc., Tokyo
Prentice-Hall of Southeast Asia Pte. Ltd., Singapore

To
Rosemary and Shabari

Contents

Part I: The Multinational Business Environment

Part II: Management Dimensions

List of Tables

List of Figures

Preface

The subject matter of multinational business is relatively new. Its academic content is not yet quite settled and its unique aspects, for the most part, remain unspecified. Yet, the literature on multinational corporations, large and small, and their activities continues to grow at a rapid rate. The number of firms emerging as MNCs is also increasing at a rapid rate. With a decade of good research and sound analysis behind it, the field of multinational business has now come into its own. Its importance is felt by all; its impact permeates almost every business activity and segment of society.

In this book, we have emphasized the problems and prospects of managing multinational business operations in a worldwide context. There are now a number of good books dealing with multinational business, some treating the subject either in a very general manner and some in a very specific way. In this volume we have focused on the management aspects—namely, planning, organization, people management, production, and marketing within the context of a multinational business environment. Yet we have limited our discussion to manufacturing firms and have not considered the problems of mining companies, petroleum companies, banks, and other nonmanufacturing enterprises.

This volume is addressed primarily to the student with some background in economics and management. We feel that many of the topics are still in the process of crystallization, yet the reader with an understanding of both the *macro* or environmental factors and the *micro* or corporate-level operational and strategic factors will be in a position to pursue specific topics in depth. As an aid in this direction, we have included suggested readings, references to selected cases, and a selected bibliography of recent books.

The book is divided into three parts and eleven chapters. Selected environmental aspects are covered in Part I. Part II deals with operational and strategic aspects, and Part III with some emerging issues. Chapter 1 is concerned with the basic nature of multinational business; Chapter 2 with its economic environment. Chapter 3 discusses both the structure and evolving patterns of direct foreign investment, the key element in multinational business. Chapter 4 is concerned with the international financial environment. Chapters 5, 6, 7, 8, and 9 focus on operational areas of multinational business: planning, organizational structure, management of subsidiary managers, production, and marketing. Chapter 10 analyzes the problems and prospects of East-West trade, and the final chapter deals with some of the factors that may influence the future of multinational corporate behavior.

Much of the work entailed in preparing this volume was supported by our respective institutions. The Office of the Vice-President for Research at Utah State University provided some financial support to Dr. Shetty, and our colleagues at both institutions were helpful in commenting on parts of the manuscript. A few deserve special mention: Dean Robert Collier of the College of Business and Professor Howard M. Carlisle, head of the Department of Business Administration at Utah State University; and Professors Robert Raymond and Azmi Mikhail of the College of Business Administration at Ohio University. We also appreciate the help of Professor Richard N. Farmer of Indiana University and Professor Stefan H. Robock of Columbia University for their suggestions for improving the manuscript. The real encouragement to develop this volume, of course, came from Earl Kivett of Prentice-Hall. To all these individuals, our sincere thanks.

The book itself would not have been possible without the cooperation and courtesy of many publishers and authors. In seeking their aid, and in consolidating the available present knowledge about multinational management, we hope that we have provided a broad picture of the issues and problems in the multinational context, one that will instil in readers a certain intellectual curiosity which will impel them to seek further knowledge in this challenging area.

S.B.P.
Y.K.S.

An Introduction to Multinational Management

1

The Multinational Corporate Phenomenon

International business has evolved from the simple idea of trade—the importing and exporting of the products of various areas—into a complex system in which multinational corporations (such as the American-based IBM, the Japan-based Matsushita, or the Canada-based Massey-Ferguson) play a major economic role in a worldwide context, often with far-reaching political and social implications. This economic role, more precisely stated as manufacturing and marketing, stems from direct investment in a number of countries.

The multinational corporation (MNC) has now become a household word. Although its definition is still the subject of debate, what distinguishes an MNC from its predecessors, companies with foreign subsidiaries or affiliates, is direct investment abroad and direct interest in the business environment in which it has such investments. As Behrman put it, the hallmarks of an MNC are *control* and *integration of affiliates*.[1]

The phenomenon of multinational business is neither purely American nor particularly new. European companies such as Ericsson, Nestlé, and Unilever have been in the multinational business for more than half a century. And some writers who include the trading activities of companies like the British East India Company and the Hudson's Bay Company suggest that the MNC has its roots far back in history.[2] But in its contemporary form, the MNC is truly a product of the twentieth century. Its evolution has been variously described, often by its role:

> The emergence of the multinational private corporation as a powerful agent of world social and economic change has been a signal development of the postwar era.[3]
>
> The multinational corporation has become well recognized as a key feature of the changing international business pattern.[4]
>
> Multinationals did not grow in a vacuum. They flourished because, after World War II, the major developed countries led by the U.S. established a framework for the world economy that encouraged the free flow of goods and private capital between countries on market principles.[5]
>
> In most cases it can be taken for granted that a multinational corporation is a change agent in its country of origin. If it is also a change agent in another country, the corporation actually becomes a medium of intercultural interaction—in effect, an exchange agent.[6]
>
> Today's multinational enterprise is a logical outgrowth of widening markets overseas, improved managerial techniques and postwar cooperation.[7]
>
> A potent agent of economic transformation and development, not only in the more laggard "developed" countries, but also in the developing countries of the world.[8]

The factors that were instrumental in sparking and sustaining the rapid evolution of MNCs, particularly American-based MNCs, as Kolde states, are in part environmental and in part "managerial."[9] The environmental factors were (1) multilateralism in international economic relations, (2) massive U.S. foreign aid, and (3) the communist threat from the USSR and China. The managerial factors were a combination of (1) lower costs of production, (2) competition, and (3) restrictions such as import restrictions and money restrictions.

A variety of studies concerning foreign direct investment has amply documented the factors that induced firms to set up facilities for manufacturing and marketing abroad: the attraction of a growing market, the stimulus of government restrictions on direct trade, encouragement by the government of the host nation, and managerial aspects of the firm and the industry group of which it is a member.

WHO ARE THE BIG PLAYERS?

Among the U.S.-based multinationals, excluding the petroleum and financial firms, as Table 1-1 shows, a variety of firms derive a substantial proportion of their profits from operations abroad. In addition to the legendary Coca-Cola and IBM, there are small appliance makers such as Hoover and large chemical firms such as Dow. Among the non-American multinationals, European and Japanese firms are the big players. Table 1-2 shows a selected list of MNCs that have subsidiary operations in the United States. Most of these MNCs are large in terms of assets, sales, and employees.

SOME CRITICISMS OF MNCs

MNCs have long been the objects of criticism. At the turn of the century, a book entitled *The American Invaders*[10] was directed at the penetration of Britain by Heinz, Singer, USM, and Westinghouse. It has been followed by a number of other assessments of direct American investment abroad.[11] One point to note is that much of the criticism is leveled against U.S.-based MNCs in a blanket fashion; that is, without any distinction, whether the MNC is a mining firm, a bank, or a farm equipment maker.

The following are some of the major criticisms from within the United States: Labor organizations, particularly the AFL-CIO, contend that MNCs ''export'' American jobs by increasing production overseas and then selling the product in the American market. The ever-increasing amount of evidence, especially that stemming from a major 1971 study at Harvard, that several thousand new jobs had been created in the United States, however, dents this argument. Congressional critics and others assert that MNCs are exporting precious technology to other nations, particularly the USSR, and are overlooking the national interest. Export they do, but American multinational corporations maintain that they do so in a way highly beneficial to the United States and within the framework set by the government. It may be, however, that the MNCs are indirectly exporting technology. The increasing number of high-technology deals between the American firms and the Soviet Union, on which some restrictions have been liberalized, has perturbed Pentagon critics. The areas involved in recent sales range from computers and communications to shipbuilding and aircraft. The inherent fear is that other nations can use these technologies to the detriment of American interests.

Some criticisms relate to the economic and political power wielded by the multinational corporations, especially abroad. Some points made by the critics are salient, yet caution must be exercised to separate facts from mere impressions. For example, Barnett and Muller in an article in *The New Yorker* characterize the multinational corporation as an institution built upon an international division of labor. Top management of the multinational corporations and their subsidiaries are drawn from the rich countries, and workers, particularly in their subsidiaries, are drawn from the poor or low-wage countries.

Such an institution, according to Barnett and Muller, wields enormous power in the developing countries, through the control of finance capital, technology, and marketing. The net result in their view is the creation and sustenance of worldwide poverty. They insist that ''In their bid for managerial power on a

TABLE 1-1

Large U.S.-based MNCs Earning More Than Half Their Profits Abroad, 1974

Company (Fortune rank)	*Assets**	*Sales**	*Employees*
Addressograph-Multigraph (321)	$ 0.462	$ 0.541	23,300
Coca-Cola (74)	1.536	2.522	31,750
Dow Chemical (27)	5.114	4.938	53,325
Ferro (457)	0.210	0.322	7,700
Gillette (160)	0.998	1.246	33,100
Hoover (334)	0.385	0.502	27,400
International Harvester (26)	3.326	4.965	110,990
IBM (9)	14.027	12.675	292,350
Pfizer (130)	1.683	1.541	39,500
Signode (403)	0.280	0.405	6,400
Uniroyal (82)	1.647	2.300	63,800

*In billions of dollars.
Source: Adapted from *Fortune,* "Gillette Swings a Mighty Blade Abroad," November 1974, p. 175, and "The Fortune Directory," *Fortune,* May 1975, pp. 208-29.

TABLE 1-2

Some Large Non-American MNCs with Subsidiaries in the United States, 1973

Company	*Base Country*	*Industry/Products*	*Assets**	*Sales**	*Employees*
Akzo	The Netherlands	Synthetic fibers, chemicals	3.240	3.384	105,800
Beecham Group	Britain	Food products, cosmetics	0.790	0.817	29,600
Feberwerke Hoest	Germany	Chemicals, pharmaceuticals	5.879	5.600	155,400
Hitachi	Japan	Electrical equip-ment, machinery	7.308	5.971	150,800
Hoffman-La Roche	Switzerland	Pharmaceuticals	2.115	1.463	34,900
Massey-Ferguson	Canada	Farm machinery, engines	1.250	1.506	51,267
Matsushita	Japan	Electrical and electronics	3.934	4.410	85,306
Michelin	France	Rubber products	1.927	2.200	100,000
Nestlé	Switzerland	Food products	3.829	5.205	127,801
Philips	The Netherlands	Electronics, chemicals	8.557	8.108	402,000
Unilever	Britain/The Netherlands	Food, detergents, toiletries	5.675	11.009	353,000

*In billions of dollars.
Source: Partly based on Sanford Rose, "The Misguided Furor About Investments from Abroad," *Fortune,* May 1975, p. 174.

worldwide scale, the men who run the global corporations must demonstrate that they have answers to the problems of world poverty.''[12]

The basic theme of criticism coming from outside the United States has been that the multinational ventures involve cynical ''exploitation'' of poor countries' workers, consumers, and resources.

Is there an easy answer to these and other criticisms of multinational corporations? One suggestion has been to bring the MNCs under the wing of the United Nations. The multinational companies, of course, do not favor a global version of the U.S. Federal Trade Commission. However, in an attempt to carve out a global corporate supervisory role for itself, the UN appears to be following a path that might ensure more favorable response from the MNCs. The milder UN concept of setting up a registry of companies pledged to follow a voluntary code was warmly received. A UN information center on multinational corporations also won some corporate sympathy. A few of the business leaders have also acknowledged the need to have guidelines. The chairman of the Xerox Corporation reportedly has said that he would welcome some kind of international or at least regional guidelines that would establish a reasonable external check and balance system for the multinational companies.[13]

Our own view about the criticisms of American multinational companies in particular is that they are often too sweeping for an intelligent evaluation. Furthermore, while assessment of multinational corporate behavior is necessary, few carefully considered and researched studies are available.

SUMMARY

The multinational corporation (MNC) has now become a household word, although the phenomenon is neither purely American nor truly new. Economic and political conditions, especially since the mid-fifties, have favored the rapid growth of these corporations.

MNCs are not always the largest corporations in a country, but often they are. The case of the Computer Machinery Corporation, a relatively small Los Angeles-based maker of key processing systems, is illustrative; so is the worldwide scope of Canada's farm machinery and engine manufacturer Massey Ferguson. Materials on these two MNCs are included in the appendixes to this chapter.

Whether large or small, MNCs are open to assorted criticisms from a variety of quarters. Exporting jobs and technology are some of the major alleged criticisms from the American side. The Third World countries have made allegations of exploitation of people and resources, and the exercise of enormous political influence that places the MNCs beyond the control of nation-states.

There is a general feeling now that a set of international guidelines endorsed by the United Nations, national governments, and the MNCs themselves is absolutely essential to lay a foundation for "good" world corporate citizenship. Some, like C. Fred Bergsten of the Brookings Institution, are said to favor the creation of a new international institution analogous to the General Agreement on Tariffs and Trade.[14]

Notes

[1]Jack N. Behrman, *Some Patterns in the Rise of Multinational Enterprise* (Chapel Hill, N.C.: University of North Carolina, 1969), p. xiv.

[2]Richard Hays, C. M. Korth, and M. Roudiani, *International Business: An Introduction to the World of Multinational Business* (Englewood Cliffs, N.J.: Prentice-Hall, 1972), pp. 260-64.

[3]Neil H. Jacoby, "The Multinational Corporation," *The Center Magazine,* May 1970.

[4]Stefan H. Robock and K. Simmonds, *International Business and Multinational Enterprise* (Homewood, Ill.: Irwin, 1973), p. 6.

[5]Stephen Hymer, in a written statement to the Group of Eminent Persons, United Nations, 1973.

[6]Hans B. Thorelli, "The Multinational Corporation as a Change Agent," *Southern Journal of Business,* July 1966, p. 3.

[7]ITT, *Multinational Corporation Fact File,* 1974.

[8]Harry G. Johnson, "The Multinational Corporation as a Developing Agent," *Columbia Journal of World Business,* May-June 1970, pp. 25-30.

[9]Endel J. Kolde, *International Business Enterprise* (Englewood Cliffs, N.J.: Prentice-Hall, 1968), pp. 230-39.

[10]A. McKenzie, *The American Invaders* (London: Grant Richards, 1902).

[11]See, for example, Francis Wilhams, *The American Invasion* (New York: Crown, 1962); J. J. Servan-Schrieber, *The American Challenge* (New York: Atheneum, 1968); E. McCreary, *The Americanization of Europe* (Garden City, N.Y.: Doubleday, 1964); Richard Barnett, and Ronald Muller, *Global Reach* (New York: Simon and Schuster, 1975).

[12]*The New Yorker,* December 2, 1974, p. 60.

[13]*Business Week,* June 15, 1974, p. 85.

[14]*Business Week,* July 14, 1975, p. 69.

Suggested Readings

AHARONI, YAIR, "On the Definition of a Multinational Corporation," *Quarterly Review of Economics and Business,* August 1971.

BEAUVOIS, JOHN, "Internationalism: A New Concept for U.S. Business?" *California Management Review,* winter 1960.

BENOIT, EMILE, "The Attack on Multinationals," *Columbia Journal of World Business,* November-December 1972.

CURRY, ROBERT L., JR., AND DONALD ROTHCHILD, "On Economic Bargaining Between African Governments and Multinational Companies," *Journal of Modern African Studies,* No. 2, 1974.

DRUCKER, PETER, "Multinationals: The Game and the Rules of Multinationals and Developing Countries—Myths and Realities," *Foreign Affairs,* October 1974.

FAYERWEATHER, JOHN, "Elite Attitudes Toward Multinational Firms," *International Studies Quarterly,* December 1972.

GABRIEL, PETER P., "Adaptation: The Name of the MNC's Game," *Columbia Journal of World Business,* November-December 1972.

———, "MNC in the Third World," *Harvard Business Review,* July-August 1972.

GAEDEKE, RALPH M., AND ALAN E. LAZAR, "How Multinational Businessmen View Trade Restrictions," *California Management Review,* spring 1972.

GALLOWAY, ROY J., AND ASHOK KAPOOR, "Asia: Problems and Prospects for the MNC," *Columbia Journal of World Business,* November-December 1971.

HELTZER, HARRY, "The World Is the Business of American Business," *Columbia Journal of World Business,* spring 1973.

HOSKINS, WILLIAM R., "The LDC and MNC: Will They Develop Together," *Columbia Journal of World Business,* September-October 1971.

HYMER, STEPHEN, "The Efficiency (Contradictions) of Multinational Corporations," *American Economic Review,* May 1970.

MASON, HAL, "Conflict Between Host Countries and the Multinational Enterprise," *California Management Review,* fall 1974.

NYE, JOSEPH S., JR., "Multinational Corporations in World Politics," *Foreign Affairs,* October 1974, pp. 153-75.

OGRAM, ERNEST W., JR., "The Multinational Corporation: Problems and Prospects in the Years Ahead," *Foreign Trade Review,* July-September 1971.

REICH, R. B., "Global Responsibility for the Multinationals," *Texas International Law Journal,* spring 1973.

ROBBINS, SIDNEY M., AND ROBERT B. STOBAUGH, "Multinational Companies," *Financial Executive,* July 1973.

ROBOCK, STEFAN, "The Case for Home Country Controls over Multinational Firms," *Columbia Journal of World Business,* summer 1974.

———, AND KENNETH SIMMONDS, "International Business—How Big Is It?" *Columbia Journal of World Business,* May-June 1970.

ROOT, FRANKLIN, "Public Policy Expectations of Multinational Managers," *MSU Business Topics,* autumn 1973.

———, "Public Policy and Multinational Corporations," *Business Horizons,* April 1974.

RUDELL, ALLAN L., "In Defense of International Business," *Advanced Management Journal,* January 1972.

SAFARIAN, A. E., AND JORL BELL, "Issues Raised by National Control of the Multinational Corporation," *Columbia Journal of World Business,* November-December 1973.

SHETTY, Y. K., "Ownership, Size, Technology and Management Development: A Comparative Study," *Academy of Management Journal,* December 1971.

SIROTA, DAVID, "The Multinational Corporation," *Personnel,* January-February 1972.

TAYLOR, GUS, "Multinationals: A Global Menace," *Atlantic Community Quarterly,* winter 1972-73.

TEAGUE, BURTON, "Multinational Corporations," *Conference Board Record,* September 1971.

TSURUMI, YOSHI, "Japanese Multinational Firms," *Journal of World Trade Law,* January-February 1973.

UTLEY, JON BASIL, "Doing Business with Latin Nationalists," *Harvard Business Review,* January-February 1973.

WAITE, DONALD C., "The Transnational Corporation Corporate Form for the Future," *European Business,* summer 1974.

———, "The Rise of the Transnational Corporation," *The McKinsey Quarterly,* summer 1974.

WEIGEL, DALE R., "Multinational Approaches to Multinational Corporations," *Finance and Development,* September 1974.

WELLS, LOUIS T., JR., "Social Cost/Benefit Analysis of MNC's," *Harvard Business Review,* March-April 1975.

WOODROOFE, ERNEST G., "The Social Role of the World Enterprise," *The McKinsey Quarterly,* summer 1974.

WOOTON, L. M., "The Multinational Corporation," *Management International Review,* 4-5, 1971.

WRISTON, WALTER B., "The World Corporation," *Sloan Management Review,* winter 1974.

APPENDIX 1-A: Computer Machinery Corporation

Computer Machinery Corporation (CMC) is a Los Angeles-based producer of key processing systems. Its products are used by different types of firms—for example, in manufacturing (Texas Instruments), in retailing (Avon), in banking (two banking groups in France), and in services (Blue Cross of Southern California). From a modest beginning, CMC has evolved into an organization employing about 1,600 people worldwide in 1975. CMC went multinational in 1969, when it was a small company with 75 employees and $2 million in total capital. The following is a brief sketch of the points Chairman of the Board James K. Sweeney made in connection with CMC's first venture abroad.*

CMC set up a sales and production facility in England in 1969. Its purpose in entering the world marketplace was to forestall fierce competition in the computer business by establishing a foothold before competitors got a chance to do so. Its market research revealed that England, France, and West Germany were significant potential markets. In their approach to Europe, CMC executives endorsed the view that their overseas ventures were not "foreign"; the location outside the United States were incidental.

CMC decided to set up operations first in England because its market for the firm's products was as large as any and its language and laws were similar to those of the United States. It should be noted that for the computer industry, markets throughout the industry tended to be quite similar with respect to product demand. CMC patterned the English subsidiary after the parent company. For motivational and political reasons, CMC insisted that the English operation be independent in pursuing its objectives once the parent company had given the subsidiary unity and direction.

During the critical period before the new operation was actually launched, in addition to adopting a low profile, CMC officials worked closely with host country officials. Long before the English subsidiary was anything but an idea, they contacted a subgroup in the British Ministry of Technology. CMC invited the group to their California facility. A special point was made of CMC's desire to do business in England, employ British nationals, and become a U.K. export company. Regular communications and progress reports helped the establishment of a good rapport.

CMC's management decided that the agent route was definitely *not* the way to enter Europe. Finding the right English national to head the subsidiary was a major undertaking. It took a great deal of time to settle on the man because he was deemed to be absolutely critical to success. In his search, Mr. Sweeney relied mostly on his computer industry contacts. In addition to the usual qualities such as industry knowledge, intelligence, and decisiveness, he was hoping to find a man who had some experience working with an American firm. Eventually, he selected a man who not only had had sales management experience with General Electric Company, Ltd., but was also an experienced computer programmer.

On December 28, 1973, CMC sold the wholly owned U.K. subsidiary along with regional manufacturing and distributor rights for $10.154 million. Concurrent with the sale of the subsidiary, the company entered into a licensing agreement with CMC Ltd. and granted it rights to manufacture and market Key Processing Systems.

WHY DID THE COMPANY SELL ITS SUBSIDIARY IN THE UK?

The reason given by the company, as noted in its 1973 Annual Report (p. 14), was as follows: Selling this subsidiary was the best way to support expansion of the company-owned lease portfolio with a minimum impact on future earnings per share.

During the early development, earnings alone could not finance a high growth rate. Therefore, to finance continued growth, the company (1) sold a portion of on-lease equipment to financial institutions, and (2) borrowed against committed revenues represented by leases.

The sale of CMC, Ltd., provided needed funding while allowing the parent company to continue to participate in the success of its former subsidiary through selling to it certain products that it manufactures more economically. In addition, the parent firm receives royalties from its previous subsidiary's sale. CMC still endorses the view that overseas ventures are not foreign and that it is simply geography tempered by common sense and national loyalty. The scope of its *foreign* operations can be gleaned from the following figures:

Assets: (000)	*1974*	*1973*	*1972*
Current	NA	$ 8,782	$10,173
Noncurrent	NA	15,533	11,639
		$24,315	$21,812
Liabilities and parent's equity: (000)	*1974*	*1973*	*1972*
Current	NA	16,555	10,209
Noncurrent	NA	6,154	5,771
Parent's equity including advances	NA	1,606	5,832
		24,315	21,812
Revenues	16,183	13,177	10,749
Net earnings (loss)	(1,840)	(511)	(1,493)

Source: Annual Reports of 1973 and 1974, CMC.

*Mr. Sweeney's pointers are extracted from his article, "A Small Company Enters the European Market," *Harvard Business Review*, September–October 1970. With permission from the *Harvard Business Review* and the author.

APPENDIX 1-B: The Concept of the Global Corporation: Massey-Ferguson*

The experiences of the company in the international environment, taken all together, and viewed in broad perspective, tell much about the fundamental character of international or multinational industrial companies in general and of the problems they encounter. This makes it difficult to resist the temptation to generalize on the concept of the global corporation from the special vantage point of the history of Massey-Ferguson.

It seems that the essence of a sophisticated international industrial corporation is that it at all times is prepared and in a position to develop markets for its products wherever on earth such opportunities exist and seeks to deploy its manufacturing and engineering facilities internationally in a way that will minimize its global production and developmental costs and will assist in the development of particular markets. Arbitrary rules guiding asset deployment can only do harm to such a corporation. Rational judgments relating to prospective rates of return, based on detailed knowledge of local, social, political, and economic conditions must lie at the heart of its international asset deployment decisions. Emotional attachments to the "home base" and misconceptions about conditions and opportunities abroad have no place.

What induces a corporation to move beyond the boundaries of its domestic market? Obviously opportunities for increased profit are of paramount importance. But this simple explanation is not very illuminating; the profit motive can express itself in various ways. Massey-Ferguson Harris discovered early in its history that export business was not only profitable but frequently even more profitable than business in its home markets. It also recognized early that expansion of sales through the development of export markets reduced manufacturing costs through increased scale of operation.

Once a company has established valuable export markets, and has geared its total organization to fit the expanded volume of business that export markets have produced, it becomes very difficult to sit idly by when those markets are suddenly threatened by local trade restrictions. Management is therefore given a compelling incentive to contemplate establishing manufacturing facilities outside its domestic market. In the process of developing export markets and embarking on some manufacturing operations outside the home country, a corporation inevitably becomes increasingly familiar with, and therefore less frightened about, the commitment of its assets to international business operations in general. Personnel with experience in international business, and with necessary language qualifications are gradually acquired, and their views are likely to be biased in favour of sustaining and expanding international operations.

Also, a corporation that does not develop business abroad when its competitors do, or when foreign companies invade its own market, may find that its smaller scale of operation places it at a cost disadvantage even in its domestic market. In other words, if full economies of scale are attained only if a corporation's activity is extended into international markets, then a purely domestic company in the industry may encounter cost disadvantages. In the manufacture of technically complicated machines, or complicated components for machines, optimum-sized production may be very large. To a certain extent, a corporation may therefore be pushed into the international environment in its fight for survival, and this may take the form of export activity, licensing agreements, or assembly and manufacturing operations.

A convenient bridge for entering manufacturing operations abroad, for Massey-Ferguson at least, has been the company's local independent distributor. Such local independent companies can often supply capital themselves and interest other local investors. They also have an incentive to participate in the project, for failure to do so could mean loss of their distribution rights. For the international company such associations are frequently invaluable as a source of both local capital and of specialized knowledge concerning negotiations with governmental authorities, the acquisition of local manufacturing facilities, and the availability of management personnel. Some local participation may be required by law, or may be desirable because it may cause governmental authorities to view a project more favourably than they would without it. Where risks are great, the international company may even be pleased to have some local contribution of risk capital. Finally, acquiring the facilities of an existing local company—often the simplest way to become established—may be possible only with some participation of former owners.

While the reasons for some form of association with local interests may, under certain circumstances, be compelling there are also major disadvantages. If profits of a subsidiary represent not merely a return on capital but also an indirect payment for managerial and technical contribution of the parent company (a point to which we shall return), then sharing profits on the basis of financial capital contributed might reduce the profitability of the project from the parent company's viewpoint. The need to heed the predilections of local shareholders may also complicate the planning procedures and operations of a world-wide corporation. For example, local Board members may have their own views as to how the local company should invest its short-term funds or plan its expansion, and these may conflict with the policy of the parent company. There are no such complications with a wholly owned subsidiary, for the parent company elects all the directors.

Massey-Ferguson has favoured wholly owned subsidiaries in the industrially more advanced countries but, unlike some corporations, it has pursued a flexible policy, elsewhere. As we have seen, there are many reasons why such a policy may be necessary or desirable. An international corporation that pursues a rigid policy of operating only through wholly owned subsidiaries is likely increasingly to deny itself access to business opportunities. In some countries Massey-Ferguson owns a majority of the stock of the local company, in others a minority of the stock, while in some cases its only association is through a licensing agreement. But it has been careful in recent years not to lose control over its corporate name through permitting it to be incorporated into the name of a company that it does not control. We shall see shortly that one reason why an international corporation may profitably compromise with a policy of operating only through wholly owned subsidiaries is that its income from such operations need not and frequently is not confined to its share of the profits.

What is the fundamental role of a global corporation? What is it that the international company provides that justifies the profits it receives on its foreign business? The obvious answer is that it provides capital. This is also an incomplete answer. Indeed, it is so incomplete as to be largely incorrect. Massey-Ferguson, as so many other international corporations, generally depends heavily on local sources for loan capital. Its equity contribution, even where it operates through a wholly owned subsidiary, is minimized, commensurate with giving the local company an adequate credit standing in the capital market.

Providing funds is not, therefore, the unique contribution of the international corporation. Its unique contribution is the provision of advanced technology and managerial skills. It is much more a seller of "know-how" than a provider of funds, even though the funds it provides are at times substantial in amount. To us the most impressive characteristic of the global corporation is the speed with which it channels advanced technology into the far corners of the world. It is a characteristic that distinguishes it clearly from mere international "lending" agencies; it is also one that seems not to be clearly understood by all emerging nations. The profits a global corporation receives from the operations of a subsidiary constitute payment not merely for capital contributed but also for "know-how" provided. The same is true for the gains it may make through appreciation in market value of the investments it has in operations abroad.

But the income that an international corporation receives from operations abroad comes from more directions than this discussion implies. Besides the total profits of subsidiary companies, or the share of profits from companies in which it has merely a majority or minority interest, an international company may at times receive additional income from technical assistance agreements or royalties, from licensing agreements, and from the sale of component parts to the local company. It also not infrequently happens that import licenses for whole machines are more generously given to companies with local manufacturing projects than to those without such a stake in the country. For all these reasons the reduction in income implied in an international company not being sole owner of a local company may to a degree be offset by other forms of income from the operation. Indeed, one would expect in theory that it would be entirely offset in the long run, and in practice it probably is.

This possibly is of considerable importance to international corporations because of the strong feeling in many countries over non-resident ownership of industry. Ideally, it seems that international corporations would in most cases wish to see local investors invest in the stock of the parent company rather than in stock of the local company. However, habits of local investors and sentiment surrounding ownership of industry have not become sufficiently "internationalized" in most countries to permit this to happen. Consequently international corporations are at times forced to deviate from operating only through wholly owned subsidiaries or forgo opportunities for expansion.

At the same time the possibility that local investors will begin more and more to be interested in parent company stock should not be entirely discounted. As the relative size of Massey-Ferguson in the United States market has increased, so has the relative amount of its total stock held by United States investors. While the exemption of the United States withholding tax on new issues has had a significant effect, it is none the less interesting that after the company's 1966 rights offering of one share for every five shares held, United States investors acquired about two-thirds of the rights issued, buying many of them from Canadian investors. Consequently United States investors now own just under 40 per cent of the common stock of the company, compared with just over 20 per cent in 1964.

The total commitment to the international environment implied in the concept of the global corporation outlined earlier has significant implications for the organizational structure of a company and for the system that is devised to control its many operations. Indeed, some writers have even defined international corporations in terms of their organizational structure rather than in terms of the nature of their commitment to the international environment. It does seem apparent that an organizational structure suitable for a purely domestic corporation is not likely to be suitable for world-wide operations.

There are several reasons for this. First of all permanent differences between nations demand that international corporations learn to cope with diversity while yet achieving efficiency through careful planning, co-ordination, and control of world-wide operations. The problems posed by international diversity are reduced if nationals predominate in the operations of local subsidiary companies and if they are given maximum responsibility and authority for achieving the defined objectives of the parent company. Such executives are more likely to have the language requirements, the knowledge of local conditions, and the cultural background that is necessary for being effective in the local business environment. All this suggests that there is merit in moving towards maximum separation of corporate or parent company executives from line responsibilities in local operations units, and in avoiding the temptation of sending executives from the "home base" to manage operations abroad.

Not that this is typically any easy task. The experience of Massey-Ferguson has been that managerial skills, while scarce around the world, are less scarce in the United States than elsewhere. The temptation to send North Americans abroad is therefore always great, and only a conscious and determined effort to seek out and develop local managerial talent will prevent it. It may be recalled that when, in 1956, Massey-Ferguson, a Canadian company, suddenly required a number of senior executives quickly, it found most of them in the United States. A managerial talent "gap" seems to be a major problem in most countries, and it is one gap that the international corporation is in a unique position to fill—given a chance.

Maximum separation of corporate executives from operating responsibilities seems desirable for other reasons. The executives of local operations units must be able to feel satisfied that each operations unit will be treated fairly when world-wide decisions concerning, say, capital expansion and export activity are made. If corporate executives are more closely associated with some operations units than with others, this feeling of confidence is difficult to create. Such an association may also make it difficult for corporate executives to appraise objectively the operations of each subsidiary and it may leave them mentally unprepared for planning the global strategy of the corporation. Detailed attention to operational matters might also mean inadequate attention to long-term planning. Finally, it is difficult to hold local subsidiaries substantially responsible for operations if corporate intervention in local operations is detailed and continuous.

Massey-Ferguson has accepted the principle that operations units should enjoy maximum responsibility and authority and that exceptions to this principle should be defined and understood. Massey-Ferguson Limited, the parent company, has been transformed into a holding company and its executives constitute the corporate group. The North American operations unit has the same relationship with the corporate or parent company executives as do operations units in the rest of the world. True, corporate executives retain some detailed line responsibilities and, in emergency cases, temporarily assume others in individual operations units. But generally their role is to examine and eventually approve annual plans of operations units, to examine performance against plans, and to plan long-term strategy for the continuing development of the company's world-wide operations.

Long-term planning of a global corporation involves considerations that are not encountered by a domestic company. Efficient location of plant requires a knowledge of conditions in a number of countries. Massey-Ferguson produces various types of tractors at Detroit (United States), Coventry (England), Beauvais (France), Sâo Paulo (Brazil) and (with associates) at Madras (India), Barcelona (Spain), and Queretaro (Mexico). It has centred combine production at Brantford (Canada), Kilmarnock (Scotland), Marquette (France), Eschwege (West Germany), and Sunshine (Australia). Decisions regarding the number of units and the models that should be produced at each factory, and where expansion should occur, involve strategy on an international plane. By pursuing a policy of maximum interchangeability of component parts—particularly for tractors and combines—Massey-Ferguson has increased its flexibility in international production strategy and has reduced its costs of production.

This global strategy in plant location gives the international corporation flexibility not enjoyed by a domestic company. Over the years, for example, Massey-Ferguson has come to locate its labour-intensive North American operation in Canada where wages are lower than in the United States. Some operations are located in the United States partly because of the relationship that is believed to exist between local plant location and local market penetration. As a consequence, and in spite of over two decades of free trade and substantially increased company penetration of the United States market, the proportion of Massey-Ferguson's total North American employees located in Canada was about the same in 1966 as it was in 1939. Also, when the company required more combine capacity in Europe, it had to choose between expansion at Kilmarnock or Marquette. Marquette was chosen partly because of the long history of labour difficulties at the former. The international corporation is also in a position to acquire technology and new products quickly by considering the purchase of existing companies outside its home base. Massey-Ferguson did this on a number of occasions. For an international corporation, therefore, plant location decisions can be heavily influenced by relative cost differences, by the political environment, and by the opportunity for acquiring technology and products quickly wherever in the world they are available.

An international corporation must make similar global decisions in its financial operation. In what currencies should it assume new liabilities, and where should it invest its liquid assets? Appropriate strategy involves making assumptions about future exchange rates, interest rates, political stability, and about what constitutes a tolerable risk. Global tax liabilities may be minimized by taking full advantage of national tax structures by being aware of changes in them and, to the extent legally possible, by shifting profits to subsidiary companies facing the lowest tax rates. Unfavourable tax treatments in particular countries can more easily by minimized by international corporations than by domestic ones, and the possibility that even parent companies might shift locale for that reason, or for other ones, is not entirely remote. In the case of Massey-Ferguson, since the parent company is essentially a holding company with global management responsibilities, its staff is relatively small—numbering just over 100 in 1967 out of a world-wide total of about 46,000. The physical obstacles to shifting Head Office staff are therefore very small. There can be no doubt that the bargaining position of an international corporation in its relations with individual governments is inherently stronger than that of purely domestic companies. Much parochial legislation will face its moment of truth when it first encounters the international corporation.

The deep involvement of the corporate group in planning, co-ordinating, and controlling worldwide operations has rather interesting implications for the potential development of Massey-Ferguson in future. By acquiring the skills and developing the organizational and control procedures that are specifically suitable for supervising the operations of relatively independent and far-flung operations, it should become increasingly easier to add to the number of such operations units. Nor is there any inherent reason why such operations units should in future be confined to agricultural machinery and the industrial and construction equipment business. Indeed, the development of the Perkins organization with its large "external" sales of engines, the establishment in North America and Italy of distinct industrial equipment operations, and the acquisition of an interest in truck manufacturing in Spain may confirm that the organizational structure does lend itself to industrial diversification as well as to geographical diversification of corporate activity. A corporation of this kind is more properly thought of as being a highly competent managerial group than a segment of a specific industry. Now that Massey-Ferguson Limited is a holding company without fixed assets, this point is illustrated by its legal structure.

The corporate group cannot exercise adequate supervision and control over world-wide plans and operations without a comprehensive system of reporting. In Massey-Ferguson the required information is generated through the gradual adoption by each operations unit of the company's integrated planning and control system, by the submission of annual plans, and by the monthly submission of control reports that compare performance against approved plans and that highlight variances. This approach makes it virtually mandatory for executives in all the operations units to become intimately acquainted with essentially North American concepts of business planning and control. The application of this approach to operations units abroad, operations units that may previously have been quite unfamiliar with it, is time-consuming, frequently frustrating, and almost never completely successful until some new managerial personnel have been introduced into them. But experience has shown that it is not an impossible task.

To achieve adequate communication and co-ordination is a difficult task in any large corporation. These difficulties are compounded in a global corporation and require detailed attention. In the case of Massey-Ferguson, its operations units are located in countries with marked political, social and economic differences and with a variety of languages. The development of uniform organizational structures and reporting systems is only one way in which internal communication is improved. It is also improved by the practice of hiring local senior executives who have a working knowledge of English. At present almost all of the company's senior executives in each of the operations units abroad speak English even though many of them are nationals of the countries in which they work.

Co-ordination is achieved in a number of ways. It is achieved by the requirement that each operations unit must submit an annual plan to the corporate group and by the further requirement that the plan must be approved by corporate executives. It is enhanced by the organizational structure of the corporate group which ensures that there will be corporate executives with specialized knowledge of each one of the major functional divisions of the operations units. Co-ordination is also improved by the corporate group retaining certain defined line responsibilities, particularly engineering or product development, part of finance, and export activity. The corporate group also arranges conferences attended by executives of the various operations units. For example, there is an annual world-wide product planning conference. Occasionally there are also world-wide conferences for engineering, manufacturing, marketing, finance, personnel and industrial relations, and public relations. Corporate executives make frequent trips to the operations units and, to a limited extent, are transferred from operations units to the parent company, and from the parent company to the operations units.

This approach to managing a worldwide organization has important implications for the kinds of corporate executives that are required. A senior staff executive of such a group is in some respects in an unnatural position. To a large extent he exists to give advice. He must be careful not to give orders to operations units if the company's concept of decentralized responsibility is to be preserved. Accolades for increased profits must go not to him but to local line executives who chose to accept, or reject, his advice. Yet because of his background and because of the necessity of his having qualifications that will permit him to assume line responsibilities temporarily if serious trouble arises in particular operations units, his instincts may frequently be "line" rather than "staff." The borderline between "advising" and "ordering" can be thin—as thin as the tone of the voice, perhaps. But that borderline must be identified and respected at all times if a drift—often hardly observable in the short term—towards centralization is to be avoided. An international corporation is therefore particularly likely to have to devise means that will cause it to pay constant attention to the organizational principles that it has chosen, just as it must pay constant attention to introducing evolutionary changes into its organizational structure as the size and complexity of its operations increase.

A corporate executive must take it for granted that he will spend much of his time travelling by air and that he will frequently be away from his home and family. Permitting wives to accompany their husbands on such trips from time to time is a corporate necessity, not an act of friendly corporate paternalism or charity. Not all tax authorities see the problem quite this way.

In time the executive of the international corporation will probably develop a much more international outlook than an executive of a purely domestic corporation. His national economic loyalties are likely to be more diffused, and his views on trade more liberal than those of executives in domestic companies. Nor is one likely to find rabid nationalists among parent company executives of international corporations, although they can be found among the executives of the local companies of such a corporation. A corporate executive, for example, often can make a decision on capital allocation only after an objective examination of opportunities in several countries. His responsibilities and decisions force him into becoming an international man just as they force him to move physically in the international environment. Increasingly the parent company group to which he belongs will be drawn from a diversity of operations units and a diversity of countries. At that point the process of "internationalizing" the corporate group will attain its logical maturity.

The international industrial corporation is in many respects a remarkable phenomenon. It reflects the effect on business of a world that is getting smaller and of a technology that is becoming very complicated and universally demanded. It mirrors the remarkable adaptability of business institutions and businessmen in a rapidly changing international environment. It widens the horizon of businessmen contemplating new business opportunities and transforms them until they are more international than national. And in the course of all this it becomes intimately involved in distributing the advanced technology and managerial skills that so many nations seem to require. It is not a phenomenon that should be dismissed with superficial generalizations in the world that lies ahead.

*Reprinted from *A Gobal Corporation: A History of the International Development of Massey-Ferguson Limited*, by E.P. Newfeld, by permission of the University Press. © University of Toronto Press, 1969.

APPENDIX 1-C: International Organizations and the MNC

During the past several years there have been a number of efforts to examine the activities of multinational corporations (MNCs). The studies indicate that, with few exceptions, the MNCs do not present unique problems, but only different aspects of the general problems associated with international investment. The key studies are these:

1. UN Economic and Social Council (ECOSOC), Eminent Persons Group. The Eminent Persons Group was created by a July 1972 ECOSOC resolution requesting the Secretary-General of the UN to appoint a group to (1) study the role of multinational corporations, (2) formulate conclusions to be used by governments in making decisions on national policies, and (3) submit recommendations for appropriate international action.

2. The UN Commission on International Trade Law (UNICITRAL). The General Assembly asked UNICITRAL to (1) collect information relating to legal problems created by MNCs and the implications for unification and harmonization of international trade law and (2) consider what steps (including uniform legal rules) might be necessary to deal with these problems.

3. International Labor Organization Activities. A meeting of experts convened by the governing body of the ILO in the fall of 1972 recommended that the ILO study the usefulness of social policy guidelines relating to MNC activities. A number of research projects are underway.

4. OECD Activities. Various standing committees and working parties of the OECD have been considering aspects of the activities of multinational enterprises, among them (1) improvement of information and improved exchange of information on the activities of multinational enterprises; (2) the role of multinational enterprises in international financial flows; (3) internal transactions and marketing policies of multinational enterprises and their impact on competition, national economics, and trade; (4) evaluation of the extent of, and examination of possible solutions to, taxation problems related to the activities of multinational enterprises, in particular as regards transfer pricing, use of tax havens, and investment incentives; (5) impact of multinational enterprises on industrial relations, employment (in both home and host countries), and wages (in host countries); and (6) technological transfer through multinational enterprises and its

impact on the national scientific and technological potential, as well as on other factors such as employment and trade.

5. Joint Committee of the United States Congress and the European Parliament. Delegations from the American Congress and the European Parliament met in October 1973 in Washington, and one of the results was a directive to the rapporteurs to draft an international agreement with respect to taxation, standards of conduct, and control of mergers of MNCs.

6. Tripartite Business Task Force on International Investment Codes. A Tripartite Task Force composed of American, Japanese, and European businesspeople met in October 1973 and submitted a draft report on international investment codes.

7. The International Chamber of Commerce. In November 1972, the Council of the International Chamber of Commerce adopted a set of comprehensive Guidelines for International Investment that cover many of the areas now being looked at by the various groups listed above.

8. The United States Chamber of Commerce. This organization has a special panel on MNCs that has been considering such issues as the impact of MNCs on host countries, foreign investment in the United States, and international investment codes.

9. Atlantic Council of the United States. The Special Advisory Panel on International Institutions to the Trade Committee has included the topic "Multinational Enterprises" in its work program.

Part I: The Multinational Business Environment

2

The Economics of Multinational Business

International economics provides the essential tools for understanding the risks and uncertainties arising from balance of payments considerations, foreign exchange regulations, tariff policies, and trade restrictions at a theoretical and highly abstract level. The major thrust is still on trade flows rather than on firms and their business operations. Such enormous worldwide organizations as Exxon, General Motors, Matsushita, Nestlé, Philips Gloeilampen, and Unilever, for example, with assets and life expectations paralleling those of nation-states, transcend the competitive market assumptions on the basis of which international economics rests.

The development of the multinational corporation through which multinational business undertakings and transactions take place is a fairly recent one. The world business environment is complex and dynamic. The multinational economic forces that affect the MNCs are primarily policy changes and regulations pertaining to such areas as balance of trade, tariffs, GATT, and the United States Trade Reform Act of 1975. But first a few words about a viable *theory* of comparative advantage.

In an abstract way, the theory sheds light on the trade flows among countries. Direct foreign investment, which is the hallmark of the present-day MNC, follows trade, so that an understanding of trade flows through the theory is a good place to begin.

The possibilities of trade between two countries, P and Q, depend on the opportunity cost advantage; that is to say, trade would be possible between P and Q if each could gain by expanding its output in its least-cost product and trading to import desired amounts of the other's product. Whether this theory, or more complicated versions of it, has any real-world validity is debatable. Earlier empirical studies did not show clear evidence for or against the basic theory. MacDougall's study,[1] which related labor productivity to export performance in the pre-World War II era, showed that the United States exported the products in which it was relatively more efficient than the United Kingdom. However, Leontief[2] in 1953 demonstrated that the United States tended to export products that were labor-intensive and to import items that were capital-intensive. The Leontief paradox has not yet been fully resolved by economists working at high levels of abstraction.

The comparative advantage theory, as offered in the field of international economics, does not seem to be of much use to international managers who seek profitable investment opportunities on a worldwide basis; yet there appears to be some value in being familiar with it. Mason and others[3] suggest some ways in which such knowledge might be useful to MNC managers. First, the manager should know the general characteristics of the production function (that is, the production-possibilities schedule) of his own operations;[4] the implication here is that if he is able to determine the entire spectrum of available technological configurations for his domestic production, he can then extend this analysis to the foreign environment from the point of view of his firm's international competitive position. Furthermore, if he can analyze trends in labor productivity in the domestic setting and compare them on a multinational basis he can more easily discern competitive problems abroad. Mason and colleagues conclude by saying that "much research remains to be done before comparative cost doctrines of international economics can be directly applied to planning activities of large MNCs."[5]

BALANCE OF TRADE

All countries of the world, large and small, collect data on their international trade transactions. The two basic types of transactions are (a) "real" transactions, those involving trade in goods and services, and (b) financial transactions. Statistics on balance of trade are the major segment of the balance of payments. The balance of payments position of a country in a year and over a period of years reflects its internal economic strength or weakness.

For the United States as well as for many other industrial nations, imports and exports of finished goods constitute the largest proportion of real transactions. Trade transactions in goods and services also involve a method of payment, and consistent deficits do bring about changes in government policies. Also, the economic conditions summarized in a country's balance of payments accounts are generally mirrored in its currency exchange rates.

Trade deficit suggests international competitive weakness in one or more major goods; conversely, trade surplus points to the international economic strength of a nation. No country manages to be continuously on the surplus side insofar as its international trade transactions go. Many of the less developed countries ended on the deficit side during the post-World War II era; and in the post-oil embargo period, (1973 onward), many industrial nations also have fallen victim, with one exception among the big oil importers, West Germany. The estimated trade deficit for the United States in 1974 was in the neighborhood of $10.58 billion, however, recent reports indicate the 1975 figure may well be a surplus of $12 billion.

Hard hit by the rise of foreign oil prices, the United States posted a merchandise trade deficit of about $3 billion in 1974. Figures showed that exports climbed 40 percent to about $98 billion while imports rose 45 percent to about $101 billion; the resultant deficit was a sharp reversal from the $1.35 billion trade surplus of 1973. The value of petroleum imports soared from $17 billion in 1974 to $24.5 billion. Besides this, steel shipments into the United States were expected to expand again in 1975, as were aluminum imports. As for exports, such items as coal, agricultural products, machinery, data-processing equipment, and aircrafts and parts held the most promise.

In sum, although the payments position of a country is brought about by a complex interplay of economic and political forces, the summary results presented in technical terms can be of some value to decision makers in the realm of multinational business.

TARIFFS AND TRADE RESTRICTIONS

That free trade maximizes world output is an oft-quoted maxim; yet free trade is more of an ideal than a reality. Since the mid-1930s the United States has been the principal advocate of freer trade, albeit with varying degrees of zeal. There can be a number of reasons why nations impose trade restrictions via tariffs, exchange controls, and even quotas: as a source of revenue, as a stimulus to domestic economic development, in the interest of national defense, as a retaliatory tool, and as a means of protecting domestic industries and employment. While economists debate the pros and cons of tariffs in terms of flow of goods (or merchandise) in the contemporary world, one can see the significance of restrictions imposed by national governments on the flow of human resources, of technology, and of money capital.

The General Agreement on Tariffs and Trade (GATT), first formulated in 1947, has served as the main forum for multilateral negotiations to reduce barriers to international trade. GATT is a framework for nations to manage their international commercial policy. Its main provisions cover three areas: discriminatory trade controls, quantity restrictions, and settlement of trade-related disputes between countries. Multilateral bargaining, under the purview of GATT, generally takes place in long sessions. Six bargaining sessions since 1947 have produced considerable tariff reductions. The sixth session in 1967, referred to as the Kennedy Round, produced weighted-average tariff cuts of around 35 percent, making it the most sweeping tariff reduction agreement.

The less developed countries are not altogether satisfied with the working of GATT as it affects them. From the start, it has diluted the objective of most favored nation treatment for all parties: countries were allowed to set up customs unions or free trade areas. The most significant such union is the European Economic Community (EEC), popularly referred to as the Common Market. Since its inception in 1959, the Common Market has had two significant effects on American multinational business. First, as a result of high tariffs on agricultural products, some American exporters were displaced by suppliers from within the trading area. This tendency has intensified now that there are three new Common Market members: Britain, Denmark, and the Republic of Ireland. Second, as a consequence, there has been an incentive for American multinationals to invest directly behind the common tariff barrier.

THE UNITED STATES TRADE REFORM ACT OF 1975

The international economic environment has been considerably modified by the Trade Reform Act of 1975. The United States is perhaps the only major trading nation in which tariff schedules are part of national legislation, and changes in them require legislative approval. An American administration must seek congressional authorization before making tariff reduction offers to other countries, whereas in most countries, tariffs can be fixed up to a certain level without additional legislative action.

Scope

Under Title I of the 1975 act, the President is authorized during a five-year period to enter into trade agreements for modifying tariff rates and liberalizing other barriers to trade. His authority extends to both reducing and increasing existing rates. Tariff-cutting, however, is limited. Duties higher than 5 percent ad valorem can be reduced only up to 60 percent, while duties of 5 percent ad valorem or less can be eliminated. When the reduction exceeds 10 percent, it takes effect over a period up to ten years at an annual rate no more than one tenth of the total reduction, or 3 percent ad valorem, whichever is greater. Duty raising is limited to no more than 50 percent of the column 2 rates of January 1, 1975, or

20 percent above the current ad valorem (the most favored nation [MFN]) rates, whichever is higher.

The act lists the revisions in GATT considered necessary to promote the development of an open, nondiscriminatory, and fair world economic system. These revisions involve decision-making procedures; safeguard procedures; extension of GATT to cover trade conditions not now covered; adoption of international fair labor standards and of public petition and confrontation procedures; treatment of border adjustments for internal indirect taxes; changes in balance of payments provisions to recognize import surcharges as the preferred method of import restraints; improvement of provisions relating to export controls, access to supplies, and consultation procedures on supply shortages; inclusion of multilateral procedures for access to supplies; establishment of procedures for regular consultations on international trade and for adjudication of commercial disputes; elimination of special and reverse preferences; and international regulation of the use of subsidies.

The act gives the President authority to proclaim import measures for a period of up to 150 days for balance of payments purposes. Under certain circumstances, he is required to impose import restrictions unless he informs Congress that they would be contrary to the national interest. For example, he must impose import restrictions (1) to deal with large and serious U.S. balance of payments deficits; (2) to prevent an imminent and significant depreciation of the dollar in foreign exchange markets; or (3) to cooperate with other countries in correcting an international balance of payments disequilibrium. Under other conditions, he is authorized (rather than obligated) to take measures to increase imports (1) to deal with large and persistent U.S. balance of trade surpluses or (2) to prevent significant appreciation of the dollar in foreign exchange markets.

Measures to expand exports consist of a temporary duty reduction of up to 5 percent ad valorem and a temporary increase in values or volumes of goods that may be imported under any import restrictions, or the temporary suspension of any import restriction. For all restrictions, product coverage is to be broad and uniform unless liberalization will cause or contribute to material injury of a domestic industry or will be contrary to the national interest.

Relief for Domestic Industries

Title II of the act provides for import relief and adjustment assistance for industries, firms, and workers injured by import competition. A petition for import relief may be submitted by a trade association, firm, union, or group of workers representative of an industry. The subsequent investigation must consider all relevant economic factors. If increased imports are attributable in part to dumping, the International Trade Commission may recommend antidumping action. Duties may not be raised more than 50 percent ad valorem above the existing rate, and quantitative restrictions or marketing agreements may not lower imports below the level of the most recent representative period.

Although the duration of import relief may not exceed five years (with one possible three-year extension), to the extent feasible relief must be phased out after three years. Relief measures must be kept under review, and the President may terminate them at any time. No further investigation may be made of an article that has received import relief until two years have passed since relief was last provided.

Unfair and Illegal Trade Practices

Title III deals with unfair and illegal trade practices adversely affecting United States commerce. This portion of the law has four chapters, as described below.

Foreign Import Restrictions and Export Subsidies. The President is given broad authority to take retaliatory measures against "unreasonable" as well as "unjustifiable" practices of trade partners, such as prohibitive tariffs, import restrictions, discriminatory policies, export subsidies, and "restrictions on access to supplies of food, raw materials, or manufactured or semi-manufactured products." The President must provide for the presentation of views concerning such practices and actions that may be taken in retaliation unless the national interest requires expeditious action. Prior to taking retaliatory measures against export subsidies, the President must ensure that (1) the secretary of the treasury has found that such subsidies exist; (2) the International Trade Commission has found that the exports enjoying the subsidies reduce the sales of competitive American products; and (3) the provisions embodied in previous acts are "inadequate to deter such practices."

Antidumping Activities. These provisions amend and update the Antidumping Act of 1921. Some amendments are designed to improve the enforcement of the 1921 act by requiring, for example, the secretary of the treasury to conduct more prompt investigations of alleged dumping practices. The investigation procedure is simplified, and equal hearing rights are guaranteed to interested parties. Other amendments are intended to update the 1921 act's definitions of "purchase price," the "exporter's sales price," and so on. The "purchase price" is defined as the f.o.b. price less export taxes, plus rebated import duties imposed by the country of exportation, plus any taxes rebated for exportation that would have been levied if the product had been sold in the country of exportation. This new definition amends the Antidumping Act by providing that export taxes will be subtracted, rather than added, to the purchase price. The purchase price is used as a reference price in determining dumping practices by comparing it to the foreign market value. The "exporter's sales price," which can be used in lieu of the purchase price, is adjusted by subtracting the value added to the merchandise after importation into the United States.

The earlier antidumping legislation was inadequate in these three areas: below cost sales, state-controlled economy dumping and multinational corporate dumping. In these three cases, the secretary of the treasury is required to determine the fair value either by reference to a foreign market outside the country of exportation where the sale price is not subject to distortions, or by adjusting the price in the country of exportation for the difference between the costs of production in other countries and in that country. Under the 1921 law, the foreign market value was measured by two alternative criteria. The primary criterion was the price at which such or similar merchandise was sold or offered for sale in the principal markets of the country from which it was exported. The second criterion covered situations in which there were no home market sales; in this event, the foreign value was determined on the basis of the price for similar merchandise in other countries.

Countervailing Duties. This section of the 1975 law amends some provisions of the 1930 Tariff Act and obligates the secretary of the treasury to enforce, within strict time limits, the provisions of the countervailing duty law. In circumstances where dumping is proved, importers will be required to pay duty equal to the margin of dumping. The secretary of the treasury must report to the Congress whenever he has determined that progress made or underway toward the elimination of barriers to international trade (or other distortions) warrants a suspension of countervailing duties. Procedures are set forth to allow an American manufacturer to request the secretary of the treasury to reassess the value on which countervailing duties are levied.

Unfair Import Practices. The International Trade Commission is required to investigate "unfair methods of competition and unfair acts in the importation of articles into the United States or in their sale" that may injure an industry operating in the United States, prevent the establishment of such an industry, or restrain or monopolize trade and commerce in the United States. The commission is required to seek advice within the government and to conduct its investigation promptly. It may order the suspension of importations violating the provisions of the act. Commission findings must be transmitted to the secretary of the treasury and to the President. (These provisions do not apply to imports affected by or for the United States government.)

Most Favored Nation Treatment

Title IV allows the President to extend most favored nation (MFN) treatment, grant Export-Import Bank credits, provide guarantees for credit and investment, and conclude commercial agreements with a nonmarket economy country if that country does not restrict emigration or assures the President that its emigration practices will henceforth meet his approval. Before these benefits can be granted, the President must submit a report to Congress and must receive approval of both the House and the Senate. Nonmarket economy countries receiving MFN treatment before the passage of the act (Poland and Yugoslavia) will continue in that status. MFN treatment will be given and will remain in effect only as part of a bilateral commercial agreement. Such agreements will be limited to an initial period of three years and must allow for suspension for national security reasons, include safeguards against market disruption, and ensure the protection of trademarks, patent rights, and copyrights of American nationals.

MFN treatment extended to a foreign country within the framework of a bilateral commercial agreement will be applied only if the country is not in arrears in the repayment of its Lend-Lease obligations. If the exports from a Communist country are suspected of causing market disruption, the International Trade Commission will make an investigation and recommend necessary action to the President. If the President finds grounds for believing such disruption exists, he may also initiate consultations with the country concerned.

Tariff Preferences

Title V gives the President authority to extend duty-free treatment to imports of eligible articles from beneficiary developing countries for a maximum of ten years. Specifically excluded from the list of potential beneficiary countries are developed countries listed in the act; any Communist country unless it is a member of the International Monetary Fund and a contracting party to GATT, members of the Organization of Petroleum Exporting Countries, or countries party to any action that causes withholding of supplies of vital commodity sources from international trade or raising of prices of such commodities to an unreasonable level; and countries granting reverse preferences to developed countries other than the United States unless such preferences are to be eliminated before January 1, 1976. A country that has appropriated American property without adequate compensation loses its beneficiary status.

All manufactures and semimanufactures are included, with the expection of textiles, shoes, watches, and some import-sensitive electronic, steel, and glass products. The last of eligible articles is to be published periodically.

Under the act, the President may withdraw, suspend, or limit the duty-free treatment of any article from any country, except that no rate of duty may be established other than the MFN rate applicable to the article. In order to provide safeguards for domestic industry against competition from preferred imports, the act provides for a "competitive need" formula that limits imports from important beneficiary suppliers. If a country supplies more than 50 percent of the value of total imports of an eligible article, or supplies to the United States a quantity of it valued at more than $25 million per year, that country shall then lose its beneficiary status not later than sixty days after the close of the calendar year with respect to such an article, unless the President decides otherwise. An automatic adjustment to the $25 million ceiling is provided by allowing it to adjust proportionately to changes in gross national product as compared with 1974 GNP.

Other Provisions

Among the other provisions of the act are a requirement that the President submit an annual report to Congress on international drug control, a section authorizing the President to initiate negotiations for a trade agreement with Canada to establish a free trade area covering the United States and Canada, and a limitation on total loans, guarantees, and insurance relating to exports to the Union of Soviet Socialist Republics (apart from operations of the Commodity Credit Corporation) of $300 million without prior congressional approval.

SUMMARY

International economics helps us to understand the elements of international trade flows. The statistics of imports and exports that demonstrate the relative trade position of a country are in turn reflected in such things as exchange rates and exchange control restrictions of direct concern to multinational business. The international economic environment has been considerably modified by the United States Trade Reform Act of 1975, which affords specific power to the President, provides for import relief and adjustment assistance, and discourages dumping. Furthermore, under the Act, most favored nation treatment can be extended to China and the USSR.

Notes

[1]G. D. A. MacDougall, "British and American Exports: A Study Suggested by the Theory of Comparative Costs, Part I," *Economic Journal,* 59, 244 (December 1951), 697-724.

[2]W. W. Leontief, "Domestic Production and Foreign Trade: The American Position Re-examined," in R. Cave and H. G. Johnson, eds., *Readings in International Economics* (Homewood, Ill.: Irwin, 1968), pp. 503-27.

[3]R. Hal Mason, R. R. Miller, and D. R. Weigel, *The Economics of International Business* (New York: Wiley, 1975), pp. 48-67.

[4]See, for example, Richard Hays et al., *International Business: An Introduction to the World of the Multinational Firm* (Englewood Cliffs, N.J.: Prentice-Hall, 1972), pp. 55-59.

[5]Mason, *op. cit.*

Suggested Readings

BALDWIN, ROBERT E., ''International Trade and Economic Growth: A Diagrammatic Analysis,'' *American Economic Review,* March 1975.

JOHNSON, HARRY G., ''Technological Change and Comparative Advantage: An Advanced Country's Viewpoint,'' *Journal of World Trade Law,* January-February 1975.

MULLER, R., AND R. D. MORGENSTERN, ''Multinational Corporations and Balance of Payments Impacts in LDCs: An Econometric Analysis of Export Pricing Behavior,'' *Kyklos,* 27, 2 (1974).

SHETTY, Y. KRISHNA, AND S. B. PRASAD, ''Comparative Advantage Theory and American Investments in Developing Nations,'' *Foreign Trade Review,* January-March 1973, pp. 420-38.

3

The Dynamics of Direct Investment

"As the chairman of a worldwide corporation, let me try to make my company's motives overseas clear so that you can better evaluate the charges of economic isolationists. There is no question about it: the opportunity to make a profit is central to any decision we at General Motors make to invest overseas." So said Thomas A. Murphy, chairman of General Motors, in a recent speech.[1] He was referring to General Motors direct investments.

The field of international economics covers investments or international capital movements, which have occurred throughout recorded history. Foreign capital, for example, provided the base for the industrial development of the United States. There are generally two types of foreign investment: direct and portfolio. Economic theory posits that capital flows from one nation to the other in response to its marginal productivity. True; but that is not the entire story. Firms may base their investment decisions on future market opportunities, pressure of competition from MNCs, and a host of other factors in addition to an opportunity to make a profit. Our focus in this chapter is on direct investment—that is, investment in physical assets—plant, equipment, machinery, laboratories. (The United States government defines direct investment as an ownership interest in foreign enterprises of at least 10 percent.)

Direct investment has its ebbs and flows. In recent years, though, it has been a two-way street—American investment in foreign countries, and foreign investment (mostly European and some Japanese) in the United States. There is not always an actual flow of capital from one geographic area to the other; capital *formation* abroad may take place instead of capital *remittance*.

UNITED STATES DIRECT INVESTMENTS ABROAD

Although U.S. corporations had made fairly substantial direct investments abroad since the mid-1800s, during World War I the United States became a creditor country, and since then investment capital has flowed in the direction of Europe. The real expansion came in the 1960s. For the ten-year period between 1949 and 1958, total capital outflow was $10.44 billion, or a yearly average of about $1 billion; comparable figures for the ten-year period between 1959 and 1968 were $20.9 billion and $2 billion, a twofold increase. As a proportion of total U.S. investment, direct investment by corporations was just about half. Between 1960 and 1965, U.S. direct investment rose from $32.8 billion to $49.4 billion—an increase of 50 percent. The increase between 1965 and 1968 was from $49.4 billion to $64 billion—an increase of 29 percent. In 1974, an increase of 14 percent was due to record net capital outflow of $7.4 billion and reinvested earnings of $7.5 billion.

Direct investment outflows and income for the years 1965 to 1972 are shown in Table 3-1. What is interesting in addition to notable increases in capital outflow and in total income is the fact that funds borrowed abroad through security issues and used to finance direct investments have become substantial since 1965. The direct investment position of American corporations currently is in the neighborhood of $150 billion, a figure thought alarming by many people. Much of the addition to this stock came about during the 1960s. The year-end values of direct investment (in billions of U.S. dollars) were as follows: 1960, $31.9; 1969, $71; 1970, $78.2; 1971, $86.2; 1972, $94.3; 1973, $107.3; 1974, $118.6, and an estimated $130 billion by 1975.[2] Of course, affiliates of American MNCs are expected to show the biggest rise in capital outlay in the Mideast in 1975.

Rates of return on foreign investments for American-based MNCs were handsome. In 1973, as *The Wall Street Journal* put it, on top of a profitable 1972 for foreign operations, many American-based companies expected 1973 to wind up even better.[3] Union Carbide, for example, earned $44.7 million abroad in 1971 and $62.9 million in 1972. International Harvester's foreign profits nearly doubled in 1972 to $86.6 million from $45.2 million in 1971. As a proportion of overseas assets, this meant an increase to 22.3 percent from 12.6 percent against a rise in the domestic return on assets from 4.4 percent to 6.5 percent. The major reasons for this increase in profitability were the European business surge and the 1971 devaluation of the dollar. Capital spending by American affiliates abroad, including Canada, is to go up to $27 billion. In 1975, expenditures by U.S. units

TABLE 3-1

Direct Investment Outflows and Income, 1965-1972*

Year	*Capital Outflow*	*Less: Foreign Borrowing*	*Net Capital Outflow*	*Interest, Dividends, & Earnings*	*Fees & Royalty*	*Total Income Value*
1965	3,468	52	3,416	3,963	1,199	5,162
1966	3,661	445	3,216	4,045	1,329	5,374
1967	3,137	278	2,859	4,517	1,438	5,955
1968	3,209	785	2,424	4,973	1,546	6,519
1969	3,254	631	2,623	5,658	1,682	7,340
1970	4,400	378	4,022	6,001	1,919	7,920
1971	4,765	331	4,434	7,286	2,169	9,455
1972	3,339	259	3,080	7,948	2,345	10,293

*In millions of dollars.
Source: Survey of Current Business, October 1972 and August 1973.

in developed countries are expected to rise a slim 2 percent, in contrast to a 20 percent jump in developing countries in Africa and Latin America.

The explanation for the rapid expansion of United States industry abroad is simply that there are markets to be served and profits to be made. In some cases the most important attraction is the availability of raw materials; in other cases, it is relatively low wage rates or the opportunity to develop a market for products not yet introduced in that particular market. Also, local content regulations often make direct investment the only way to do business in the host country.

Investment attractions in the host countries also lure experienced MNCs. Recently, pharmaceutical MNCs such as Merck, Pfizer, Smith-Kline, and Warner-Lambert flocked to build plants in Ireland. In 1975 the Irish Industrial Development Authority reported that in the past eighteen months new investment in pharmaceutical production totaled nearly $200 million.[4] The surge partly reflects investment attractions offered by Ireland and her new membership in the Common Market.[5] The success, measured in terms of profits or earnings, is due to the comparative organizational advantage that many American firms have over their counterparts abroad: access to the most modern technology, background and experience in the high U.S. market, and ability to develop management processes that make the best use of potentials in modern technology.

The fear that large American investments would come to dominate the economy of a country with the result that nations would become mere satellites of the United States has led to efforts to discourage investment in many countries. The foreign stake in West German business, and particularly that of the United States, has risen sharply in the past few years after a period of stagnation at the end of the 1960s. However, steps are being taken to introduce controls on foreign investment in German industry, partly as a reaction to the Kuwait purchase in

1975 of almost 15 percent of the prestigious auto manufacturer Daimler-Benz and the 25 percent Iranian participation in Krupp.

Between 1970 and 1973, direct foreign holdings in the nominal capital and reserves of German companies rose by 45 percent or 13.6 billion marks to 43 billion marks, according to a recent survey by the West German Bundesbank. The American share in the 13.6-billion-mark rise in the period was 45 percent; in other words, its stake in the 31.6-billion-mark total of such foreign investment rose slightly from 41.7 to 43 percent. The increase came chiefly in four areas: auto manufacturing, electro-technology, holding companies, and banking. The European Common Market companies raised their share by almost 40 percent to 11 billion marks at the end of 1973, while nonmember Switzerland also increased its holding by 1 billion marks to 4 billion to remain second largest foreign holder of German capital after the United States.

The oil industry is the one most concentrated in foreign hands, with this sector in West Germany, as in most other countries, dominated by a few multinational companies. At the end of 1973, 76 percent of the capital of companies in this sector was controlled from abroad. The electrotechnical sector was also a strong magnet for foreign investment with the foreign—again primarily American—lead in computer technology an advantage here. The chemical sector has always been the domain of the German industrial giants, with one of the big three, Hoechst, doing its bit to reverse the flow with its recent $100 million takeover of Foster Grant in the United States.

FOREIGN INVESTMENTS IN THE UNITED STATES

The considerations that induce foreign corporations to make direct investments in the United States seem similar to those that impel American firms to go abroad. Most American companies embarked on foreign ventures with a clearly perceived strategy of linking their own competitive advantage (which may stem from superior technology or management or corporate image) with a market advantage in a given geographical region.

During the 1960s, while U.S. firms were investing extensively in foreign countries, there was very little by way of a foreign-based multinational invasion of the United States. One good reason for this was that there was a wide gap between the resources and the capabilities of American firms and those of European and Japanese firms. It is evident that now the gap has narrowed. An additional factor is that labor costs in the major industrial countries have begun to equalize.

Scope of Foreign Investment in the United States

The majority of foreign investment in the United States has come in the wake of that which began in the early 1960s. Total foreign direct investment (that is, in manufacturing as well as nonmanufacturing) in the United States in 1960 stood at $6.9 billion. In 1969, it rose to $11.8 billion. During the 1970s the figures were 1970, $13.3 billion; 1972, $14.3 billion; 1973, $17.7 billion; and 1974, an estimated $22 billion. Foreign firms have placed the bulk of their investments in the United States in such nonmanufacturing sectors as insurance, petroleum, and retail trade. As noted above, the book value of total direct investment in 1974 was in the neighborhood of $22 billion, but of this total about $9.3 billion constituted investment in the manufacturing sector.

Historically speaking, the principal foreign investors in the United States have been the British and the Canadians. Although in 1971 Britain still had the largest number of firms investing in the United States (437), France, Japan, and Germany had bypassed Canada (143).[6] In recent years, German and Japanese companies have come into the United States in increasing numbers. Although states such as New York, New Jersey, and California have long served as locations for foreign-owned enterprises, South Carolina appears to have attracted many new enterprises. Ten of the largest foreign-owned manufacturing companies are listed in Table 3-2. These were among the *Fortune* 500 in 1974 (this short list does not include petroleum companies such as Shell or Sohio, retail firms such as Gimbels, or banks and insurance companies.

While direct investment in U.S. corporations is done primarily by foreign individuals or companies, foreign central banks hold U.S. government securities. At the end of 1974, total foreign holdings of U.S. stocks and bonds reached $80 billion.

OPEC

It comes as a bit of a shock to realize that there is one powerful economic institution in the world which is neither American nor European, and that is OPEC. Its Persian Gulf members have actually made sizable, albeit much less than earlier estimated, direct investments in the United States. A U.S. Treasury Department study in 1974 found no evidence to suggest that there had been any inundation of foreign investment. It concluded that any concerns are, for the most part, based on the potential for future investment by members of OPEC. Let us briefly examine the scope and influence of this new force in the international economic arena.

Since its establishment in 1960 under the leadership of Venezuela and Iran, OPEC espoused two cardinal goals: (1) to raise taxes and royalties earned by member countries; and (2) to assume control over production and exploration from the major international oil companies. OPEC began life as a means of protecting the interests of petroleum-exporting nations from the dominance of international oil companies. This leads us to a debatable point—namely, whether or not OPEC is a cartel and whether or not it is a viable cartel.

TABLE 3-2

Manufacturing Firms Owned by Foreigners, 1974

Company	*Assets**	*Sales**	*Investor*	*Country*	*% Owned***
Airco	$ 661,147	$760,178	British Oxygen	Britain	35%
Akzona	624,426	753,861	Akzo	The Netherlands	65
Alumax	377,221	464,085	Mitsui	Japan	45
Certain-teed Products	391,682	559,129	St.-Grobain Turner & Newall	France	39
				Britain	12
ESB	315,140	436,002	International Nickel	Canada	100
General Cable	363,014	518,690	British Insul.	Britain	20
Indian Head	353,544	615,446	Thyssen-Bornemisza	The Netherlands	90
Lever Brothers	310,500	669,200	Unilever	Britain-The Netherlands	100
Libby, McNeill & Libby	307,845	464,710	Nestle	Switzerland	61
Seagram & Sons	1,383,826	750,019	Seagram	Canada	100

*Figures in thousands of dollars.

**Ten percent ownership, according to the U.S. Department of Commerce, constitutes control.

Source: Adapted from *Fortune,* May 1975, p. 174.

OPEC members include Arab and non-Arab countries. They are: Algeria, Ecuador, Indonesia, Iran, Iraq, Kuwait, Libya, Nigeria, Quatar, Saudi Arabia, United Arab Emirates, Venezuela. Some like Algeria, Iran, Iraq, Nigeria, and Venezuela have populations of more than 10 million. Some like Ecuador, Kuwait, and Saudi Arabia have ample reserves extending to more than fifty years. These nations jointly interact with the petroleum companies, and the result is felt all over the world.

TABLE 3-3

Size and Profitability of International Oil Companies

Company	*Sales**	*Assets**	*Return on Equity*		*Return on Total Capital*		*Net Profit Margin*
			1970-1974	*1974*	*1970-1974*	*1974*	*(1974)*
Continental	$ 7.04	$ 4.67	13.5%	23.4%	10.1%	16.6%	6.3%
Exxon	42.06	31.33	16.3	22.4	13.5	18.2	7.4
Gulf	16.45	12.50	11.9	18.8	9.6	15.1	6.3
Mobil	18.93	14.07	14.3	20.5	11.9	16.9	6.3
Occidental	5.71	3.32	11.9	38.5	6.9	15.4	4.9
Phillips	4.98	4.02	11.2	21.0	8.6	15.5	9.2
Standard (Calif.)	17.19	11.64	13.7	20.0	12.0	17.2	7.6
Texaco	23.25	17.17	16.6	23.6	12.8	17.4	9.2

*In billions of dollars.

Sources: Data on sales and assets from *Fortune,* May 1975, pp. 210-29. Data on profitability from *Forbes,* January 1975, p. 218.

The international oil companies are listed in Table 3-3. Their size is characterized by assets and sales; their profitability by net margin as well as returns on equity and capital. Data are as of 1974.

OPEC has more than succeeded in its first objective, and may well be on its way to reaching its second goal. What has happened in this process is not just a post-1973 phenomenon and what portends for the future is not only limited to the belligerent region known as the Middle East. Among other things, in purely economic terms a few poorer countries are becoming richer at the cost of wealthy industrial countries. Because their methods are disliked by the petroleum-consuming nations, it is only natural that in these countries OPEC is a villain. Some of the consequences, however, have brought numerous multinational business opportunities, including a surplus payment position for the U.S. in 1975.

The Cartel

The earliest known example of an international cartel is the salt cartel of 1301, whose members were King Philip of France and Charles II, king of Naples. Cartels are just one species of the broader category of oligopolistic market structures. What distinguishes a cartel from a looser form of oligopoly is the presence of a formal, explicit, and detailed plan for sharing the market and for controlling output and prices. Given these descriptive characteristics, OPEC looks like a cartel and acts like a cartel, although its Arab members dislike the label. The London *Economist*, however, has made reference to the "old cartel"—that of the major international oil companies which allegedly engaged in market-rigging.

According to the *Economist*, the old cartel was (a) hurting all consumers to the benefit of producers in the sense that it kept selling prices above marginal cost, but (b) kept most of the gravy from the most efficient producers (Arabs) to finance the digging of oil from uneconomic areas on which these companies got both a producer's and distributor's profit. At the same time, the companies (c) cannily did not push selling prices so high as to induce substitution or indeed even (d) so high as to maximize monopoly profits.[7]

Cartel or not, OPEC's strong points have so far outweighed its weaknesses, and it should have staying power at least through the decade of the 1970s. Some of OPEC's features are these:

1. The top six members control well over 50 percent of total world reserves of crude oil, and all have more than two-thirds
2. Members provide more than 85 percent of world trade in oil and thus exercise control over the world market
3. Industrialized countries depend, in various degrees, upon OPEC oil. For example, the United States meets a third of its needs from OPEC sources, and Japan relies almost entirely on OPEC for her needs
4. Joint Arab influence is dominant in the cross-cultural OPEC, although Iran now and then makes important moves. Whatever solidarity there is of the trade union sort was no doubt reinforced in 1973 and 1974 with the organization's success in raising its members' revenues through a sudden and drastic rise in the official price of crude oil from a little above $2 to nearly $10.50 per barrel.

Oil Pricing Stategy

The official price for OPEC member nations is based on a benchmark crude oil called Arab light that is produced by Saudi Arabia. In March 1975, the benchmark price was $10.46 a barrel. There are many speculations about what is likely to happen to the price of OPEC crude. There are no cogent reasons to believe it will go higher; if anything, it is likely eventually to go down. But no matter what changes there are, crude will remain expensive. No one but OPEC executives knows what the pricing mechanism has been or is, although there are some indications that it is based on refined arithmetic.

The price elasticity of petroleum has been estimated at −0.15, which means that, in the short run, a 100 percent rise in the price of crude leads to only a 15 percent cut in consumption. Also, the lowest-cost alternative to a barrel of crude oil is said to be in the neighborhood of $8 to $11 per barrel. This alternative is a barrel of oil made from coal.

Some economists have pointed out that OPEC is following a *price discrimination through time*. That is to say, charge a high price now (possibly considering the price elasticity and the cost of substitute origins), and when actual massive investment by others is made to develop alternate sources, start to lower the price just enough to induce uncertainty about where the price will end up. The economics of such a strategy appears workable in view of some of OPEC's strong points, but the politics of the Middle East and the imminent decline in world demand because of global recession might counter it.

The beginning of 1975 showed a sudden softness in the international petroleum market. Apparently as a consequence of the market slump, production was cut in some of the OPEC countries (in Abu Dhabi by a third, in Kuwait by a fourth, and in Libya by half). U.S. Secretary of State Kissinger advocated a floor of a minimum (guaranteed) price. This scheme may give a push to an already mounting drive for world commodity agreements covering a wide range of products and aimed directly at compelling the Western industrial world (and Japan) to bear the burden of higher commodity prices.[8] With OPEC's September 1975 decision in Vienna to raise the oil price by 10 percent, the once-hoped-for demise of the cartel and a sharp drop in oil prices appear more out of reach than ever.

Surplus Buildups

There has also been much speculation about the buildup of the surplus revenues of OPEC members by 1980. The original estimate of the World Bank was a staggering $650 billion, but this figure was revised downward. The OECD (Paris) came up with a figure of $300 billion. Which number one picks, for purpose of counter strategies if not for gunboat diplomacy, depends upon one's view of (a) how much crude oil the OPEC countries actually sell, a function of world demand; (b) how much of oil revenues they spend on imports of goods, services, and technologies; (c) how much of revenues they give away as grant aid; and (d) how much of revenues they invest, which means how big a burden they will place on world money and capital markets.

The first step in thinking about the pros and cons of foreign investment in the United States is to distinguish between portfolio and direct investment. In 1973, portfolio investment (mostly in the form of net purchases by foreigners of

American securities) came to $4.7 billion. The other category (including purchases of real estate, establishment of subsidiaries by foreign companies, and acquisition of 25 percent or more of the voting stock of existing American companies) came to about $14 billion. As of 1974, the value of direct foreign investment in the United States was placed at $22 billion. Comparatively speaking, direct American investments had a book value of more than $120 billion (total foreign investment at the end of 1972 was $94 billion).

SUMMARY

There was much more commotion about Arab direct investment in the United States than recent German or Japanese investment. A Conference Board Survey showed that the oil-rich countries shun investing in American plant and equipment. In other words, they tend to stay out of manufacturing and marketing but tend to get into real estate, banking, and possibly insurance—the traditional commercial ventures. As an editorial in *Fortune* expressed it: "When Arab money goes into real estate, it is simply following an investment strategy long favored by foreigners."[9] According to one estimate, deployment of oil exporters' surplus in the United States was about $11 billion.[10]

It is fair to say that while some Americans vehemently oppose foreign investment, especially new Arab investment, most are uncertain about the impact of the inflow of foreign capital. The job-creating possibilities, especially when the unemployment rate in the United States is above 8 percent, appear to mold their thinking. In the long run, as Sanford Rose observes, the long-term foreign contribution to United States capital formation is probably quite limited.[11]

Although one would expect a continued inflow of foreign investment into the United States, a survey by the Conference Board (NICB) found that, during the first half of 1975, foreign firms announced 79 new investments compared with 133 in 1974. The survey also showed that Japanese investors led the list in 1975, followed by West Germany, The Netherlands, Britain, and Canada, in that order. The slight slowing down may be due to (a) a deepening of the recession in many foreign countries, and (b) a sharp increase in the stock prices of many American corporations. We tend to subscribe to the view, well expressed by *The Wall Street Journal*,[12] that it is clearly in the interest of the United States to be the financial hub of the world, which gives it superior access to capital and the political power of a lever on foreign investments and enterprises.

Notes

[1]Thomas A. Murphy in a speech to the Chamber of Commerce, Flint, Michigan, May 1, 1975.

[2]IMF Survey, February 17, 1975, p. 61.

[3]*The Wall Street Journal,* November 1, 1973, p. 10.

[4]*The Wall Street Journal,* March 31, 1975, p. 10.

[5]For an extensive treatment, see S. B. Prasad, *Enterprise in Ireland* (Milwaukee: Stein Publishing Co., 1969).

[6]J. L. Angel, *Directory of Foreign Firms Operating in the U. S.* (New York: Simon and Schuster, 1971). See also J. Arpan and D. Ricks, *Directory of Foreign Manufacturers in the United States* (Atlanta, Ga.: School of Business Administration, Georgia State University, 1974).

[7]*The Economist,* ''The North Sea Bubble,'' March 8, 1975, pp. 15-17.

[8]For an interesting discussion, see Ray Vicker, ''Cartelizing Commodity Prices,'' *The Wall Street Journal,* March 6, 1975, p. 10.

[9]*Fortune,* October 1974, p. 116.

[10]*Bank of England Quarterly Bulletin,* March 1975.

[11]S. Rose, ''The Misguided Furor About Investments from Abroad,'' *Fortune,* May 1975, p. 294.

[12]*The Wall Street Journal,* ''Controlling Foreign Investment,'' April 16, 1975, p. 16.

Suggested Readings

ALIBER, ROBERT Z., ''Impending Breakdown of the OPEC Cartel,'' *The Wall Street Journal,* March 20, 1975.

Business Week, ''OPEC: The Economics of the Oil Cartel,'' January 13, 1975.

COOPER, RICHARD N., ''The Invasion of the Petrodollar,'' *Saturday Review,* January 25, 1975.

The Economist, ''The North Sea Bubble,'' March 8, 1975, pp. 15-17.

Fortune, ''The Shah Drives To Build a New Persian Empire,'' October 1974.

MANCKE, RICHARD B., ''The Future of OPEC,'' *The Journal of Business,* 48, 1 (January 1975), 11-19.

MAZZOLINI, BENATO, ''Creating Europe's Multinationals: The International Merger Route,'' *The Journal of Business,* 48, 1 (January 1975), 39-51.

TANNER, JAMES, AND K. SLOCUM, ''Petroleum Power—Oil Gives Mexico a Boost,'' *The Wall Street Journal,* February 11, 1975, p. 1.

VICKER, RAY, ''The OPEC Test an Uneasy Unity,'' *The Wall Street Journal,* February 27, 1975, p. 12.

APPENDIX 3-A Multinational Joint Ventures

In recent years the world economy has suffered gigantic problems of inflation and material shortages, not to mention food shortages and hunger in some parts of the globe. The short time span between 1972 and 1974 can be characterized as global boom in the sense that prices of industrial commodities such as copper and rubber went up, to the limited advantage of producing countries. But the aftermath of the oil crisis has come to mean further inflation and declining industrial activity and output.

Although the rate of increase has slowed at present, inflation is still a global problem. A variety of single-cause explanations have been offered; the monetarists, for example, hold that excessive money supply is the sole cause. Others point to the cartel behavior of the OPEC. For individual firms and countries that have to bear the brunt of economic maladies such as inflation and material shortages, there is little comfort in the explanations offered, however enlightening they may be. For the first time since World War II, output in all the world's major industrial countries has been either falling or growing more slowly than capacity. Unemployment is on the rise almost everywhere. The interdependence of today's economies and the constraints on government policies may mean that the international business cycle is now more important than politics or diplomacy.

In an unsettled environment such as the one the world is now experiencing, we believe that the global firms, whether American-, Japanese-, or European-based, have an important challenge to meet and a positive contribution to make by pursuing well-thought-out and mutually beneficial joint ventures based on new management philosophies. Because of the importance of what the MNCs have to offer to the less developed nations, which are seriously handicapped by increasing inflation and unemployment, our focus here will be on the hurdles, conflicts, and problems associated with multinational joint ventures.

The first point to remember is that governments all over the world are endeavoring to obtain for themselves a bigger share of the markets, the jobs, the technology, and the managerial skills MNCs create or control. To accomplish this objective, governments tend to expect the MNCs to help promote collaborative or joint ventures. Saudi Arabia, for instance, has asked the multinational oil companies to set up joint venture refineries and petrochemical plants in return for long-term supplies of crude oil. Given the new expectations of developing (and some developed) countries, near-saturation in domestic markets, and new opportunities in the oil-rich nations, a rethinking by the MNCs about joint ventures is in order.

MUTUAL BENEFITS

As a mode of multinational investment, the joint venture has shortcomings as well as advantages. American business people generally do not favor joint ventures, and the tenor of the argument is that "a divided ownership results in a tangled skein of corporate relations."* That is to say, it is difficult to control operations, technology, and proprietary rights such as patents and trademarks. In contrast, the intrinsic value of the multinational joint venture lies in sharing financial, technical, managerial resources with an acceptable quid pro quo. Joint ventures can facilitate training of managers and stimulate local entrepreneurship; they can increase the effectiveness of technology and management knowhow; they can reduce the vulnerability of foreign private investment to nationalistic policies of host countries. Recognizing the economic benefits of joint ventures, many American-based MNCs do provide technology, knowhow, and management to local partners all over the world. What most countries aspire for is more of the same at less cost.

AREAS OF CONFLICT

Management attitudes toward equity participation in joint ventures vary from one country to another as well as from one company to another. Some MNCs insist on majority interest in all their joint ventures; others seem to be more flexible. In setting up joint ventures, some MNCs tend to place undue emphasis on controlling interest. In a pragmatic sense, though, the degree of ownership makes little difference from the point of view of effective functioning of the joint venture *if* there is conflict among partners. It has become increasingly clear that statutory and contractual safeguards are no substitute for mutual understanding and useful collaboration. What gives rise to conflicts?

Unless the partners have common goals, the joint venture may run into serious trouble. An MNC may be primarily interested in establishing operations so that it can enter the market in a country that may forbid wholly-owned foreign subsidiaries. At the same time, a local firm may eagerly seek collaboration with a foreign firm so that it can strengthen its own market position. Faced with foreign exchange shortages, the domestic government may endorse the joint venture. What we have here is a simple case of partners with different objectives often not clearly defined or understood. The predictable outcome is one of conflict of goals, and the consequent ineffectiveness of the joint venture.

In addition to objective factors such as quick market entry or increased profitability, subjective elements also appear to contribute to the conflict. The conclusion Friedman reached from his analysis of joint venture enterprises was that "In such matters, unconscious attitudes are understandably present— attitudes toward familial patterns, hierarchical and impersonal relationships. . . ."** Day-to-day operational problems stemming from cultural and interpersonal relationships and modes of decision making with respect to resource allocations may bring about conflicts just as much as policy regarding the disposition of the venture's profits.

A major source of conflict between partners, and a matter of keen interest on the part of the host country, is in the area of technology transfer. One of the major incentives for a domestic firm to team up with a foreign firm is to derive the benefits of the advanced technology the foreign firm controls or possesses. At least three key issues surround the problem of technology transfer in a multinational joint venture: cost to the domestic unit and the country, the type and level of technology the foreign firm actually transfers, and the capacity of the domestic unit to absorb and effectively employ the technology. The seriousness of these questions is generally correlated with the nature of the joint venture itself; that is to say, if it is a joint enterprise between an MNC and a domestic firm in a poor and industrially less advanced country, the questions posed above become crucial sooner or later. If, however, the joint venture is between a firm in India and one in Malaysia, these questions may not take on disruptive proportions. The preconditions for sharing knowledge are normally better fulfilled among industrially advanced countries where the collaborating parties are skilled bargainers of technology transfer on a bilateral basis with clearer understandings of the quid pro quo.

Developing countries are more and more demanding that foreign investors bring advanced technological knowhow. Among these countries, some have more clout than others. Brazil, for example, has more bargaining power with MNCs because it has a big and a fast-growing market. Thus, for instance, an MNC like ITT is aware that if it does not bring in new technology, Brazil can turn to its Swedish rival, L. M. Ericsson.

One country that has looked carefully into the issue of transfer of technology and its costs as well as benefits is Mexico. Its 1973 Law on the Transfer of Technology is a good example, and perhaps an indicator, of regulations to come in the realm of multinational joint ventures. Under this law, Mexico set up a government commission to rule on contracts involving royalties for technology, trademarks, and even management aid. As *Business Week* reported, it has pared royalty levels from a range between 5 and 15 percent to less than 3 percent in a number of cases.†

FRUITFUL APPROACHES

In a number of cases, multinational joint ventures have proved to be less than satisfactory for a number of reasons. Providing a broad framework within which approaches are flexible enough to respond to changing developments is generally the first step to avoid failure in joint ventures. The prerequisite for a sound framework is ability to identify potential conflict areas and to institute specific processes to deal with them when and if they arise. Some of the fruitful questions to be raised and resolved are (1) Is the collaboration of mutual benefit to the parties? (2) Is it possible to define the objectives of the partners in operational terms? (3) Is there a common approach to attaining these objectives? (4) Is there an acceptable mode of resolving unforeseen conflicts?

Within the framework of specifically defined objectives and identified modes of accomplishment, it is possible to institute methods and policies to resolve conflicts emanating from operational issues such as the disposition of the net profits, maintenance of product quality, marketing effectiveness, internal pricing of products and services, and so forth. Although the choice of the partner and the formulation of an operating agreement are fundamental to the success of joint ventures, they do not necessarily guarantee success. Potential conflicts can be reduced substantially by timely and skillful top management action at the corporate level. But this calls for a multinational management philosophy that incorporates the needs and aspirations of the host countries into the economic objectives of the MNC.

*Frederick Donner, "Worldwide Corporations in a Modern Economy," *Canadian Chartered Accountant,* January 1973, p. 37.

**W. G. Friedman and G. Kalmanoff, *Joint International Business Ventures* (New York: Columbia University Press, 1961), p. 125.

†*Business Week,* July 14, 1975, p. 69.

4

Multinational Financial Resources

Management of an MNC's financial resources is, needless to say, perhaps the most complex aspect of running an international organization. When firms transcend national boundaries and national financial systems, they confront a multiplicity of situations often difficult, if not impossible, to evaluate. Multinational finance managers constantly face choices about the timing of intercompany payments, where to hold liquid funds, and where to borrow to finance operations in various corners of the world. The right choice depends on careful consideration of "institutional" factors such as tax considerations, exchange rates, exchange restrictions, and inflation. None of these stand still. The purpose of this chapter is to acquaint the reader with the nature of the financial environment in which the MNCs operate and the nature of problems they invariably encounter frequently. It should be borne in mind that multinational banks do offer a wide range of services to firms engaged in multinational operations; the choices, however, must be made by the MNCs themselves.

THE MULTINATIONAL FINANCIAL ENVIRONMENT

The financial environment, in a narrow sense, consists of four important elements, almost always in a state of flux: tax structures, exchange rates, exchange restrictions, and price levels or inflation. Operating in multiple financial environment with a global outlook means constantly scanning changes and portents, and being on the alert to minimize risks and maximize rewards. The basic decisions of the firm in a multinational setting are affected by these elements. As one writer put it, "As more and more companies practice the fine art of international finance, there is a corresponding growth in the need to know more about the future international financial environment."[1]

Tax Considerations

The net effects of taxation on any specific investment depend on the interplay of the laws of the two countries involved—the source country in which the income is earned and the destination country to which it goes.[2] Different tax laws and different treatments of foreign investment tend to make taxation of a multinational firm extremely complex. We may consider first the fashion in which the United States government taxes a company with foreign operations and then move on to consider taxation by foreign countries.

If a U.S. corporation carries on business abroad through a *branch* or *division,* the income from that operation is reported on the company's U.S. tax form and taxed in the same way as domestic income. If business is carried on through a foreign *subsidiary,* however, the income normally is not taxed in the United States until it is sent to the parent in the form of dividends. In certain cases, income of a foreign subsidiary is subject to taxation prior to its actual remission in the form of dividends. In order to prevent tax havens, by which American taxes are deferred through transfer price and other arrangements between an American company and its foreign subsidiary, Subpart F of the Revenue Act of 1962 was passed. Under this provision, an American stockholder owning more than 10 percent of a foreign company is taxed on certain types of income from that company.

In order to encourage exports, the United States government provides favorable tax treatment for certain types of operations; for example, the Western hemisphere trade corporation, which is a domestic company whose business is entirely in the Western hemisphere and at least 95 percent of whose gross income comes from sources outside the United States. The maximum marginal tax rate for such a company is 34 percent instead of the regular corporate rate of 48 percent. A domestic international sales corporation (DISC) also receives a tax incentive to encourage exports.

Every country taxes the income of foreign companies doing business in that country, although the type of tax imposed varies. Most of the larger industrial countries impose taxes on corporate income that correspond roughly to the corporate rate in the United States. Some differentiate income distributed to stockholders from undistributed income, with a lower tax on distributed income. Less developed countries frequently have lower taxes and provide certain other tax incentives in order to encourage foreign investment. One method of taxation that has become very important in Europe is the value-added tax. In essence, the value-added tax is a national sales tax in which each stage of production is taxed on the value added. In order to avoid double taxation, the United States gives a federal income tax credit for foreign taxes paid by an American corporation. If a foreign country has a tax rate of less than 48 percent, the American corporation would pay combined taxes at the 48 percent rate. Part of the taxes would be paid to the foreign government and the other part to the United States. Large accounting firms such as Ernst and Ernst provide special services in the area of taxes in foreign countries.

Foreign Exchange

Foreign exchange problems add an important dimension to multinational financing.[3] In the international arena, where currency exchange occurs between countries, a national monetary unit has no legal tender. Transactions between countries must therefore be made by conversion of one currency into another, and this process is called foreign exchange. The market in which claims to foreign currencies are bought and sold in terms of domestic money is known as the foreign exchange market. The basic function of the foreign exchange market is to transfer purchasing power from one country to another. This is done through various foreign exchange bankers and the foreign exchange departments of commercial banks who buy and sell foreign exchange.

The framework for exchange rates and convertibility has been the International Monetary Fund agreements. After World War II, an international agreement put together in Bretton Woods, New Hampshire, created the International Monetary Fund (IMF) and formulated a system of fixed exchange rates with the U.S. dollar serving as the system's linchpin.[4] IMF's purposes were to (a) foster a worldwide system of stable exchange rates; (b) provide a source of monetary reserve for a currency whose stability is threatened; (c) provide orderly changes, when necessary, in par value; and (d) encourage free currency convertibility.

Under the IMF agreements, most countries of the world were committed to maintaining fixed par value for their currencies. According to the original system, a currency was allowed to float between ± 1 percent of its par value. When the fluctuations exceeded the limit, the government of the country concerned would intervene to keep the changes within the agreed-upon bounds. IMF provided a source of monetary reserve to assist nations whose currency was threatened. If the government concerned could not prevent fluctuations because of serious economic maladjustments, then the country was expected to devalue or revalue its exchange rates to a reasonable par. A government could alter the par value of its currency by as much as 10 percent in correlation with the IMF, but any change exceeding 10 percent required approval of the Fund.

In 1971, the limits of 1 percent were widened so that a currency could fluctuate by 2¼ percent on either side of parity. The major objective of such a fixed exchange rate is to bring about exchange stability and avoid competitive exchange depreciation. Also in 1971, the United States devalued the dollar and severed its tie to gold. The crisis following the dollar devaluation resulted in a series of devaluations and revaluations and made the fixed parities of the Bretton Woods pact a thing of the past.[5] A new system with greater flexibility in exchange rates was waiting to be developed. A second dollar devaluation came in 1973, matched by another series of currency adjustments in other parts of the world. Since then, theoretically, world currencies have been floating.

Apart from fixed, floating, and crawling currencies, the intervention strategies used by different governments to defend their currencies when values are fluctuating also differ. Some governments intervene only when their currencies reach the allowable limits; others intervene well before these limits are reached. These and other diversities in exchange rate changes introduce a high degree of complexity and uncertainty into the system of managing financial resources in a multinational context.[6] Recent exchange rate developments are shown in Figure 4-1.

Exchange Controls

Exchange controls, imposed in a number of countries around the world and particularly in the less developed countries, are a formidable obstacle to multinational financial managers. Normally, exchange controls are directly related to a country's balance of payments position. Many countries, less developed as well as developed, perennially experience balance of payments difficulties. In the less developed countries, the balance of payments problem is caused by a number of economic factors peculiar to these countries.

First, in order to develop economically through industrialization, the developing countries need an increasing volume of capital goods, most of which are obtainable only in the industrialized Western countries. This requirement adds a new item to the balance of payments and tends to product a deficit. Second, in most of the developing countries, industries are less diversified with respect to both internal production and external trade. Agricultural products as a whole have been lagging far behind manufactured items in the growth of international trade. Last, the less developed countries are more prone to inflation than industrialized countries; the development process has some degree of built-in inflation. With the advent of the energy crisis, the oil-producing countries of the Middle East have become the surplus area of the world (see Figure 4-2). Rising oil prices have not only worsened the situation of many underdeveloped countries that import oil but have also added new pressures.

In order to correct the adverse balance of payments problems, most of the developing countries employ exchange controls. Under this system, the government maintains a desired exchange rate. The available foreign exchange is rationed on the basis of some standards devised for the purpose. The main reason for the restriction of foreign exchange for use in importing foreign goods or

FIGURE 4-1

Exchange Rate Developments

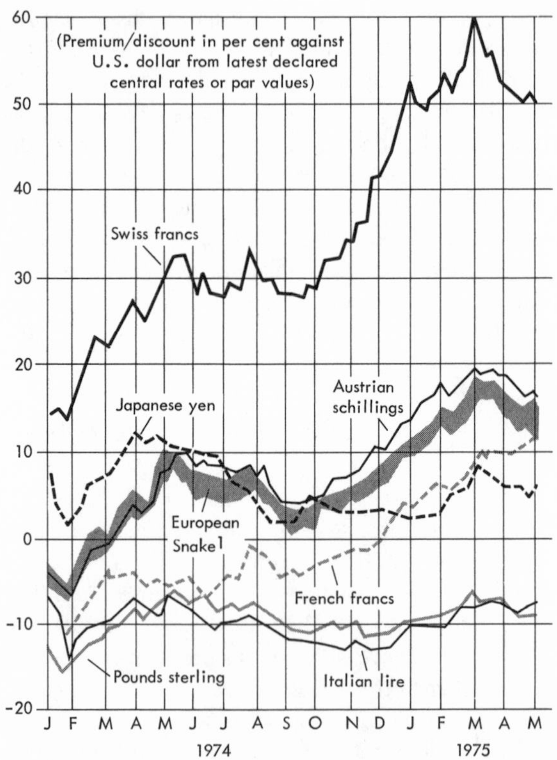

[1]Belgian francs, Danish kroner, Deutsche mark, Netherlands guilders, Norwegian kroner, Swedish kronor.

Source: IMF Survey, May 12, 1975, p. 141.

traveling abroad has been to reduce the demand of residents for foreign currencies. Almost all the developing countries today have this kind of restriction. Such controls take many forms, but usually involve controlling the entry of capital for investment or lending, restricting the exit of funds, or controlling imports. The exchange controls may prohibit or restrict altogether the importation of certain required parts or components.

Because of exchange controls, some companies find it impossible to lend surplus funds accumulated in one country to a subsidiary in another. The greatest problem, however, is encountered with respect to the withdrawal of funds. Restrictions on convertibility through various types of exchange controls limit profits, dividends, royalties and/or repayment of principal on intracompany loans. They also put limitations on transfers of working capital. They may tie up funds within a particular company for which there is no attractive investment opportunity to earn a satisfactory rate of return. Often exchange restrictions block funds within a country so that the parent company cannot have immediate access to them.

Occasionally exchange controls take the form of multiple exchange rates, one rate being applied to certain external payments and another to all other external and internal payments.[7] In recent years, there has been a growing tendency in certain Latin American countries to use this system to deal with the foreign exchange problem. Such rates usually represent a partial devaluation and are often aimed at giving premium rates of exchange to exporters and penalizing importers. For investors from abroad, this often means that dividends, royalties, and other receivables are paid at a discount, and additional capital must enter the company at unfavorable exchange rates. And multiple exchange rates that discriminate against imports can be expected to increase the cost of imported supplies and components.

Generally speaking, the imposition of exchange controls and the application of multiple exchange rates can have two kinds of effects: they can restrict the freedom of business decision making in certain types of transactions and increase the cost of conducting business. Exchange controls may often lead to devaluation that places the currency in question in a more realistic relationship to those of the rest of the world.

Even in countries that have had a free exchange system, an analysis of the nation's international trade may cause investors to doubt whether a free exchange system can be continued indefinitely. Adverse balance of payments along with inflationary pressures in the economy lead to lack of confidence in the particular currency. Under these conditions, the constant possibility of depreciation in the value of a currency poses a threat to the worth of foreign investment in it.

FIGURE 4-2

Disposition of Major Oil Exporters' Current Surplus, 1974

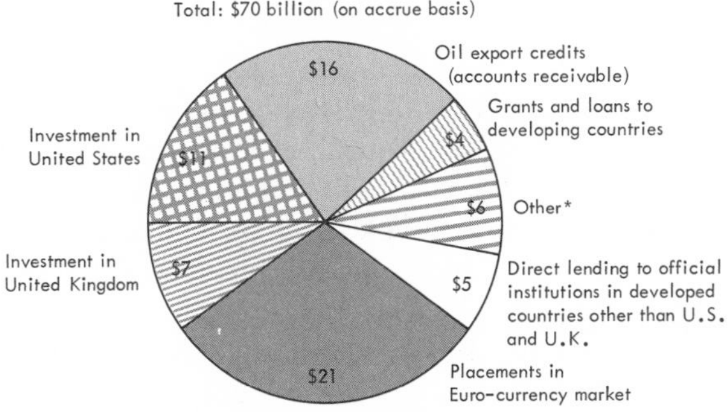

Source: Federal Reserve Bank of Chicago, *International Letter,* No. 218, April 18, 1975.

TABLE 4-1

Currency Depreciation in Selected Countries

Country	*Currency Unit*	*Unit per U.S. Dollar*		
		Nov. 1948	*Oct. 1969*	*June 1975**
Argentina	Peso	3.73	350.00	26.66*
Belgium	Franc	43.83	50.50	35.71
Brazil	Cruzeiro	18.50	3,660.00	7.87*
France	Franc	214.71	494.00	3.98*
India	Rupee	3.31	7.53	8.19
Mexico	Peso	4.86	12.50	12.49
Spain	Peseta	11.22	69.50	55.55
The Netherlands	Guilder	2.65	3.64	2.43
The United Kingdom	Pound	0.25	0.42	.44

*Not comparable to 1948 or 1969 figures.

Sources: Bernard A. Lietaer, "Managing Risks in Foreign Exchange," *Harvard Business Review,* March-April, 1970, p. 128; *The Wall Street Journal,* June 20, 1975, p. 18.

Since World War II, currency values have been gradually depreciating throughout the world. Table 4-1 indicates the magnitude of depreciation in selected countries. During the period 1948 to 1970, nearly one hundred countries underwent one or more rounds of devaluation of their exchange rates. Even the dominance of the American dollar has been seriously questioned in recent years. The deteriorating U.S. balance of payments and the international reserve position caused the dollar to sink nearly 50 percent in value from 1969 to 1974. Britain and France experienced similar problems. Britain devalued the pound in 1949 and in 1967; France devalued the franc in 1957 and again in 1969.

Declining currency values and devaluations have serious implications for financial management abroad. Depending upon the amount of imported materials and services utilized in the manufacturing process, devaluation will affect different firms differently. If a foreign firm uses more imported materials and services than local firms, devaluation will immediately increase the cost of production by increasing the local currency cost of imported items. Second, devaluation will also increase the local currency cost of foreign indebtedness, whether borrowed from financial institutions or through intracompany loan, by the amount of devaluation. For the parent company, devaluation of a foreign currency will reduce the dollar value of the foreign subsidiaries' and affiliates' local earnings unless profits in the local currency are simultaneously raised to cover the devaluation. More important, devaluation reduces the dollar value of the foreign subsidiary's assets by the magnitude of the change in exchange rates (the opposite happens if the dollar is devalued).

Inflation

Of course, this depreciation is both a consequence of and a contributing factor to the inflationary process throughout the world. The inflationary pressure has been universal throughout the postwar period, although it differs in intensity in different countries. Although the less developed nations are the hardest hit by inflation, recent price trends (wholesale and consumer prices) in industrialized countries showed tremendous increases between 1971 and 1974. However, the year 1975 witnessed a slowing down of inflation, largely due to continued weak overall economic conditions. According to recent OECD data, consumer prices in the twenty-four member countries, taken as a group, rose at an annual rate of 9.5 percent during the three months ending February 1975.[8]

The price performance of individual countries, however, was mixed. While the inflation rate dropped in some countries, it accelerated in others. In Italy, consumer prices rose 23.3 percent in the twelve months ending February 1975, compared to a 19.1 percent rise in 1974 as a whole. In Britain, the rise was 19.8 percent (compared to 16 percent in 1974); in Belgium, 15.4 percent (12.6 percent); in France, 13.9 percent (13.6 percent); and in the United States, 11.1 percent (11 percent). Countries showing a marked deceleration in prices were Japan, where the inflation rate fell to 13.9 percent (compared to 24.4 percent in 1974); Switzerland, 8.4 percent (9.8 percent); and Sweden, 8.2 percent (9.4 percent). Germany, with the lowest rate of inflation among major countries (7 percent) registered a decline to 5.8 percent in the twelve months ending February 1975.

For foreign affiliates, the impact of inflation may stem from one or more of the following situations. Inflation, resulting in general price increases in the local economy, may increase the costs of domestically acquired raw materials, components, parts, and labor. If the company is exporting some of its output, it will be in an unfavorable position in the world market because of the difference between internal and external prices. Local governments may impose price controls in order to curb further inflation, which might reduce the foreign firm's profit if prices are restricted more than costs.

Inflation often increases the possibility of exchange controls, devaluation of currency, and higher tariffs and taxes, measures that have several implications for MNCs. As local governments attempt to curb inflation, higher tariffs and taxes may be expected. Increased tariffs, particularly when the import content of the operation is high, will hurt domestic operations. Similarly, higher taxes on business as a measure to contain inflation affects the company's financial planning and profit position. Inflation also discourages business savings and thereby accentuates the shortage of capital resources (which are already scarce in less developed countries) and increases the cost of capital. Uncertain import supplies, prices, and availability of liquid funds have the most damaging effect on cost considerations, sales forecasting, and financial planning.

When measures taken to curb inflation include tightening credit availability, efforts of subsidiaries and affiliates to balance liquid assets with local currency debt become more difficult. Not only does inflation erode the purchasing power of firms' financial assets, but it also weakens the external value of the currency—a process that, coupled with other factors, frequently leads to various sorts of exchange controls and devaluation. Under these conditions, the local government may impose restrictions on transfers of funds abroad that may limit movement of profits, dividends, and capital.

Depreciating currencies and devaluations may lead to substantial losses for multinational companies. For example, Exxon wrote off $55 million in 1971, and as long-term debts in revalued foreign currencies come due, will write off an additional $70 million through 1978. Goodyear Tire and Rubber wrote off $12 million in 1971. Hoechst, the giant German chemical company, announced a $26 million exchange loss in 1971. Gulf Oil wrote off $25 million in 1972. Of course, devaluation has the opposite effect on an exposed liability, and the company may realize a foreign exchange profit in this area. Gains may also occur on conversion of foreign earnings into home-country currency. For example, the sharply increased 1973 profits reported by the major American-based international oil companies were heavily influenced by gains on conversion of foreign earnings into dollars at the higher 1973 dollar exchange rates: Exxon gained $150 million; Mobil, $150 million; and Texaco, $116 million.[9]

MULTINATIONAL FINANCING

Multinational firms have a wide range of alternative sources for financing foreign operations. These sources range from the internal resources of the parent company, domestic sources in the parent country, and local sources of foreign subsidiaries to many regional and international sources. In other words, another major facet of multinational financial management involves raising funds to finance foreign affiliates.

Parent Firms' Domestic Sources

Internal financing is comprised of equity investment and loans from the parent company and its own retained earnings and depreciation. Recently, internal sources of funds have accounted for somewhat over 70 percent of the total financing of American-owned foreign affiliates.[10]

Apart from these, multinational firms have access to many sources of financing in the parent country. For example, there are a number of sources within the United States for loans and equity capital that can be utilized by American multinational firms. One such source is the Export-Import Bank, which was established to finance the foreign trade of the United States and is the single largest source of direct financing for private American international traders and investors. The export activities of the bank consist of financing, guaranteeing, and insuring payment for goods and services of American origin.

Affiliates of United States commercial banks chartered under the Edge Act to engage exclusively in foreign operations, provide both loans and equity capital to multinational concerns. They provide venture capital to new enterprises as well as capital to assist in expansion and modernization of established enterprises. The loans provided range from short- to intermediate-term. In recent years, a new type of merchant and investment bank specializing in equity financing of multinational ventures and in development loans has emerged. These banks may invest in business in the form of equity and may underwrite stock issues. Some of them may also make direct loans for working capital and refunding purposes. Some of the firms in this category are American Express Company, American Investment Corporation, International Basic Economy Corporation, and Overseas Investors, Inc. Similar facilities are also available in many developed countries—Belgium, England, France, Germany, Italy, The Netherlands and so on.[11]

International Sources

One of the major sources of finance for multinational firms is the Euro-currency market.[12] Any currency deposited outside the home country can be called Euro-currency. The Euro-currency market is truly an international capital market undisturbed by the regulations of any national state. Although many currencies are included in its operations, Eurodollars represent about 50 percent of the transactions. The other major Euro-currencies are British pounds, German marks, and French and Swiss francs. Eurodollars are dollar deposits held with European banks but expressed in dollars instead of local currencies. This practice, started by the European banks, involves accepting dollar deposits and making dollar loans to give owners of dollars a non-American alternative for banking their holdings, and to enable borrowers to satisfy their requirements through European sources. The major reason for depositing dollars outside the United States is so that the depositor can earn higher interest on his Eurodollar deposit. In the United States, the Federal Reserve Bank forbids interest on demand deposits and limits interest on time deposits.

Euro-currencies are available for short- and medium-term financing and to some extent for long-term financing. The long-term financing is usually achieved through Eurobonds.[13] Eurobonds are securities expressed in Euro-currencies and floated in international capital markets. Interest on these currencies depends on a number of factors, such as general money market conditions, the credit standing of the borrowing company, and the duration of the loan itself. Eurobonds are available for terms of five to fifteen years, and exist in any internationally traded currency such as German marks or Swiss francs. Significantly, though, the bulk of the market is in American dollars.

A number of international agencies directly or indirectly engage in limited and selected financing of international trade and investment. Among them, the International Bank for Reconstruction and Development (World Bank or IBRD), the International Development Association (IDA), and the International Finance Corporation (IFC) are the important ones. The purpose of these agencies is to assist the economic growth of less developed countries by making direct loans, providing technical assistance, subscribing to shares, and underwriting financial commitments. Some of these facilities are available to foreign firms, joint ventures, local firms, and government bodies. Multinational companies that can (a) demonstrate the benefits of their project to the economic growth of less developed countries, (b) document that normal financing is not available, and (c) show that the project is acceptable to the host government often have a good chance of obtaining some of their capital requirements through these sources.

Another source of financing multinational business ventures is international private capital. ADELA Investment Company, S.A. (The Atlantic Development Group for Latin America) is one of the newest and most publicized investment companies jointly formed by multinational corporations and banks from the United States, Western Europe, Canada, and Japan. The basic purpose of ADELA is to promote the development of local economies by making minority investments in both national and international business enterprises in Latin America. ADELA is an investment company and derives its income from interest, dividend, and capital appreciation. The company also engages in debt financing and underwriting activities, with or without the assistance of other national and international financial institutions. Its debt financing usually involves equity participation or some equity features such as stock options, conversion rights, or profit incentives. ADELA also provides management and technical assistance.

ADELA has added another possible source of financing for business operations in these countries. Currently, ADELA is supported by more than two hundred multinational enterprises and has about $350 million of outstanding loans and investments to nearly 400 companies ranging from agricultural processors to capital goods manufacturers in more than twenty countries. One indication of the success of ADELA is the formation of similar institutions in other parts of the world—for example, the Private Investment Corporation for Asia (PICA), formed to facilitate capital investment in private enterprises in the less developed nations of Asia.[14]

Subsidiaries' Local Sources

Another major source of finance for multinational firms is their subsidiaries' local sources. Throughout the world, commercial banks provide short-term financial resources to business enterprises. Both local banking institutions and branches of foreign banks are primary sources of local currency financing. It is possible to obtain local loans by overdrafts, factoring receivables and customers' drafts, or pledging inventories. Opportunities to obtain secured financing using assets other than receivables and inventories are also expanding in a number of countries. On the whole, overdrafts are the most common short-term borrowing instrument in Europe. Overdrafts, discounted bills, and short-term loans are the most common instruments in Asia and Latin America.

Local banks also extend medium- and long-term credits in a number of forms—renewable drafts, bridge loans, medium-term loans, and rediscountable medium-term loans. In granting medium-term loans (loans maturing in one to several years), commercial banks pay particular attention to the borrowing company's anticipated sources of repayment and examine critically the cash flow generated from operations. Real estate or equipment is commonly pledged to secure the medium-term loans, and the lending bank is more likely to impose conditions on the operations of the borrowing subsidiary. Medium-term loan facilities are available in Belgium, Germany, the United Kingdom, The Netherlands, Switzerland, and other countries.

Long-term financing is available primarily in connection with the purchase of fixed assets such as plant and equipment. When granting a long-term loan, commercial banks analyze the borrowing subsidiary's long-term market potential, management capability, technological position, and so on. Security is usually required. Long-term debt financing in the form of promissory notes is usually secured by a pledge of specific assets such as plant, real estate, and equipment, in addition to a parent company guarantee.

Equity is another form of direct long-term financing available from commercial banks in certain countries. Through equity participation, commercial banks become part owners of enterprises and are entitled to a share in earnings. The bank shares in both the risk and the profitability of the company being financed under this system. Commercial banks are also important intermediaries between the company and investors when the securities of the multinational concern are being placed on the market. Depending upon market conditions, it is sometimes possible to make a private placement of notes or debentures through banks, finance companies, or brokerage houses.

If the company does not insist on a wholly owned arrangement or if local conditions make it necessary, the sale of common or preferred stock can be an excellent source of local currency financing. In countries such as Japan, Mexico, Argentina, and Brazil, and in most European countries, there are fairly well-developed stock markets (or bourses) that facilitate such equity financing.

Group Cash Reserves

Surplus liquidity frequently exists in various parts of the multinational corporation. Some affiliates may have excess cash or near-cash assets that can be relied upon as a source of short-term financing. For example, Mobil Oil's practice of coordinated deployment of network cash resources has resulted in substantial cost savings to the company.

Top financial managers of MNCs are constantly searching for some measure of centralized control over cash while leaving their subsidiaries some freedom to "optimize" the financial choices open to them. As *The Economist* noted, it is the European-based multinationals (mostly those in Britain, Holland, and Switzerland) that tend to be more centralized than their American counterparts when it comes to managing group cash reserves.[15] Multinationals such as Shell and Unilever, which are based in London, apparently keep their central cash in sterling in London. Since these two giants also have a second base in Rotterdam, they have a second central pool there.

Holding liquidity in foreign currencies means running a risk in terms of the balance-sheet currency of the parent firm; holding it in home currency does not. Doing so, however, may mean missing some opportunities to make handsome profits.

FORECASTING THE ENVIRONMENT

Having considered the multinational financial environment and alternative sources of financing operations, we now shift our focus to the task of forecasting future changes so that appropriate measures can be taken to minimize financial risks. Since there is considerable diversity and uncertainty in managing financial resources in a multinational context, the forces underlying these uncertainties in each country must be studied by multinational firms. In other words, multinational managers must be able to understand the forces at work when exchange controls and devaluations occur.

High inflationary trends are a leading indicator of exchange controls and/or devaluation, though many other factors are also involved. The forecasting of inflation is more or less an estimate of future price levels. The estimate is reached by an analysis of the determinants of the general level of prices, especially of what might well be called the leading indicators of inflationary trends:[16]

1. Continuous deficit spending by the host government
2. Substantial increases in business spending
3. Changes in private expectations about prices
4. Restrictions on imports
5. Government attitudes toward inflation as a tool of growth
6. Pressure of wage increases
7. Government's political and technical ability to curb inflation
8. Possibility of wartime inflationary pressures
9. Local employment

A number of measures are available to multinational firms for minimizing foreign exchange losses.[17] To reduce exposure, local cash, receivables, inventories, and other current assets should be minimized.[18] Receivables should be reduced to the extent local operating circumstances permit under inflationary conditions. Companies can promote rapid payment through discounts for early payment as long as the value of the discount does not exceed the expected loss. It may be worthwhile to minimize investments in inventories. If the affiliate depends on imported materials, it may be profitable to buy surplus materials before anticipated exchange controls, higher tariffs, and devaluation come into force. At times, foreign suppliers' insistence on prepayment is a convenient excuse to move money out of the country while there is still a favorable exchange rate. Prepaid expenses, such as deposits on materials, insurance premiums, and other business expenses, except deposits on imported materials, should be kept as low as possible. In reaching a decision on inventory level, managers should consider these factors against inventory carrying costs.

Another alternative is to utilize, as much as possible, local sources of debt capital so that home country costs will be less after devaluation. Apart from local financial sources, it is possible to use locally denominated funds, which are available to some United States firms. For example, Cooley funds are generated by the sale of surplus U.S. farm commodities. It is also beneficial to arrange all or most short-term borrowing from local sources. Use of local sources could take the form of outright bank loans, issuance of bonds, and so on. The choice of the form in which local capital will be used will depend on availability and cost.

Accelerating remission should be actively pursued if local authorities appear likely to institute exchange restrictions. Whenever possible companies should prepay—or at least hedge—foreign currency obligations through future contracts and "swaps," including anticipated dividend payments. Minimizing vulnerable balances through prompt remission of earnings in inflation-ridden countries may be another means to reduce losses from depreciation.

If the net rate of return is higher than the rate at which a currency loses its value, then the company is ahead of the depreciated value. This means the local profit margin must be high enough to absorb the decline in currency value and still provide a good return on investment. Pricing and sales terms should be adjusted frequently enough to keep ahead of, or at least up to, the rate of inflation. Pricing must reflect estimated replacement costs, not existing inventory cost. Changes in pricing must provide enough lead time to cover the cycle from purchase to collection. Cash discounts and past-due interest charges must relate to local money costs, or they will not be effective in speeding up collections.

The task of forecasting environmental conditions, then, is an exceedingly difficult one. Frequently fluctuating market conditions and lack of readily available statistical information are crucial problems. Nonetheless, there must be constant effort on the part of corporate management to collect and analyze whatever information is available in the area of the financial environment. Moreover, there must be constant effort to compare the cost of utilizing different techniques with the value of achieving the improvement. Appropriate measures will vary from situation to situation, depending upon local conditions, government policies, the international financial situation, and the long-run objectives of the company. The methods and techniques given here for minimizing foreign exchange losses are only an indication of those that have been used successfully by alert companies in the multinational arena.

MULTINATIONAL FINANCIAL STRATEGY

Diversity in the economic and financial environment imposes certain costs and risks on the multinational firm, since greater knowledge and flexibility are required. These costs, however, are frequently offset by greater opportunity for higher profits and other benefits. Given the lack of convertibility of many currencies, the possibility of devaluation, several kinds of currency needs and sources, and the importance of ensuring financial success, managing a multinational enterprise obviously requires attention to many situations simultaneously and a global approach to financial planning.

Under these conditions, multinational financial strategy requires added attention. Knowing its needs, available funds, interest rates, exchange conditions, tax liabilities, and forecasting inflation and impending devaluation will help the company to channel its resources so as to provide funds at the lowest possible cost and take advantage of exchange rate fluctuations. But in order to utilize opportunities, the MNC must understand the forces that affect foreign exchange rates. This rightly suggests the need for information on many markets classified by country, the legal and political problems of fund movements, the economics of foreign exchange transactions, and the tax implications of various alternatives. The MNC's should also be familiar with markets that permit it to move funds from one country to another, or protect it against foreign exchange losses. Management's task is to be aware of what is happening in the financial systems of different countries and in the international arena and to develop plans that will minimize risk and optimize returns.

In contrast to the risks involved, multinational financing also provides opportunities for planned preventive measures and for making larger profits.[19] First, in facing foreign environments, multinational companies have advantages over firms with just one or two foreign operations—superior maneuverability and greater choice of options. If necessary, management anticipates payments to subsidiaries in different countries in order to take full advantage of market situations.

Second, a number of companies have protected themselves against loss from inflation and devaluation of other currencies vis-à-vis the U.S. dollar (or other "hard" currency) by borrowing substantially from sources within the countries where subsidiaries are located and then entering into forward exchange contracts, according to which currencies will be delivered on specific future dates. In addition, whenever possible arrangements are made for certain portions of the exports of subsidiaries to be paid for in hard currencies. As a result, devaluation has had little or no adverse effect on some MNCs, and in some cases has even been beneficial.

Multinational companies can use their multiple bases to keep money costs down, for example, by taking advantage of low interest rates in one country to supply the working capital needs of operations in high-interest areas. They can ship components or finished goods between subsidiaries on open account and take no immediate payment, thereby utilizing the excess working capital in one subsidiary for the benefit of another and taking advantage of lower interest rates. Exchange-rate planning has become a highly developed tactic in many multinational enterprises; in fact, the foreign exchange forecasting staff of one large multinational firm claims to have made more profit for the company in some years than the production and sales staffs.

This analysis implies that a multinational firm should be considered as a system and that it will perform well when the opportunities growing out of that system are fully understood and exploited. According to Robbins and Stobaugh, the system consists of units (subsystems) operating in different countries with differing environments.[20] The units are connected through a series of links made up of methods of transferring funds between them. Within certain limits—such as government regulation and financial markets—the flows within the system are subject to manipulation through corporate financial policy (for example, dividend policy, transfer price policy, lending policy).[21] The multinational firm can make use of policy tools to obtain the best results for the system or company as a whole. With such a systems approach, the financial strategy of the multinational company will maximize profit for the company as a whole rather than for its parts.

The systems approach has not yet become common in practice, although the financial systems of multinational firms develop in a predictable pattern as foreign business grows. Generally speaking, small firms, often new to multinational operations, tend to consider each subsidiary as a separate entity; the subsidiaries operate independently, with little use being made of intercompany financial links. The result is to suboptimize results for the whole company. As the multinational firm grows to medium size, managers learn how to operate in a wider environment. The importance of the foreign business grows and as a result management becomes more centralized and oriented toward optimizing results for the whole system. The large firms are generally conscious of the total system concept, but their very size hinders them from fully exploiting its benefits. These companies face the dilemma of wanting to keep tight control over foreign operations but being unable to do so in practice because of sheer size and complexity. In other words, a strategy for the whole system that takes into account all relevant objectives has usually proved too complicated to execute.

SUMMARY

This chapter has presented a selection of fundamental issues in multinational finance to pinpoint some of the key problems affecting the financial management of multinational business.

Multinational financial management is much more complex than and differs significantly from domestic patterns due to differences among countries in currencies, financial resources, institutions, government policies, and other variables. Operating in such multiple financial environments means that managers need to be constantly alert and responsive to a number of variables—inflation, exchange rate depreciation, devaluation, the availability and cost of different sources of funds, tax structures, and so forth. Multinational firms have a wide range of alternative sources for financing their foreign operations—the internal resources of the parent firm, domestic sources in the parent country, local subsidiaries' sources, and regional and international sources. The alternative sources selected will, of course, depend on the availability and cost of capital, government regulations, and risk factors. Under these conditions, a financial strategy based on company needs, availability of funds, interest rates, and forecasts of inflation and devaluation will make it possible for the company to minimize its financial risks and employ its resources most productively. On the whole, a multinational company will perform best when it is considered as a system and the opportunities growing out of that system are fully understood and exploited.

Notes

[1]Richard Kaufman, "Assessing the International Financial Environment," in S. P. Sethi and J. N. Sheth, *Multinational Business Operations: Financial Management* (Pacific Palisades, Calif.: Goodyear, 1973), p. 3.

[2]Dan T. Smith, "Tax Policy and Foreign Investment," *Law and Contemporary Problems,* 34, 1, winter 1969, pp. 146-56.

[3]For a detailed discussion of foreign exchange problems, see David B. Zenoff and Jack Zwick, *International Financial Management* (Englewood Cliffs, N.J.: Prentice-Hall, 1969); also David K. Eiteman and Arthur Stonehill, *Multinational Business Finance* (Reading, Mass.: Addison-Wesley, 1973).

[4]For a discussion of the International Monetary Fund, see Franklin R. Root, *International Trade and Investment* (Cincinnati: South-Western, 1973), pp. 455-64.

[5]See, for example, H. B. Chenery, "Restructuring the World Economy," *Foreign Affairs,* January 1975, pp. 242-63.

[6]Alan Teck, "Control Your Exposure to Foreign Exchange," *Harvard Business Review,* January-February 1974, pp. 67-68.

[7]Margret G. de Vries, "Multiple Exchange Rates: Expectations and Experiences," *IMF Staff Papers,* July 1965, pp. 282-313. For full coverage of the existing foreign exchange restrictions, see IMF Annual Report on exchange restrictions.

[8]Federal Reserve Bank of Chicago, *International Letter,* No. 217, April 11, 1975.

[9]John T. Wooster and Richard Thoman, "New Financial Priorities for MNCs," *Harvard Business Review,* May-June 1974, p. 59. For a discussion of the accounting problems of conversion of foreign earnings into home country currency, see Marvin M. Deupree, "Translating Foreign Currency Financial Statements to U.S. Dollars," *Financial Executive,* October 1972, pp. 48-68; also Edgar Barrett and Leslie L. Spero, "Accounting Determinants of Foreign Exchange Gains and Losses," *Financial Analysts Journal,* March-April 1975, pp. 26-29.

[10]James C. Van Horne, *Fundamentals of Financial Management* (Englewood Cliffs, N.J.: Prentice-Hall, 1974), pp. 504-5.

[11]For a discussion of these sources see Zenoff and Zwick, *op. cit.,* pp. 340-48.

[12]"Euro-Dollar Market," *Monthly Review* (Federal Reserve Bank of Richmond), April 1967, pp. 8-10; also Root, *op. cit.,* pp. 492-94.

[13]Gunter Dufey, "The Eurobond Market: Its Significance for International Financial Management," *Journal of International Business Studies,* summer 1970, pp. 65-77.

[14]Exxon Corporation, *Multinational Enterprise* (New York: Exxon Corporation, 1973), p. 5.

[15]*The Economist,* December 14, 1974, pp. 83-84.

[16]Zenoff and Zwick, *op. cit.,* pp. 65-96.

[17]For an interesting computerized model for hedging against devaluation, see Bernard A. Lietaer, "Managing Risks in Foreign Exchange," *Harvard Business Review,* March-April 1970, pp. 127-38; also see Teck, *op. cit.,* pp. 70-72; and Horace C. Walton, "Foreign Currency—To Hedge or Not To Hedge," *Financial Executive,* April 1974, pp. 48-53. For a discussion of the experiences of Chrysler Corporation in managing its foreign exchange, see Robert K. Ankrom, "Top Level Approach to the Foreign Exchange Problem," *Harvard Business Review,* July-August 1974.

[18]For a discussion of the problems and options open to multinational firms in managing liquid funds, see Richard K. Goeltz, "Managing Liquid Funds Internationally," *Columbia Journal of World Business,* August 1972, pp. 59-65.

[19]Sanford Rose, "The Rewarding Strategies of Multinationalism," *Fortune,* September 15, 1968, pp. 100-5, 182-83; "How a Multinational Firm Protects Its Flanks in Monetary Dealings," *The Wall Street Journal,* August 1971, pp. 1, 10.

[20]Sidney M. Robbins and Robert B. Stobaugh, *Money in the Multinational Enterprise* (New York: Basic Books, 1973); also, "Growth of the Financial Function," *Financial Executive,* July 1973, pp. 24-31.

[21]For a discussion of internal financial policies, see Michael Brooke and Lee Remmers, *The Strategy of Multinational Enterprise* (New York: American Elsevier, 1970), pp. 157-76.

Suggested Readings

FOREIGN BANKS IN THE UNITED STATES

BRIMMER, ANDREW F., "Multi-National Banks and the Management of Monetary Policy in the United States," *Journal of Finance,* May 1973, 439-54.

EDWARDS, FRANKLIN R., "Regulation of Foreign Banking in the United States: International Reciprocity and Federal-State Conflicts." *Columbia Journal of Transnational Law,* 1974, pp. 239-68 (Columbia University, Graduate School of Business, Research Paper No. 64).

———AND JACK ZWICK, "Foreign Banks in the United States: Activities and Regulatory Issues," statement prepared for U.S. Congress, Senate Banking, Housing and Urban Affairs Committee, 94th Cong., 1st Sess. *Congressional Record,* March 5, 1975, pp. 3082-90.

European-American Banking Corporation, "Sources of Capital and Methods of Financing Investments in the United States," in *Direct Investment in the United States,* ed. Leonard C. Yassen, European-American Banking Corporation, 1974, pp. 41-56.

"Foreign Banking in North America," Part 1, "The United States," *Banker*, April 1974, pp. 341-43.

GILBERT, ABBY, "Foreign Banking Operations in the United States," *SAIS Review,* Johns Hopkins University School of Advanced International Studies, winter 1971, pp. 20-33.

JOHNSON, JAMES A., "Foreign Banking in the United States," *Vanderbilt Journal of Transnational Law,* spring 1973, pp. 595-623.

KLOPSTOCK, FRED H., "Foreign Banks in the United States: Scope and Growth of Operations," *Monthly Review* (Federal Reserve Bank of New York), June 1973, pp. 140-54.

LEES, FRANCIS A., "Foreign Investment in U.S. Banks," *Mergers and Acquisitions,* fall 1973, pp. 4-15.

MACKENZIE, ROBERT D., AND ROGER D. MACKENZIE, "Penetration of the United States Market by a Foreign Bank," *International Lawyer,* 1972, pp. 876-88.

MIKESELL, RAYMOND F., "Foreign Dollar Balances in the United States," *Euromoney,* February 1972, pp. 14ff.

MIOSSI, ALFRED F., "Foreign Banking in the U.S.—Protectionism versus Competition," *Euromoney,* June 1974, pp. 28ff.

NADLER, PAUL S., "Invasion of Foreign Funds—Meaning for U.S. Banks," *Bankers Monthly,* August 1973, pp. 23-25.

STABLER, CHARLES N., "Foreign Banks Expand U.S. Operations, Stir Some Alarm, Resistance," *The Wall Street Journal,* May 10, 1973, pp. 1f.

U.S. Board of Governors of the Federal Reserve System, "Foreign Bank Act of 1974: Summary of Principal Features," press release with bill and analysis. Washington, D.C., December 3, 1974.

GENERAL REFERENCE

Pick's Currency Yearbook (New York: Pick Publishing, 1974).

CASES FOR ANALYSIS

CULLMAN, W. ARTHUR, AND HARRY R. KNUDSON, eds., *Management Problems in International Environments* (Englewood Cliffs, N.J.: Prentice-Hall, 1972), Brooke Bond & Co., Ltd., pp. 4-22; Companhia Uniao Fabril, pp. 22-39.

The time frame for the Brooke Bond case is early 1968, and the finance director of this large tea company faces the issue of a strategic diversification into the packaged meat market. Being the first diversification move for Brooke Bond, the case is illustrative of the multicountry variables to be taken into account by the firm's Diversification Committee.

The problem of debt financing is at the heart of the Companhia Uniao Fabril case. Still undecided about the denomination of the bonds, the chief executive considers three alternatives: Eurodollars, European unit-of-account bonds, or a multiple currency issue denominated in escudos, dollars, and marks.

Also see the Champion Manufacturing Company case, which deals with the problem of managing financial assets in an inflationary economy, in David B. Zenoff and Jack Zwick, *International Financial Management* (Englewood Cliffs, N.J.: Prentice-Hall, 1969), pp. 258-267.

Part II: Management Dimensions

5

Multinational Corporate Planning

As business entities transcend different national subsystems with varying environmental conditions, corporate planning must become responsive to different sets of conditions. Expansion beyond national boundaries is much more than a step across a geographical line; it is an entrance into a different realm of social, political, economic, and technological forces. Multinational corporate planning thus entails scanning the world environment, assessing a wider range of variables, and coming up with an option that enhances the company's effectiveness as a multinational business. In other words, planning in a multinational context requires attention to diverse and uncertain national and market environments. It is essential to optimizing performance abroad. An increasing number of multinationals are therefore deliberately introducing a substantial element of planning into their overseas operations.

The purpose of this chapter is threefold: First, to identify and analyze how corporate planning by multinational firms differs from that of purely domestic firms; second, to discuss the processes of planning and implementation within the multinational context; and third, to consider the value of corporate planning for companies operating on a global scale.

CORPORATE PLANNING IN THE MULTINATIONAL CONTEXT

Planning in the multinational context is concerned with (a) determining major goals for the enterprise as a whole as well as for its subsidiaries, and (b) adopting essential courses of action in terms of policies, programs, and action plans throughout the enterprise to achieve the predetermined goals. Planning can be defined in terms of the kinds of problems confronted and classified as strategic or long-range, or operational and short-range. Decisions involving issues that are basic to a multinational firm's long-term well-being and vitality can be considered strategic, whereas planning that contends with operational problems can be called short-range. Strategic and operational plans are interdependent, and both are important for multinational companies.

Strategic planning develops major goals, strategies, and programs and deploys corporate resources in pursuit of these goals. Within this framework, the company establishes short-run plans that cover in detail the targets and action programs for the immediate future. The short-range operating plans spell out the tactics to be used by the company in achieving its goals.[1]

Multinational planning differs from domestic planning because of the inherent variability of environmental conditions. Table 5-1 highlights the ways in which planning needs to be modified in multinational operations. Developing plans for business activities (operating in diverse environments) is not an easy task; it is even more arduous when numerous organizations must be utilized. More complex than planning for domestic operations, it provides an unprecedented challenge for multinational managers.[2] For example, working with people from different countries who speak different languages makes two-way communication, which is an important ingredient of effective planning between headquarters and field offices, more difficult. Added to this is the problem of physical distance as it affects transmitting and receiving information and makes it difficult to achieve the same degree of effectiveness in multinational operations as in domestic ones.

The most obvious distinction between multinational and domestic firms lies in the environmental framework in which the firms operate and make decisions. The multiplicity of market environments presents both risks and opportunities of a kind not normally encountered within the domestic sphere, for elements of unfamiliarity and complexity are inherent in multiple environments. Different environments also exhibit different rates of change. This is particularly true in such areas as economic growth, inflation, political instability, and legal restrictions. High rates of inflation tend to decrease the value of a company's investments abroad much faster than new opportunities develop. Political instability in some cases threatens investments.

Like domestic planning, multinational planning requires comprehensive information. Information is needed on environmental factors and their changing dimensions at the time of planning as well as continuously in order to monitor,

TABLE 5-1

Domestic Versus International Planning

Domestic	*International*
1. Single language and nationality	1. Multilingual/multinational/multicultural factors
2. Relatively homogeneous market	2. Fragmented and diverse markets
3. Data available, usually accurate and collection easy	3. Data collection a formidable task, requiring significantly higher budgets and personnel allocation
4. Political factors relatively unimportant	4. Political factors frequently vital
5. Relative freedom from government interference	5. Involvement in national economic plans; government influences business decisions
6. Individual corporation has little effect on environment	6. "Gravitational" distortion by large companies
7. Chauvinism helps	7. Chauvinism hinders
8. Relatively stable business environment	8. Multiple environments, many of which are highly unstable (but may be highly profitable)
9. Uniform financial climate	9. Variety of financial climates ranging from overconservative to wildly inflationary
10. Single currency	10. Currencies differing in stability and real value
11. Business "rules of the game" mature and understood	11. Rules diverse, changeable and unclear
12. Management generally accustomed to sharing responsibilities and using financial controls	12. Management frequently autonomous and unfamiliar with budgets and controls

Source: William W. Cain, "International Planning: Mission Impossible," *Columbia Journal of World Business,* July-August, 1970, p. 58. Reprinted with permission. Copyright © 1970 by the Trustees of Columbia University in the City of New York.

and if necessary to modify, goals and strategies in the light of changed conditions. However, data useful for planning purposes vary widely among the nations of the world in scope, availability, and reliability. Basic economic and social statistics are still in a somewhat primitive stage in a number of countries. Subjects such as the size of markets, growth records, industry projections, competitive standings, and profitability are difficult to discern. Companies find it difficult to conduct market research. In many foreign countries the information needed for planning is not readily available and may be impossible to develop to the same degree of reliability generally achieved in countries like the United States.

The multinational corporation must adapt to the environments of the various nations in which it operates, and to supranational environments as well—for example, the European Common Market. The nature of these environments, their particular patterns of operation and change, affect multinational corporate planning.

These and other differences make planning for multinational operations far more difficult and demanding than domestic planning. At the same time, planning is even more essential to identify threats and opportunities that can have a real impact on the company's immediate and future growth. Consequently, as Franko noted, pressures for a multinational approach to corporate planning have reached a critical level for American and other foreign-based multinational firms.[3]

PLANNING AND IMPLEMENTATION PROCESSES

Planning in multinational firms varies from company to company in terms of time dimension, process, approach, and content. Certain similarities, however, can be identified and analysed. For many American-based multinational firms, planning for global operations is a comparatively new experience. They have gone multinational only during the last two decades or so. Some corporate managements have therefore not yet fully included the multinational environment in their purview.[4] In addition, corporate planning itself is a relatively new concept for domestic American business. Experience at home has not yet developed to the point where methodology, content, approach, and tools can routinely be applied to overseas operations. As a result, multinational planning as a corporate activity is not yet fully understood, accepted, and practiced. Furthermore, it has been rather difficult for many United States firms to get overseas managers, whether nationals or expatriates, to accept or use planning with the same fervor with which it is used by domestic executives. As a result, multinational planning is only slowly attaining the level of quality achieved in the domestic sphere.

The time dimension of strategic planning in multinational companies depends on both external and internal conditions, such as the type of business, the rates of economic and social change, technical complexity, and the degree of sophistication of the company's approach. Generally speaking, a majority of multinational firms—American and foreign-based—develop long-range plans with a time horizon of about five years. A few firms plan for ten years or more, another few for three years or less. For example, Sperry Rand uses a five-year stratetic planning system. The company's rationale for developing a five-year plan is that such a period is the longest for which it can make meaningful forecasts. Short-range operational plans often encompass one year, and in a few cases, two years. For example, IBM has a two-year operational plan that is updated annually to take into account unexpected developments. Operational plans contain highly detailed information for the company as a whole as well as for its units. From this short-range plan, budgets are developed for operational activities.

The whole process of planning can be usefully categorized into a set of interrelated sequential activities.[5] A conceptual presentation of these components and their interrelationships is shown in Figure 5-1. The most effective planning would consist of (1) a realistic assessment of external environmental conditions; (2) an objective assessment of company resources and capabilities; (3) the development of strategic corporate objectives; and (4) the formulation of long-range action programs and tactical plans.

FIGURE 5-1

The International Corporate Planning Process[a]

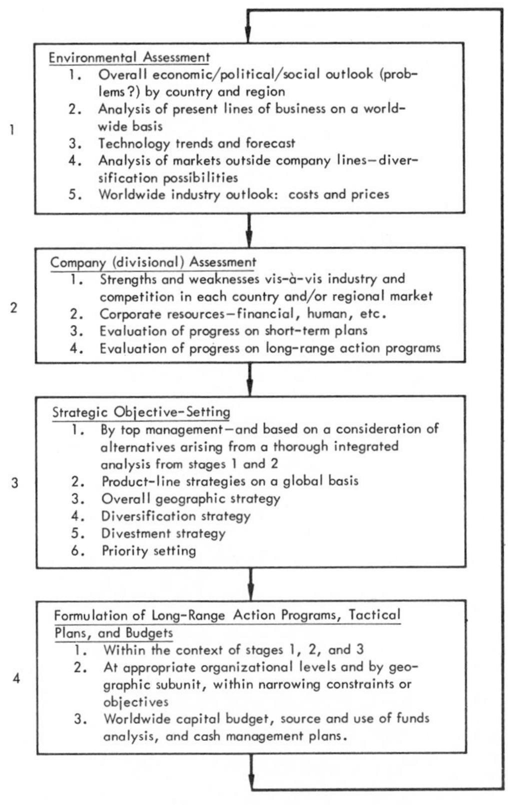

[a] This flow of activities is considered on a yearly cycle basis.

Source: John S. Schwendiman, *Strategic and Long-Range Planning for the Multinational Corporation* (New York: Praeger, 1973), p. 72. Reproduced with permission. © 1973 by Praeger Publishers, Inc., New York.

The External Assessment

The first step in developing strategic plans is to assess the environmental conditions and forecast changes in these conditions for each country or a region in which the company operates or intends to become active. The main purpose of this analysis and assessment is to identify the best opportunities throughout the world. Identifying these opportunities, of course, requires a great deal of fact gathering and analysis of a number of environmental conditions. Those that may need careful analysis are the following:[6]

General economic conditions and trends

Stages and rates of economic growth

Income size and growth pattern

Growth and pattern of world trade

International monetary conditions and trends

Sensitivity of foreign economies to fluctuations

International relations and commercial policy

Political environment and stability

Government regulation and market structure

Incentives and attitudes toward foreign investment

Exchange controls and balance of payments situation

Population growth and distribution

Education and quality of human resources

Relative availability of labor, material, and financial resources

Technological development relating to firm's products and operations

Worldwide trends in prices, costs, and so on

As an illustration, let us consider the matter of economic environment, particularly the relative stage of economic growth of a particular country. Following the system developed by Walt Rostow, it is possible to classify different countries on the basis of their particular development phase: traditional countries establishing the preconditions for take-off; countries taking off; countries driving toward maturity; and countries in the period of high mass consumption. This would provide corporate planners with some notion of where a particular company's products fit at each stage. For example, high mass-consumption products will find few markets in a pre-take-off country.

Inflation, commodity shortages, and OPEC have combined to transform the economic status and prospects of most countries for better or worse. Arguing that these changes require a fresh look at the relative strength of nations, and based upon the balance of payment prospects of particular countries, I. S. Friedman has recently developed the following fourfold classification:[7]

1. Rich-Poor (rich in financial might but poor in social and material status of people)	Equador, Gabon, Iran, Iraq, Kuwait, Libya, Nigeria, Saudi Arabia, Venezuela
2. Poor-Poor (favorable balance of payments prospects)	Algeria, Argentina, Bolivia, Brazil, Chile, Colombia, Indonesia, Malaysia, Mexico, Peru, Thailand, Zaire, Zambia
3. Poorer-Poor (reasonable, or improving balance of payments prospects)	Afghanistan, Egypt, Ghana, Kenya, Pakistan, Sierra Leone, Sri Lanka, Sudan, Syria
4. Poorest-Poor (unfavorable balance of payments prospects)	Bangladesh, Burma, India, Niger, Tanzania, Uganda

Criteria for planning foreign operations in Europe, Africa, Asia, and Latin America will differ significantly from those for domestic planning. The regional grouping of countries to obtain data for planning may be useful, but such data should be carefully evaluated before they are used. The diverse nature of each region and of countries within a region make it difficult to obtain comparable data for analysis. As an illustration, although Bolivia and Argentina have essentially the same cultural heritage, their political environments and levels of sophistication differ substantially. As a result, different marketing strategies are needed. With each group of countries, decision criteria concerning planning vary because of differences in individual national situations.[8] To derive the full benefit of corporate strategic planning, programs must be developed on a country-by-country-basis before dovetailing them into regional and global plans.

The analysis should consider the immediate factors, but it should also anticipate the development likely to occur within each country during the life of a planning cycle. Such analysis requires a thorough knowledge of the environment. The consequences of poor analysis of alternatives available abroad can be costly. Useful analysis involves a country-by-country study of inherent opportunities that can contribute to a company's objectives.

The Internal Assessment

To be sound, corporate strategic planning must also be based on a thorough analysis and assessment of the company's internal environment, plus a sensitivity to its strengths and weaknesses. The plans of multinational firms are based not on what their managements would like to do, but on what they really can accomplish. Most firms are limited to some extent by factors unique to each company.

Therefore, an intelligent appraisal of company strengths and weaknesses facilitates the development of a corporate plan for multinational operations. The company assessment may include factors such as these:

Company position in the industry and country

Financial resources and strengths

Research and development capability

Marketing organization and policy

Distribution system and facilities

Organizational structure and capabilities

Manufacturing technology

Production location, facilities, and equipment

Planning, control, and information systems

Managerial resources and skills; management values

For example, the present financial strength of a multinational company and its financial history are relatively easy to measure. They represent one of the most important controlling factors in planning for overseas operations. Expanding multinationally involves substantial investment in research and development, marketing research, plant, and machinery. A financial analysis also helps planners to consider the matter of expanding financial resources to meet demands through a systematic program. Considering alternative financial sources offers clues to different approaches to mobilizing such resources.

Evaluating company capabilities requires an inventory of available and potential resources. Any analysis of these capabilities in addition to including a physical inventory, must evaluate relative strengths. Such an analysis leads to the identification of the firm's strengths and weaknesses. Knowledge of its weaknesses allows the multinational company to avoid putting strain on certain areas; knowledge of its strengths helps to pinpoint the areas on which to concentrate future efforts.

Strategic Objectives and Action Programs

Analysis of the external environment and projected trends as well as company resources and strengths provides a sound foundation for the realistic determination of strategic objectives in crucial areas. The basic questions that should be asked are these: Which countries to select? Which markets to serve with what products? What diversification plan to pursue? What targets to specify in sales, profit, rate of return on investment, and other areas? The goals for all these areas are then set in quantitative as well as qualitative terms for the entire enterprise and for its subsidiaries. Answers to these and other related questions are neither clear-cut nor arrived at simply. But proper questions will aid in establishing clear objectives in areas such as profitability, sales, technology, management development, and acquisition.

A clear set of objectives leads to a consideration of alternative courses of action that may be used to accomplish them, and the adoption of long-range plans for divisions, countries, and each of the major functional areas—finance, marketing, manufacturing, and research and development. Within this framework, the company can establish short-range operational plans with more specific goals and action programs. The implementation of these plans then serves as a feedback loop for control purposes, which in turn may be used in adapting the plans to changing conditions.

The amount of planning and the sophistication with which these analyses are conducted varies from company to company. In order to do an effective job, multinational firms need enormous amounts of internal and external data about their business environment throughout the world. However, as Keegan's research indicates, systematic methods for information scanning are not widespread in most multinational firms.[9] Only a limited number have organized computer-based information and planning systems. For example, Bendix International gathers worldwide data on population, GNP, road miles and vehicles, and competitive market shares, as well as forecasts and trends for the sixty-four countries and the ten major product categories with which the company operation is concerned.

Approach

Differing approaches are used by multinational companies in assigning planning roles for headquarters and national subsidiaries.[10] In broad terms, these approaches can be classified as centralized or top-down planning; decentralized or bottom-up planning; and interactive planning that continuously combines the efforts of headquarters as well as subsidiaries in the planning process in an interwoven fashion.

Many argue that planning in multinational companies should be decentralized. Differences in local conditions, such as market characteristics, national institutions, the legal environment, industry conditions, government policies, and so on, make it difficult to institute a uniform planning process throughout the company. For this reason, the responsibility for planning should be assigned to the managers of operating subsidiaries who are most familiar with the local environment. Under decentralized planning, the local operating units are made responsible for formulating objectives for their operations and programs and plans of action for achieving these objectives. After analyzing the conditions prevailing in their operating environments, local managers forecast future trends in order to develop a set of objectives for their respective operations. These plans then gradually move upward in the organizational hierarchy. Each higher level makes its plans based on those of all lower levels until the results are finally combined into objectives and intended courses of action for the corporate entity.

Multinational planning at Avery Products Corporation, San Marino, California, for example, is largely a decentralized activity.[11] Local managers must submit annual plans for the following three years according to a standard format. Each manager is requested to deal with external market conditions and how he intends to meet these conditions. In the first part, he has to specify (1) the major opportunities and the anticipated actions to exploit them; (2) the critical elements upon which the present and future success of the operations under his control depend as well as the major threats that may imperil it; (3) strengths and weaknesses in existing operations; and (4) the basic assumptions or premises upon which the quantitatively oriented plans of the second part are based.

The second part of the three-year planning package consists of the following items:

1. A summary of the profit plan including certain explanatory ratios such as gross and operating profits to net sales
2. A market analysis stating market size and market share for each major product line including an analysis of the relative competitive situations
3. Sales targets for each product line
4. A sales growth plan showing anticipated sales of existing and new products
5. Total sales per country
6. A production capacity analysis showing present capacity, capacity utilization, and planned capacity expansion
7. Financing and cost data for fixed assets
8. A flow-of-funds analysis
9. Return-on-investment calculations
10. Planned manpower requirements

Corporate headquarters reviews the plans submitted by local managers and final approval is granted after some dialog between headquarters and the local managers. Subsequently, these plans are incorporated into the overall corporate plan.

Ciba-Geigy, a Swiss multinational chemical and pharmaceutical firm, also utilizes a decentralized planning system. Each Ciba-Geigy subsidiary abroad is responsible for drawing up five-year plans in consultation with corporate management. The subsidiaries are then responsible for achieving the goals they have set forth in the plan, which is updated annually. According to the company, the manager of each subsidiary is expected to know what is going on in his operating environment. Corporate headquarters exerts its influence chiefly during the consultations to focus on the business targets contained in the plans. The planning program is backed up by a worldwide management information system (MIS), and every month headquarters is supplied with data from the foreign subsidiaries.[12]

The major advantages of this approach are that (a) the expertise and intimate knowledge of local managers who are close to their operating environment can be utilized effectively; (b) incorporation of explicit factors relevant to national goals can be blended into corporate goals; and (c) managers who will be responsible for attaining the goals are allowed an active role in determining them.

Centralized or top-down planning involves the establishment of global objectives by corporate headquarters in terms of growth, profitability, and so on. Overall potential and risk factors are analyzed and objectives established for the whole company and then for the operating units. These objectives are used by the subsidiaries as a basis for developing detailed operational plans in different functional areas. Planning at Pfizer International, an American-based multinational firm, illustrates such centralized planning:

> Pfizer International relies on a heavily centralized and coordinated planning format and procedure. The major thrust of strategic planning is from top management down because of the highly technical nature and scientifically oriented research and development programs of the company. The management of Pfizer believes that research and development programs and product advancement strategies are the keys to growth and profitability. Product planning strategies have to be integrated by top management with investment, finance, manufacturing, and other policies for the entire company. On the other hand, the local operating managements of national subsidiaries assume responsibility for advising in the formulation of the strategic plan; they are also responsible for developing tactical plans within the framework of the strategic plan and for implementing the plans.[13]

Centralized or top-down planning is especially appropriate for companies with subsidiary managers who are not very familiar with the concept and practice of long-range planning. Including both approaches, however, enhances the usefulness of multinational planning.[14] A company could start out with any approach. The local managers may be first asked to develop their projections of the long-range development of the operating units under their direct management and control. Or corporate headquarters may start by setting overall objectives and allocation of contributory goals. A number of firms are using this approach, which combines top-down and bottom-up planning.

For example, Imperial Chemical Industries (ICI), a British multinational firm, combines decentralized planning by its operating units and national subsidiaries with some centralized company-wide planning. Top management provides the direction of ICI's future development and lays down the following guidelines:

1. The intention of the company with regard to its position in the world chemical industry in terms of volume of sales, turnover, share of the market, and other basic criteria
2. The types of activity in which it wishes to be involved and to what extent
3. The pattern for expansion in particular areas such as the United States and Western Europe
4. The policy for overseas investment

The eight operating divisions and two subsidiary companies and major overseas subsidiaries are responsible for short- and long-term planning in their own areas of interest. For long-term planning (five to ten years), the operating divisions assess future market conditions, product potential, plant capacity, future developments in research, and so on, to formulate long-term plans. The divisions use detailed estimates for the next year and two to four subsequent years for short-term planning. The planning process is monitored, coordinated, and supplemented at the corporate level. Top management also formulates plans for research, personnel, and organization that require an overall view.[15]

Such planning requires continuous interaction between corporate headquarters and the operating subsidiaries so that differing assumptions, inconsistencies, and conflicts can be reviewed and reconciled. Many feel that such a planning framework, which draws on the strengths of both decentralized and centralized planning, is a realistic and effective instrument for directing the complex activities of a multinational enterprise. It emphasizes the value of informational inputs from subsidiaries. The subsidiaries are in a much better position to analyze prevailing conditions and trends in their markets. At the same time, corporate management at the headquarters level provides a set of intentions and general guidelines drawn from the perspective of the position and resources of the total enterprise. Local managers develop plans against the background of their environments in the context of the overall objectives and policies. Corporate headquarters provides the stimulation of establishing and refining general guidelines and reviewing plans in depth with local management. Out of this process will emerge an agreed-upon set of goals for the company as a whole as well as for subsidiaries. This approach has the benefit of planning from the vantage point of specific markets and permits the integrated strategy necessary to promote corporate objectives in each country or region and ensure unified corporate growth.

Again, the planning orientation of a particular firm may differ depending on company size, organizational structure, length of involvement in multinational operations, diversity of product line, nature of the technology, the experience of managers, and other factors. However, as companies grow and achieve more sophistication in their planning task, they tend to combine local and global perspectives in the process.

The content of corporate planning also varies from company to company. In most multinational firms, strategic planning tends to be oriented toward (a) finance and budgeting, (b) product development and market research, and (c) acquisition and diversification.[16] These orientations often reflect the nature of the product, market characteristics, and other factors. For example, in capital-intensive industries such as mining, petrochemicals, heavy equipment, and machinery, companies often develop long-range plans on the basis of financial and budgeting considerations. Other factors such as marketing, personnel, and research and development receive relatively less attention. In addition, organizational characteristics also affect the content of corporate planning. Geographically oriented multinational firms typically place strong emphasis on production and marketing as a response to the demands of their operating environment.[17]

Implementation and Control

Irrespective of the approach used, strategic plans are meaningless unless they are effectively implemented and controlled. Planning necessitates control; the two are inseparable. Control involves making provision for monitoring the results of plan implementation and adjusting plans as necessary to ensure that the results of company and affiliate actions are consistent with planned goals. In other words, multinational managers ensure that the overall objectives of the firm and the contributory objectives of its subsidiaries are achieved by monitoring plan implementation and making adjustments. Planning and control are continuous processes of looking ahead, preparing for the future, and monitoring ongoing actions.

In order to develop a control system, the major goals established in strategic planning are divided into intermediary and short-range components. If progress toward goals is to be controlled, it will have to be measured. If it is to be measured, standards are essential. A standard takes shape as a projection of hoped-for or budgeted performance.

Once standards are established, management must devise a system for monitoring actual performance. An effective information and communication system will be needed. Multinational companies use a variety of methods to control the operations of their subsidiaries, such as financial reports, budgets, meetings, and personal visits. The reports generally contain regular financial statements on sales, costs, and profitability for all major units of the firm. Multinational companies may require these reports on a monthly or quarterly basis. Budgets are another important source of control; the actual performance of subsidiaries can be compared against the operating budgets, established for the divisions.[18]

Control is also exerted in areas such as production, market share, growth of sales, output, and costs. Additionally, personal visits, meetings, conferences, and informal contacts play an important role in any multinational control system.

The basic idea is that the control methods used generate relevant and timely data sufficient to allow management to spot unfavorable performance trends and take corrective action. A well-established control system not only provides data for monitoring and making corrections, but also generates data relevant to evaluating changes in objectives and implementation programs.

The nature of the control—tight or loose—as well as the specific techniques used vary from company to company. Some of the variables that determine the type of control are size of subsidiary and market, age of subsidiary, distance from headquarters, legal conditions, qualifications of managers, type of environment, and stability of conditions in the host country. The qualifications of the subsidiary manager, for example, can influence the looseness or tightness of control. His experience, years of service, character, and relationship with key men and staff members at headquarters all make a difference. These variations were described by a multinational executive as follows:

> There is no general pattern regarding the degree of control, even among corporations of the same size and industry. There isn't even a pattern regarding the areas or functions that are controlled. Control relationships depend on a great many variables, such as corporate history and tradition, structure and development, and personalities of top executives and their backgrounds. Therefore, each company develops its own way of conducting its international business. Identical ideas and intentions in two subsidiaries can lead to dissimilar patterns because of differences in business environment, and similar, or even the same, methods can produce quite divergent results due to different attitudes prevailing at a given time.[19]

Multinational control systems are difficult to administer because of distance, communication barriers, lack of proper understanding by headquarters of local conditions, and differing business and accounting practices. An effective control system in a multinational context should take into account the need for a well-thought-out format to be used for overseas operations with provision for adaptation to different conditions and operations.

THE VALUE OF MULTINATIONAL PLANNING

Without a strategy for overseas operations, multinational corporate decisions are likely to be based on the pressure of the moment. Much can be done to minimize risk through a systematic planning process. Such systematization can be achieved by defining and clarifying corporate objectives in terms of multinational operations, the types of products or services the firm should seek to supply, and the markets to be exploited. Strategy of this sort provides a framework for, and gives direction to, subsequent efforts and establishes a set of rational criteria to guide day-to-day decisions. It focuses attention on the type of foreign market that holds the greatest promise for the multinational firm, and it facilitates a consistent and systematic analysis of its operations with which to balance available resources against global opportunities and alternatives.

An organizational approach to the future in the multinational context introduces a degree of risk and complexity not generally experienced in domestic operations. Multinational firms have to deal with a multiplicity of environments containing varying market and political forces, levels of stability, and financial climates. Foreign operations generally imply an element of unfamiliarity and therefore complexity. Planning can minimize the negative consequences of operating in a wide variety of unfamiliar environments. Furthermore, differential rates of economic change in many countries contribute to an environment the multinational business must anticipate and perhaps respond to favorably in order to meet its growth objectives. The need for anticipating rather than merely adapting to changing conditions is the most significant element in multinational planning.

One of the objectives of multinational corporate planning is to integrate diverse activities and to realize synergistic benefits among various units operating in different environments. However, diversity of environment makes this goal difficult to attain because different operating units need to reconcile their objectives with local conditions and demands. Although multinational corporate management must think and plan on a worldwide basis to obtain effective integration and operational synergy, management abroad is inclined to think parochially in terms of local conditions. Hence integrating subsidiary plans with overall corporate plans presents a problem. Companies that can achieve a working compromise through effective planning will make a major contribution to their well-being.

Multinational corporate planning can create an effective communication system throughout the whole organization. It can ensure that all parts of the company—headquarters, regional centers, and subsidiaries operating in various countries—are striving toward the same set of goals and utilizing corporate policies and resources in ways beneficial to the corporation as a whole. Successful MNCs have learned that following a uniform, company-wide planning process is of paramount importance.[20]

Multinational corporate planning is also beneficial on other counts. It encourages systematic forward thinking by the managers at all levels and in all parts of the company's operations. Setting realistic and visible goals can inspire organizational effort. Planning develops a consciousness in management of the evnironmental forces that can generate the need for change in organizational responses. It also serves as an effective mechanism for decentralization and control. It encourages the development of alternative plans so the multinational firm can respond positively to changing environmental conditions.

SUMMARY

Multinational planning is essentially concerned with determining major goals for the enterprise as a whole as well as for its national subsidiaries and with the adoption of courses of action for achieving these goals. Planning in a multinational context differs from domestic planning because of environmental diversity, physical distance, communication barriers, and elements of uncertainty. Although these differences make planning for multinational operations more difficult, greater diversity and complexity make it even more essential for identifying opportunities and threats that have real impact on an MNC's survival and growth.

Although the multinational planning process varies from one firm to another, depending on a number of internal and external conditions, a majority of firms develop strategic or long-range plans for about five years, and operational plans for one year. The basic process of planning includes assessing the external environmental conditions; evaluating company resources and competence; developing strategic objectives on the basis of opportunities and resources; and formulating action programs and tactical plans to achieve these objectives.

Multinational corporations differ in the kind of planning process they use. With centralized planning, headquarters sets global objectives and assigns subobjectives to national subsidiaries. With decentralized planning, the operating units are responsible for formulating objectives for their operations and these objectives are then combined for the company as a whole. The final approach combines both centralized and decentralized planning; both headquarters and the subsidiaries continuously interact throughout the planning process. The last approach has the unique advantage of planning from the vantage point of specific markets and allowing the integration of strategy to promote overall corporate goals. Planning should be accompanied by a well-designed control and monitoring system to generate relevant and timely data sufficient to allow multinational managers to uncover deviations in performance and take corrective action when needed.

In today's highly competitive and dynamic industrial world, the ability to compete in world markets depends upon a well-thought-out and planned program of finding, evaluating, and properly matching markets to company capabilities. Considerable emphasis should be placed on the need for developing company strategy to avoid pitfalls and poor decisions.

Notes

[1]For a discussion of the definition of planning, see George Steiner and W. M. Cannon, eds., *Multinational Corporate Planning* (New York: Macmillan, 1966), pp. 8-16.

[2]William A. Dymsza, *Multinational Business Strategy* (New York: McGraw-Hill, 1972), pp. 501-51; William W. Cain, "International Planning: Mission Impossible?" *Columbia Journal of World Business,* July-August 1970, pp. 53-60; Thomas H. Bates, "Management and the Multinational Business Environment," *California Management Review,* spring 1973, pp. 37-45.

[3]Lawrence G. Franko, "Strategic Planning for Internationalization—The European Dilemma and Some Possible Solutions," *Long Range Planning,* June 1973, p. 59.

[4]Cain, *op. cit.,* pp. 54-55; Irwin Goldman, "Special Problems of International Long-Range Planning," *Management Review,* April 1965, p. 37.

[5]John S. Schwendiman, *Strategic and Long-Range Planning for the Multinational Corporation* (New York: Praeger, 1973).

[6]Y.K. Shetty, "Evaluating Foreign Investment Opportunities," *Journal of Economics and Business,* fall 1970, pp. 46-51.

[7]Irving S. Friedman, "The New World of the Rich-Poor and the Poor-Rich," *Fortune,* May 1975, p. 246.

[8]Millard H. Prayor, Jr., "Planning in a Worldwide Business," *Harvard Business Review,* January-February 1965, p. 131.

[9]Warren J. Keegan, "Multinational Scanning: A Study of the Information Sources Utilized by Headquarters Executives in Multinational Companies," *Administrative Science Quarterly,* September 1974, pp. 411-21.

[10]Hans Schollhammer, "Long Range Planning in Multinational Firms," *Columbia Journal of World Business,* September-October 1971, pp. 80-84.

[11]This description is based on Schollhammer, pp. 82-83.

[12]"Ciba-Geigy Reassures Its Global Futures," *International Management,* March 1973, p. 18.

[13]Dymsza, *op. cit.,* p. 59.

[14]Schollhammer, *op. cit.*

[15]W. A. M. Edwards, "Organizing for Planning in Imperial Chemical Industries Limited," in Steiner and Cannon, *op. cit.,* pp. 61-80.

[16]Schollhammer, *op. cit.*

[17]Peter Lorance, "Formal Planning in Multinational Corporations," *Columbia Journal of World Business,* summer 1973, p. 85.

[18]For a discussion of planning and control systems in Continental Can International Corporation, see D. J. Cuddy, "Planning and Control of Foreign Operations," *Managerial Planning,* November-December 1973, pp. 1-5.

[19]Robert J. Alsegg, *Control Relationships Between American Corporations and Their European Subsidiaries* (New York: American Management Association, 1971), p. 6.

[20]Ralph Z. Sorenson and U. E. Weichmann, "How Multinationals View Marketing Standardization," *Harvard Business Review,* May-June 1975, pp. 38ff.

6

The Organizational Structure

Multinational operations add a new dimension to the task of designing organizational structures. The environmental diversity facing multinational firms poses unique organizational problems not normally encountered by companies operating domestically.[1] Added to this fact is that of physical distance, which makes the relationship between different operating units and headquarters more difficult. The company involved in overseas operations should be able to structure its organization to take into account these peculiarities. Furthermore, the diversity of foreign business and the dynamics of organizational development should continue to generate changing operating designs.

Organization is a mechanism designed to accomplish corporate objectives. It defines the key tasks to be performed; assigns the authority and responsibility to make decisions to ensure achievement of goals; and provides a coordinating system to integrate the separate tasks. In other words, organization defines the relationship between different personnel and task units in terms of decision-making authority, communication channels, and control of various activities. The usual way in which organizational structure is evaluated is in terms of the quality of managerial decisions and the quality of their implementation.

The purpose of this chapter is to examine some of the key concepts relevant to the structuring of multinational companies. After examining the evolution of a multinational structure, we will analyze alternative modes of organization, such as the international division and the more global structural forms. Finally, the cardinal issues concerning managerial decision making—centralization versus decentralization—will be explored.

ORGANIZATIONAL DEVELOPMENT IN MULTINATIONAL FIRMS

Most structures for multinational operations evolve. At certain stages, design or redesign takes place due to a number of elements in the internal and external environments of the company. Size of multinational operations, company history, top management orientation, product-market diversification, and many other factors influence the organization and its continuous evolution. The degree and diversity of multinational involvement, however, play a paramount role. For example, for many firms the traditional avenue of entry into foreign markets is through exports. Exporting does not, strictly speaking, entail "management abroad," except that the export-related activities of the company need to be organized and coordinated. In other words, as a firm begins to export, it establishes an export department to develop and implement effective strategies to get its products into the hands of consumers abroad. As exports grow in value and volume, the department may become a division.

When the company finds it necessary to expand and diversify its business activities abroad, it enters into the area of licensing, joint ventures, and foreign production. For example, the company may be exporting to one country, entering into a licensing agreement in another, and operating production facilities in still another. From an organizational point of view, the existing structure may be less than adequate to meet the needs of increasing involvement in foreign operations. For as the foreign involvement gets deeper, decisions concerning overseas operations become a significant part of the total operation, and hence more and more critical to the success of the company.

Many American companies have created international divisions headed by high-ranking officials to unify all the international activities of the firm. This international division is concerned with all aspects of business abroad, such as production, marketing, R&D, personnel, and so on, whereas the export division is basically a marketing organization. As Robock and Simmonds point out, some companies pass through an intermediate organizational stage before moving to an international division structure.[2] During this period, the parent firm acts as a holding company for largely autonomous foreign subsidiaries. Such an arrangement, however, does not last long. Because of progressively greater involvement in foreign operations, many companies soon realize the need for better coordination and integration.

The rapid growth of multinational business and management's desire to develop a unified global perspective leads in most cases to the development of an integrated global organization structure. The multinational firm may establish any one or a combination of the following arrangements: (a) a functional structure, in which division of responsibility at headquarters is organized by functions such as production, marketing, and finance; (b) a geographic structure, in which primary operating responsibility is assigned to area managers, each of whom is made responsible for a specific geographic area of the world; (c) a product structure, in which each division is responsible for the production and marketing of certain products on a global scale; or (d) mixed structures with overlapping responsibilities for products, areas, and functions. The process of organizational evolution in multinational firms does not necessarily include all these stages. Some firms may bypass certain stages; others may go through several other in-between stages. What are some of these organizational forms? What are their strengths and weaknesses for effective management of multinational corporations?

THE INTERNATIONAL DIVISION STRUCTURE

Some American multinational companies that have gone through the evolutionary process of export to international division emphasize and retain the distinction by referring to one segment of their international business as international operations and to the other as exports. The former coordinates manufacturing operations in foreign nations, whereas the latter is in charge of sales through exports. The basis for such an organization is the nature of the business. Of course, there is economy, specialization, and immediate attention to operational problems with such an organizational format. But this simplicity in itself may cause problems of coordination in the contemporary multinational business environment. Nonetheless, it can be the most workable format if the MNC's activities are unifunctional—exporting to West Germany, licensing in Australia, manufacturing in Brazil.

Most American multinational firms combine these two endeavors into one international division which is market-oriented and handles all product lines throughout the world. Figure 6-1 is an example of the structure of an international division of a large American firm. At the headquarters level, the international division is usually headed by a vice-president with defined responsibilities in the area of multinational business who reports to the president or the chief executive officer of the company. He is generally responsible for directing and coordinating multinational business activities such as exports, licensing, joint ventures, and foreign manufacturing and sales; for developing company strategy and policy for foreign operations; and for providing an organizational link to corporate headquarters and the rest of the firm. In some firms, the international division, at least initially, develops its own staff to advise management on specialized matters. Later, it begins to use the domestic corporate staff, though maintaining some of its own. This change is crucial in the sense that now the

FIGURE 6-1

International Division Structure

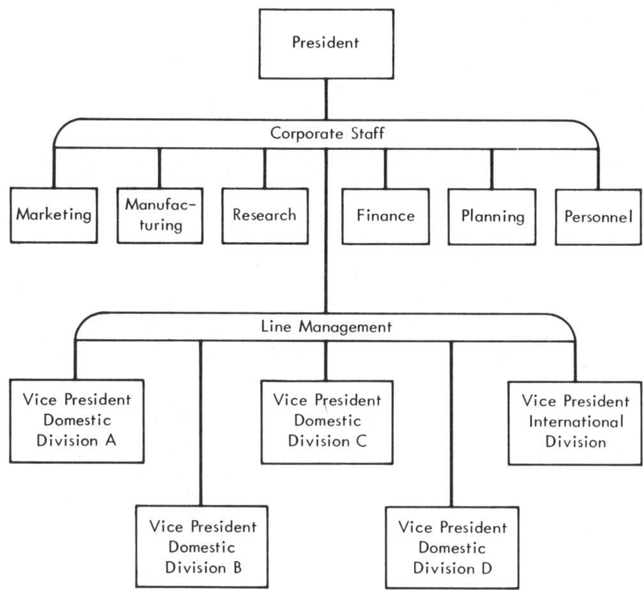

company has taken steps to globalize its staff functions and to achieve better coordination between the domestic and international divisions.

At the operations level, the international division may be organized along many lines—geographic, product, or functional.[3] For example, in American Cyanamid, regional directors for Europe, Africa, Latin America, and Far East-Oceania report to the managing director, who in turn reports to the international division vice-president responsible for foreign operations. Such an arrangement at the operational level enables the firm to concentrate on country or regional needs.

Some companies are organized on the basis of product lines at the operating level. For example, A.M.F. International is organized on the basis of product lines to parallel the product divisions of the parent organization. The firm finds it advantageous to organize this way in order to take advantage of the specialization required for the production and marketing of its complex and diversified products. Lastly, a few firms adopt a functional organization. This type of structure enables the firm to apply functional specialization to its multinational operations. In general, the international division is most commonly organized along geographic lines, with regional or country managers having line responsibility for a specific region or country.

Advantages and Disadvantages

The international division structure has many advantages for the operation of a multinational business. The multinational activities of the firm now assume an integral place in the corporate map along with the domestic divisions. Such an arrangement facilitates specialization in international problems, definition of responsibility, and a coordinated, efficient response to a large number of increasingly complex business issues. Use of the international division structure is the easiest way to concentrate scarce managerial expertise in one central place. It ensures that multinational matters receive due consideration in the overall strategy and policy of the company. A management position that has adequate organization status helps guarantee full articulation of the corporate implications of multinational business. Further, such an organizational unit can progressively cultivate expertise in multinational matters, help globalize staff functions at the corporate level, and develop organizational capability for dealing with opportunities in multinational markets.

On the other hand, the international division structure has some limitations. The problem of effectively coordinating international with domestic business tends to persist. This is particularly true if the interdependence of international and domestic operations is pronounced. Such coordination also becomes difficult when the international division begins to rival domestic divisions in sales and profits. The main reason for this can be found in the following observation by experts at Booz, Allen and Hamilton, Inc., a well-known international management consulting firm:

> In the majority of cases, organization difficulties emanate from appending international business to the domestic business instead of integrating the two parts into a world business. Typically, the organization structure just evolves rather than being carefully planned. Most businesses, for example, tend to be organized along a product or functional line. Where the foreign business is added, it is usually geographically oriented at the first two organizational levels.[4]

There may be poor cooperation between the domestic divisions and the international division. Interdivisional conflicts may develop. For example, the domestic divisions may place a low priority on servicing the international division. Additionally, the separation of international and domestic business may lead to less than an optimal use of company resources on a global scale. The establishment of manufacturing plants abroad makes product knowledge more important; but that knowledge remains stored in the domestic divisions. Because of these limitations, the international division structure often develops into a globally oriented structure.[5]

THE INTEGRATED GLOBAL STRUCTURE

Integrating the domestic and foreign business of a company into a global business entity is crucial to the development of a truly multinational corporation. Companies with extensive involvement in multinational activities soon reach a stage at which all of corporate management must be globally oriented. The usual response at this stage is the equalization of domestic and foreign operations. Corporate management becomes willing to allocate resources on a global scale without regard to national political boundaries in its effort to maximize returns on its investment.[6] Under this system, key management personnel assume worldwide responsibilities for their respective functions.

Consider, for example, Canada's Massey-Ferguson. Like some American multinational companies, it has operated under the world or global enterprise concept for some time (see Appendix 1-B). Massey-Ferguson manufactures in forty-four factories scattered in fifteen countries; sells tractors, combines, hay balers, and other farm machines in about 170 nations; and borrows long-term funds in nine different currencies. In the last decade, Albert Thornbrough, president of Massey-Ferguson, has molded the company into a corporation totally committed to worldwide production, marketing, and financing. Massey-Ferguson has been organizing for world markets since 1867, when it started exporting reapers and mowers to Germany. Since then, the company has built up an exceptionally strong dealer-distribution network. Until 1925, the company was managed by the Massey family. After World War II, it was in financial trouble because of its failure to digest Ferguson Tractor of Detroit, acquired in 1953. Thornbrough, who was the executive vice-president of Ferguson Tractor, emerged as president of Massey-Ferguson in 1960 and committed the company to global marketing and production by creating the following corporate policy:

1. Integrated plants producing interchangeable parts (A French-made transmission, a British-made engine, and a Mexican-made axle can be assembled with U.S.-made sheet-metal parts in a Detroit tractor plant and sold in Canada.)

2. Complete decentralization of operating subsidiaries (There are nine of these in major market areas, plus an export subsidiary that oversees operations in more than 150 smaller markets.)

3. Home rule in subsidiaries (To a degree often professed but seldom practiced by many other firms, Massey-Ferguson insists that nationals run subsidiaries from top to bottom.)

4. Overseas financing. (Massey-Ferguson borrows long-term funds where major assets are located, thus avoiding the bind in which some American companies have been caught in recent years.)

5. Effective direction and control from Toronto (From Toronto a staff of ninety people directs planning, financing, and product design.)

Companies adopting this orientation make no distinction between domestic and foreign business. They organize to take advantage of opportunities wherever they may exist. The global outlook is meant to apply to investment decisions as well as other activities. In other words, such an organization structure provides a mechanism to optimize corporate performance on a global basis.

Generally speaking, European-based and Canadian multinationals have moved more quickly and spontaneously to a global structure than most American firms.[7] The organization structures of well-known multinationals such as Nestlé, Royal-Dutch Shell, Unilever, Olivetti, Philips, Pirelli, and Massey-Ferguson substantiate this point. Almost no European firms have the international division structure found in some American firms. They perfer an organization that does not dichtomize international and domestic operations. In general, the European preference for a global structure may be traced to the size of their domestic markets. Faced with comparatively smaller home markets, European companies began to expand foreign operations much earlier in their organizational lives and achieved a global orientation quite rapidly.

When a company takes the global approach to organization, it has to decide whether to organize on a geographic, product, or functional basis. Multinational business decision making requires expertise in each of these three areas. Geographic expertise or input involves an understanding of the basic economic, social, and political dimensions of a market or a country in order to understand the dynamics of the market environment. Product and technical knowledge is required to match the product with the market environment. Skills in the area of finance, production, marketing, personnel, and research are needed to provide functional input. A global orientation leads to the development of one of the following organizational forms:

1. Global geographic divisions, each responsible for all products manufactured and marketed within a given geographical area
2. Global product divisions responsible for producing and marketing a product or a group of products worldwide
3. Global functional divisions such as manufacturing, marketing, and finance responsible for worldwide operations in their own functional area
4. Mixed structures with a combination of geographic operations, worldwide product divisions, and multiple functional links

Geographic Structure

Companies that have adopted the geographic structure assign operational responsibility for certain geographic areas of the world to line managers. These line managers report to the president or the chief executive officer of the company. World markets are divided into major geographic areas such as North America, Latin America, Africa, Europe, and so on (see Figure 6-2). Under this system, the company makes no distinction between domestic and foreign operations. There are different markets in different parts of the world, the home market becomes simply one of a number of markets being served by the company. All activities such as marketing, production, and finance are grouped into geographic units. These divisions receive assistance and support from corporate staffs that have global responsibility. Corporate headquarters retains the responsibility for

FIGURE 6-2

Area Structure

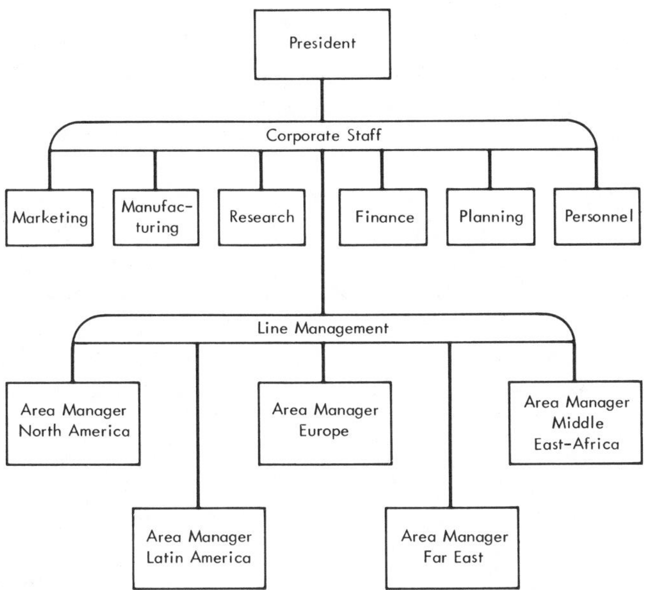

worldwide planning and control. The central staff group at the headquarters level is the main coordinating force, providing both managerial direction and functional balance.

International Telegraph and Telephone (ITT) provides a good illustration of this mode. It has its operations organized under North American, Latin American, Europe-Africa, Middle Eastern, and Australian-Far Eastern divisions. It has product and functional specialists at headquarters who are responsible for operations on a global basis. For the corporate management of ITT, there is no such thing as a foreign market, there are only different markets in different parts of the world. ITT's corporate management knows as much about the European and

Latin American markets for its products as it knows about the United States market. Such geographic designs are also common in the case of major multinational oil companies.

Multinational companies employing the geographic design have two salient characteristics: (a) the great bulk of sales revenues is derived from similar end-use markets, and (b) local marketing requirements are critical—that is, the variation in the product to meet local requirements is minimal and can be done locally; the product is highly standardized, but the techniques for penetrating local markets differ widely.[8]

One of the main advantages of the geographic structure is that it emphasizes the differences in national and regional market characteristics, placing the responsibility for all activities in a given region in the hands of an executive who is familiar with the region. Such a structure helps develop logical lines of authority and responsibility with easier communication channels between the headquarters and widely dispersed companies with many functions and products. The company can achieve profit decentralization at the operations level while holding each of its operational units accountable for its own total performance. Finally, it allows for broad management training and experience for top management personnel.

On the negative side, the geographic organizational setup causes operating problems when a firm has diverse product lines with differing marketing characteristics. Under this structure it is difficult to transfer new ideas and experiences across regional boundaries. A geographic structure with its regional segmentation also interferes with the flow of products from manufacturing facilities to markets. In order to overcome this problem, some multinational firms appoint product managers at the headquarters level who are assigned worldwide responsibility for particular products or product lines with authority over the area line managers. This structure may also lead to duplication of product and functional staff specialists at the regional level, particularly when regional management centers are located far from corporate headquarters.

Product Structure

Under this system, worldwide responsibility is assigned to product groups or divisions with senior executives in line management positions (see Figure 6-3). They coordinate all product activity through corporate staff groups such as marketing, finance, personnel, and area specialists at the corporate staff level. This means that the company's overall objectives and those for each product group are established at corporate headquarters. The product divisions have primary responsibility for planning and controlling all activities for company products on a multinational basis.

Typical of the product line organization is the Bell and Howell company. It has made organizational changes whereby international responsibilities have been placed within the company's three product groups. Prior to the change, the international division had responsibility for foreign operations. The reason for the change, according to the company, was this: "Initially, the job of structuring and getting an international operation started required the full attention of a specialized group. Once this was established, the more important problem was to have each product group think of its markets on a worldwide basis."[9] The three

FIGURE 6-3

Product Structure

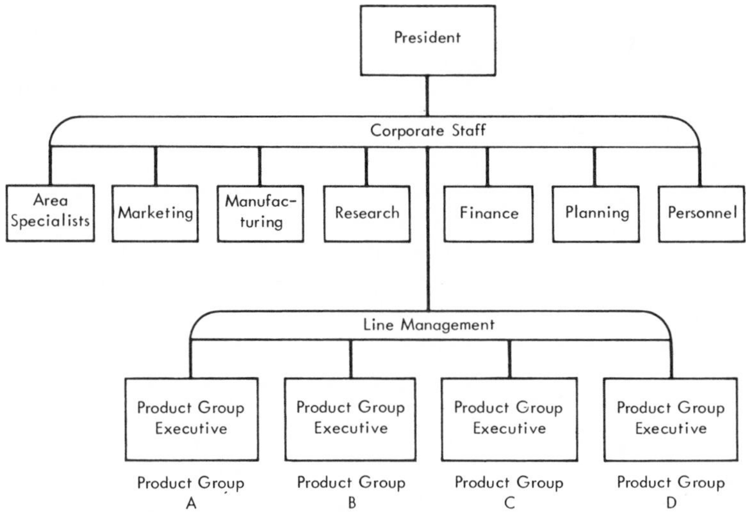

product groups—photo products, instrument products, and business equipment products—now have responsibility for domestic as well as international operations.

Product organization is most popular in multinational firms with a diversified range of products going into a variety of end-use markets.[10] Differences in marketing such products make this organization appropriate. It is easier to achieve product and marketing integration. The product structure is also beneficial for a firm that engages in overseas manufacture of products requiring relatively high technology because it brings the foreign operations into close contact with the latest technological developments. This type of organization encourages the utilization of more detailed product and marketing knowhow in the conduct of multinational operations.[11] Product organization is also advantageous when high shipping costs, tariffs, or other considerations demand local manufacture of the product. It also encourages better coverage of all product lines overseas. In this respect, the product structure may be more appropriate for companies contemplating rapid growth. Lastly, it provides some flexibility for diversified companies in that the company can add a new product division without disturbing the existing ones if the firm diversifies into another product line.

On the negative side, the product structure has several potential limitations. One is the inherent problem of coordinating and controlling the product groups in any given part of the world. Each product group may be going in different directions, and company-wide coordination becomes difficult. Lack of adequate regional knowledge is also a common weakness of this type of structure. If each product division maintains a complete international staff, there will be duplication of effort. Another limitation is that corporate executives may have had little or no experience with multinational operations. A multinational firm with a facility in a country or region manufacturing different product lines can encounter serious problems of communication and coordination. Lastly, such a structure fails to provide a uniform company image to foreign governments, banks, distributors, and the general public.

Functional Structure

With a functional structure, the division of responsibility at headquarters is organized by function—production, marketing, finance, and so forth. The vice-presidents who head these divisions have worldwide responsibilities in their own functional area. The marketing division, for example, has worldwide marketing responsibility, with direct control over all sales-related activities. Likewise, the production division has line authority over domestic as well as foreign subsidiaries' plants.

Structuring on the basis of function is most suitable for firms with narrow, standardized product lines for which product knowledge is a significant variable. A functional structure allows specialization in marketing, manufacturing, and other functions. Emphasis on such specialization may be especially important in the initial stage of developing the firm's multinational business, because it is possible for a relatively small group of executives to maintain centralized control of operations. United States MNCs consider the functional structure inadequate for widespread multinational operations and have abandoned it.

The separation of marketing, manufacturing, and other functions may prevent the full range of product and market knowhow from being applied to the company's multinational operations. Such a structure may also prevent the fullest use of national regional expertise. In order to overcome this problem, each functional division may need to have its own area specialists, and this overlapping may tend to duplicate effort. Finally, functionally oriented organization structures can create serious coordination and control problems because each division lacks a dominant overall objective, such as making a success of a particular product line or geographic area. Generally speaking, dividing multinational management responsibility on the basis of major functions or types of activity is far less common than dividing it on the basis of geography or product lines, though a few American firms do maintain such structures. In European-based multinationals, the functional structure is more prevalent.

Mixed Structural Forms

A number of multinational firms are also developing mixed or overlapping organizational structures. Some have combined functional divisions with global product divisions. Others have retained the international division in a coordinating role when operations were reorganized on a global basis. Still others have developed organizations that combine geographic and product lines. For example, in the General Electric organization, worldwide business responsibilities are assigned to product groups. The international group, however, works with the product groups. The departments under the product groups are responsible for developing appropriate relations with governments, banks, major customers, and other firms with whom General Electric does business in their area. They have their own staff experts who assist operating departments on a given problem in a particular country. Through a grid or matrix arrangement, GE emphasizes product expertise but achieves coordination on an area basis.[12]

Another combination is to assign responsibility for products, areas, and functions. For example, at Union Carbide, three executive vice-presidents head the company operations, each responsible for one or more major product lines and one or more overseas operating areas. Previously, the foreign operations of the company were split into three geographic groups—the Africa and Middle East group, the Far East and Latin American group, and the Canada and Europe group. Each of these units along with three separate domestic product line groups reported to the chief executive officer. The new setup blends managerial responsibilities for product line and regional operations. According to the company, the new structure is expected to help resolve the conflicts that develop between domestic product managers and geographic area managers who each run their own profit centers.[13]

A number of factors contribute to the adoption of mixed structures. The history of the company's foreign involvement, uneven development of its business by product or region, the size and complexity of the business, the unavailability of experienced multinational executives, and the problem of effective coordination of operations are some of the important ones. One of the main reasons for using the mixed form is probably the problem of optimum integration of regional, functional, and product inputs. There must be an appropriate degree of cross-fertilization and interaction in all three areas. The optimum way to combine area knowledge with product and functional skills is, however, an evolving concept. The most experienced companies organize to bring out these competences on a worldwide basis even though one consideration, such as product, may dominate their structure. Other competences are attained through foreign subsidiary corporate staffs with worldwide responsibilities, regional staffs, mixed structures, and other organizational devices.

THE REGIONAL MANAGEMENT CONCEPT

An impressive list of American-based multinational companies have moved in the direction of the regional management concept. In essence, a regional headquarters is created and held responsible for coordinating product, geographic, and functional activities in that area. This is an additional level of management between the local organization and corporate headquarters.

The pressure for the creation of a regional headquarters comes from two sources: the scale and complexity of a company's operations within a given region, and the nature of the region. Size as well as complexity create pressure on the multinational firm to respond at the regional level. Size also facilitates such a center because the company can now cover the cost involved in maintaining it. When a particular region is characterized by certain similarities in economic, social, political, and geographic conditions, the desire to create such a center is further strengthened. Although the majority of multinational companies have organized their operations on a regional basis, it should be noted that the European region tends to receive the greatest emphasis, partly because of the size of most multinational firms' European operations in relation to their total foreign activities. Table 6-1 gives some examples of American multinationals that have established European regional management centers.

TABLE 6-1

Examples of American Firms Having Regional Management Centers in Europe

Firm	*Industry*	*European Location*
Caterpillar Tractor	Construction equipment	Geneva, Switzerland
Colgate-Palmolive	Cleaning products	London, England
Corn Products	Processed foods	Brussels, Belgium
Dow Chemical	Chemicals	Zurich, Switzerland
Hewlett-Packard	Electronics	Geneva, Switzerland
IBM*	Computers	Paris, France
Johnson's Wax	Cleaning products	London, England
Monsanto	Chemicals	Brussels, Belgium
Procter & Gamble	Cleaning Products	London, England
U.S. Rubber	Rubber fabricating	Geneva, Switzerland

*IBM World Corporation was recently divided into two units.
Source: Annual Reports of various companies.

One reason for establishing regional headquarters is that increasingly complex overseas business activities can no longer be managed exclusively from corporate headquarters. The regional headquarters is a method of spreading the management group and placing it closer to operational problems. It helps to make a more appropriate division between policy problems that should be brought to corporate headquarters and those that apply only at the regional level. The regional headquarters also helps to achieve better coordination of regional operations, better application of company knowledge on a regional basis, and regional optimization of company resources.[14]

The advantage of such a structure is that it brings some part of the headquarters into closer contact with the local operations and makes it more responsive to the kinds of problems found on that level. One of the main disadvantages is the problem of reconciling product emphasis with a geographically oriented management approach. This problem can reach serious proportions if a company's product line is diverse and if marketing channels and techniques are varied. Such a structure also adds one level of management between the operating companies and headquarters, which has the potential of reducing communication effectiveness. Another major disadvantage of such a center is its cost.

SELECTING AN ORGANIZATION STRUCTURE

There is no one best way to organize a multinational enterprise. The structure of a multinational firm is not an independent entity, but rather an interdependent system—the result of complex interactions between the enterprise and its global environment. The type of organization most suitable for a particular multinational firm depends on its internal and external environments. Organizational designs appropriate for one multinational firm with given product-market characteristics may not be appropriate for another. Likewise, the structure suitable at one point in time may not be suitable at another. Structure must be tailored to fit the particular product-market characteristics and the long-run objectives of a multinational firm at any given point in time.

A number of factors influence the organizational design of the multinational firm. Some of the more important are these:[15]

1. The degree of involvement in multinational business
2. Its history and experience in multinational operations
3. Its product-market characteristics
4. Its capacity to effect major organizational changes
5. Its long-term strategy

Degree of Involvement. The design of an organization for a multinational firm will be influenced by the relative size of its foreign operations. For firms that are minimally involved in multinational business, the international division may be adequate. For companies with extensive foreign involvement, the separation of domestic and foreign business may not be desirable; probably they need to integrate domestic business with foreign operations to develop a unified organization posture and decision-making structure to allocate resources on the basis of worldwide opportunities.

Company History. The choice of structure is by no means unaffected by the history of the firm and its past experience. In the early stage of multinational business development, a company possesses few managers who are experienced in coping with complex, worldwide problems. At a more advanced stage, organizational decisions will be increasingly influenced by the years of overseas experience and availability of a large pool of executive manpower. A global structure requires a substantial number of internationally experienced managers. In the short run, an international division may be the only feasible structure because it provides the easiest way to marshall limited managerial skills.

Product and Market Characteristics. The product-market characteristics of a multinational firm are the focal point of concern in any type of organization design. For example, the greater the diversity of product lines, the more likely it is that a global product structure is desirable to achieve product and marketing integration. For companies with high-technology products, the product organization structure is preferable because it encourages close contact with the latest technological developments. Product diversity implies that the success of the firm depends on different trends in different markets. On the other hand, a functional structure may be effective when there is less diversity.

A multinational firm reaching diverse markets requires an organizational structure quite different from that needed by a firm facing homogeneous markets. Under such conditions, intimate knowledge of local conditions and closer contact with local operations becomes critical. A geographic structure concerned with regional differences may be an appropriate form for such a firm.

Capacity to Adjust. Another factor influencing structure is the capacity of the company to adjust to major organizational changes. Such changes, particularly the major ones, disrupt the relationships between different divisions. The manager of a domestic division may be unwilling to accept a new role when the organization is changed from a company with an international division to a unified global entity. Similarly, corporate staff personnel may be unprepared to take on worldwide responsibilities because of lack of training or inadequate incentives.

Long-term Objectives. There is general agreement that the organizational structure of a firm must be continually adaptable to changes in the company's objectives, strategies, and resources. Sound planning in the area of multinational operations is therefore essential to determine the form best suited to achieve the company's goals. Unless such planning is done, the structure appropriate for changing objectives cannot be predicted, carefully planned, and systematically developed. The strength of these and other factors will, of course, vary from instance to instance, but the multinational corporation sensitive to them can better assess the problems that face it and determine which mode of organization is most appropriate.

LOCUS OF DECISION MAKING IN MULTINATIONAL COMPANIES

Whichever form of organization is developed, as the company's foreign commitment grows, it becomes difficult to make all managerial decisions involving foreign operations at the top. One of the key considerations in deciding on the form of organization is the locus of decision making or the degree of centralization or decentralization of authority required or desired by a given firm. Decentralization refers to the extent to which authority and responsibility are delegated by the headquarters management to divisions and subsidiaries operating worldwide. Authority is concerned with the right to decide, implement, coordinate, and control; responsibility relates to accountability for producing results and achieving goals.

One form of decentralization is most important to multinational firms: profit decentralization. Under this system, operating divisions are responsible for their own profit or loss. Most American multinationals—General Electric, Kodak, Pfizer, Miles Laboratories—utilize the profit center concept in their foreign operations. However, this concept has not been favored by the European multinationals. European companies shy away from formalized role definitions, performance requirements, and authority specification. This may be the reason for the lesser popularity of this concept among the European firms.[16]

The question of how much authority corporate executives should retain and how much they should assign to subsidiaries and affiliates has not been completely resolved by multinational enterprises. The growing size of companies and the ever-increasing complexity of managing them have placed severe burdens on top executives. The demands on their time, energy, and resources cannot be effectively met by any single individual or a small group of individuals. In order to overcome this problem, many multinational companies have decentralized their managements. Well-known multinationals like Massey-Ferguson took an early lead in this direction. As a result, each division of that company operates relatively independently of corporate headquarters and is responsible for earning adequate profits and meeting other performance measures. The company's policy is to avoid involvement of parent company executives in local operations. The system has a number of advantages.

First, with a decentralized structure in which decision-making authority is placed closer to the environment where operations occur, subsidiaries and affiliates can effectively adapt to the changing environments facing their respective operations. They can make more timely decisions than management at the headquarters level. In other words, decentralization provides a built-in flexibility at the operating level. Second, decentralization can be a useful tool in motivating local managers. When decision-making authority is decentralized, initiative and creativity are encouraged.[17] Such an organizational structure also facilitates the training and development of managers at the subsidiary level. It can give the company a local image and develop a positive image in the host country. Lastly, communication obstacles due to distance, cultural, and national barriers favor maximum delegation of authority to subsidiaries.

On the other hand, many multinational companies feel that unified corporate strategy requires substantial centralization of decision-making authority at headquarters. The retention of decision making at the corporate level often makes a major contribution to the realization of economic benefits in such areas as product policies, research, and logistic plans. There can be uniformity in major policies. An attempt by headquarters to integrate and control all foreign operations would also encourage the company to centralize a substantial amount of decision-making authority. A shortage of managerial resources at the subsidiary level may also justify centralization.

Concepts of centralization and decentralization vary from company to company, from function to function within the same company, and within the same company from time to time. An optimum strategy in the area of decision making would vary with two major variables: company characteristics and the area of decision making.

Among the company characteristics that influence the degree of centralization or decentralization are the size of the firm, the profitability of the specific subsidiary, the local environment, the nature of the industry, the degree of integration of multinational operations, and the managerial talent available. For example, large, long-established, and profitable subsidiaries are likely to have a maximum degree of decision-making authority. Likewise, subsidiaries operating in countries with strong national controls that require frequent and unique local decisions may desire and attain a higher degree of autonomy.

The relative degree of decentralization or centralization will also vary with the specific area of decision making. Decisions most intimately and directly related to local conditions are likely to be decentralized, whereas decisions most directly related to central direction and system-wide optimization are likely to be centralized. For example, decisions relating to marketing, purchasing, and industrial relations tend to be most decentralized. Research, product, and financial decisions are likely to be centralized. The example of Philips illustrates this point. Decision-making authority in the area of budgets, accounting, and new product development is centralized; in the area of advertising and personnel administration, the degree of autonomy available to subsidiaries is much greater. Overall long-range planning and control functions are generally centralized.

On the whole, there is some indication that multinational firms, particularly the large, well-established ones, are moving in the direction of centralizing authority to a greater extent as well as integrating foreign operations.[18] The centralization of authority is prompted by the desire to maximize the benefits of multinational operations for the company as a whole, rather than to maximize the profit performance of individual subsidiaries. Two fundamental advantages of operating in a multinational environment are the potential for shifting resources and the emphasis on operating according to opportunities and threats perceived with a global perspective, and the ability to transmit and apply lessons and experiences from one region to another. In order to take advantage of these benefits, multinational enterprises are subject to pressures for more centralization.

For some U.S. companies relatively new to multinational business, however, the proper mix of centralization and decentralization is still an unresolved question. The uncertainty can be sensed in the following statement, made by a business executive: "We're not sure whether we ought to be tighter or looser in our organizational relationships. We don't know whether to treat our foreign operation as completely unique, with its own systems and structures, or as just another plant in Pocatello, Idaho."[19] In other words, the firms relatively new to multinational operations go through a trial-and-error stage of structuring decision-making authority.

But for many MNCs that have now gone through the process of organizational learning, one broad guiding principle has emerged: Centralize responsibility for corporate planning and control; decentralize operations. Corporate management will determine the overall strategy in terms of objectives and policies, allocate resources, and develop effective control systems to monitor the results. Managers at the operating level will have the autonomy to develop and implement specific courses of action for achieving the goals of their respective divisions. Accordingly, decision-making authority in multinational firms is conceived of as two vertical spheres.[20] One is a nationally and culturally decentralized base structure designed to deal with diverse conditions through semiautonomous subsidiaries at the operating level. The other is a centralized superstructure to provide direction, coordination, and control for the whole organization at the multinational level. Such a framework provides a flexible mechanism for developing effective multinational organizations.

SUMMARY

Organizational structure is a means for achieving company objectives. Designing organizational structures for the effective functioning of multinational firms involves unique problems emanating from diverse economic, political, social forces as well as physical distances. Organizational development in most multinational firms follows an evolutionary process. Starting with an export division, many companies then set up an international division and finally adopt a global structure with a geographic, product, or functional orientation. Each of these organizational forms has its own special operational characteristics, and there is no one structure suited to all firms. The structure must match the particular internal and external environments of the firm. Among the most important variables influencing structure are the size of foreign involvement, the history and experience of the firm, the company's product-market characteristics, the capacity of the firm to effect major organizational design changes, and the long-term strategy of the company in question.

One of the crucial considerations in designing organization is the degree of centralization or decentralization of authority desired at the headquarters and operating levels. The locus of decision-making authority seems to vary from company to company and from function to function. Though there is no precise formula available for dividing decision-making authority among headquarters and operating subsidiaries, one general principle seems to emerge: Centralize responsibility for planning and control, and decentralize operations. There is some indication that well-established multinational firms are gradually moving toward greater centralization in managing their foreign subsidiaries.

Notes

[1]Richard D. Hayes, Christopher M. Korth, and Manucher Roudiani, *International Business: An Introduction to the World of the Multinational Firm* (Englewood Cliffs, N.J.: Prentice-Hall, 1972), pp. 265-68.

[2]Stefan Robock and Kenneth Simmonds, *International Business and Multinational Enterprises* (Homewood, Ill.: Irwin, 1973), p. 429.

[3]William A. Dymsza, *Multinational Business Strategy* (New York: McGraw-Hill, 1972), pp. 23-26.

[4]Booz, Allen, and Hamilton, Inc., *The Emerging World Enterprise* (Chicago, 1962), pp. 14-15.

[5]Lawrence E. Fouraker and John M. Stopford, "Organizational Structure and Multinational Strategy," *Administrative Science Quarterly*, June 1968, pp. 47-64.

[6]Richard Robinson, *International Management* (New York: Holt, Rinehart and Winston, 1967), p. 153.

[7]For a detailed discussion of the organization structures of European-based multinational companies, see Andrew J. Lombard, Jr., "How European Companies Organize Their International Operations," *European Business*, July 1969, pp. 37-48.

[8]Gilbert H. Clee and Wilburn M. Sachtjen, "Organizing Worldwide Business," *Harvard Business Review*, November-December 1964, p. 62.

[9]Enid B. Lovell, *The Changing Role of the International Executive* (New York: National Industrial Conference Board, 1966), pp. 11-12.

[10]J. William Widing, Jr., "Reorganizing Your Worldwide Business," *Harvard Business Review*, May-June 1973, p. 158.

[11]David B. Zenoff, *International Business Management* (New York: Macmillan, 1971), p. 262.

[12]W. D. Dance, "An Evolving Structure for Multinational Operations," *Columbia Journal of World Business*, November-December 1969, pp. 29-30.

[13]"Cure for a Chemical Giant," *Business Week*, July 14, 1973, pp. 90-91.

[14]Charles R. Williams, "Regional Management Overseas," *Harvard Business Review*, January-February 1967, p. 91.

[15]Zenoff, *op. cit.,* pp. 259-60; Robock and Simmonds, *op. cit.,* pp. 440-43; Widing, *op. cit.,* pp. 158-59; Michael Brooke and H. Lee Reemers, *The Strategy of Multinational Enterprise* (New York: American Elsevier, 1970), pp. 23-43.

[16]Hans Schollhammer, "Organization Structure of Multinational Corporations," *Academy of Management Journal*, September 1971, p. 359.

[17]Endel J. Kolde, *International Business Enterprise* (Englewood Cliffs, N.J.: Prentice-Hall, 1973), p. 226.

[18]J. N. Behrman, *Some Patterns in the Rise of the Multinational Enterprise* (Englewood Cliffs, N.J.: Prentice-Hall, 1970), p. 62.

[19]Spencer Hayden, "Problems of Operating Overseas: A Survey of Company Experiences," *Personnel*, January-February 1968, p. 10.

[20]Thomas Aitken, *The Multinational Man* (New York: Wiley, 1973), p. 58.

Suggested Readings

BROOKE, MICHAEL, AND ALAN MITTON, "How to Manage Multinationals," *Management Today*, July 1974.

DAVIS, STANLEY M., "Two Models of Organization: Unity of Command versus Balance of Power," *Sloan Management Review*, fall 1974.

GRANICK, DAVID, "Use of Corporate and Divisional Headquarters: A Peculiar American Innovation," *MSU Business Topics*, autumn 1974.

REIMANN, BERNARD, "Organizational Effectiveness and Management's Public Values," *Academy of Management Journal*, June 1975, especially pp. 227-28.

ZEIRA, YORAM, "Overlooked Personnel Problems of Multinational Corporations," *Columbia Journal of World Business,* summer 1975.

APPENDIX 6-A: Eaton Corporation

Eaton Corporation is a diversified, worldwide company. For more than sixty years, the basic strength of Cleveland-based Eaton has been its ability to design, engineer, and manufacture products that "move man, materials, and energy." Industry, construction, and forestry are its target markets. Worldwide sales in these markets reached $425 million in 1973, and $505 million in 1974. Eaton caters basically to two markets: capital goods and consumer goods. Its capital goods market consists of trucks, industrial power transmission equipment, industrial vehicles, and construction equipment; its consumer markets include components for automobiles, appliances, and security systems.

Stanley Davis of the Harvard Business School has written a three-part case whose focus is the organization of Eaton's European operations (ICCH nos. 4-475-047, 4-475-048, and 4-475-049). We recommend this case for analysis and for gaining insight into the dynamics of structuring multinational organization.

7

Management Personnel Abroad

The management of human resources is of crucial importance to any company whether it is operating domestically or multinationally, for everything depends on how well this resource is developed and utilized. The multinational firm may possess enormous technical and material resources, but they will be ineffectively employed unless it possesses the human resources, particularly in the area of management, to realize their full potential.

With the growing emphasis on multinational operations, companies must begin to appreciate some of the problems associated with staffing a multinational firm. Staffing tends to become particularly important in the realm of multinational business for a number of reasons.[1] Activities are physically dispersed, so the problem of effective top management attention and control becomes more difficult. The multinational manager must be able and willing to make on-the-spot decisions without consulting or relying on the advice of the home office. Personnel selection, training, and development processes in countries outside the Western world are far from satisfactory. Furthermore, multinational operations are likely to involve ventures, products, and markets new at least to the parent firm. And, the current growth of multinational business often requires that home-country nationals be sent abroad to staff new overseas operations, at least in the initial stages. Since the environment is likely to be considerably different overseas, new and particular skills are required to guide these operations. There is also a higher degree of financial and business risk involved in sending people abroad. If, at the same time, the manager responsible for selection is not fully aware of the circumstances and requirements that prevail overseas, the problems are compounded.

These conditions add uncertainty and complexity to the firm's staffing function. The management of human resources, particularly managerial manpower, becomes important for the continued success of a multinational firm. The human resource function includes those activities essential to attract, retain, and motivate qualified personnel. It thus involves determining the personnel requirements for the jobs to be performed, recruitment and selection of candidates for positions, training and developing these employees for improved performance, and providing adequate compensation so that they contribute effectively to the organization. This chapter will present an overview of managerial manpower problems in multinational business enterprises.

MULTINATIONAL MANPOWER PLANNING

The first phase of an effective human resource management strategy starts with manpower planning—forecasting future personnel requirements in terms of different regions and different functions. With these requirements as a basis, the company can then identify all available current personnel who have the potential to fill future positions. The gap between the two provides data for scheduling recruitment. The recruitment plan can then be drawn up in terms of time required for recruitment, selection, and training. The appraisal of the staff serves as a diagnosis for prescribing training and development for both existing personnel and potential replacements.

The manpower planning program at Royal Dutch-Shell, a multinational firm, follows this approach.[2] The company utilizes a fifteen-year manpower forecast based on its long-range planning cycle. This forecast estimates future needs in different parts of the world and for different functions. The forecasts are then matched against an inventory of those with potential to qualify for projected positions. The gap between the two provides targets for recruitment. The prediction of management replacement needs and the scheduling of recruitment to fill the gap between existing management abilities and future requirements contributes to the smooth functioning of the entire organization.

SOURCES OF MULTINATIONAL MANAGERS

In general, there are three sources of recruitment open to most multinational firms for staffing foreign operations. One is to recruit a suitable person in the home country (expatriate) and send him or her on an overseas assignment; the second is to find a suitable person in the country of operations (host country) and hire him or her for the managerial position; and the third is to find a third-country national. For example, Oxy-Dry Sprayer of Chicago sent an American to be the manager of its subsidiary in Shannon, Ireland; General Foods recruited a Mexican national to manage its operations in Mexico; Eaton Corporation selected an Austrian to be the manager of its Argentine axle operations. We will briefly discuss the pros and cons of filling managerial positions abroad with home country personnel or foreign nationals versus third country nationals.

Home Country Nationals (Expatriates)

There is generally a strong desire on the part of many multinational firms to employ personnel from the parent country. For example, most United States firms feel that American business should be represented and managed abroad by Americans. The argument for this is that, in the event of a difference between national policy and the interests of the firm, native personnel will naturally favor national policy over company interests in order to remain in good standing with their government and fellow citizens. There is also a strong argument that communication between headquarters and operating units is easier and more effective if management positions are held by Americans. They will also be able to translate parent company policies more effectively than foreigners, who presumably have comparatively little knowledge of parent company points of view and ways of doing business. Furthermore, the United States enjoys a comparative advantage in educational facilities for management that is unequaled around the globe.

Host Country Nationals

The strategic advantages of giving assignments to host country personnel, on the other hand, are becoming increasingly important. Many observers feel that multinational companies should give first preference to nationals of the country in which they are doing business. These people will be familiar with the local language, the environment, and the culture, and can be more effective than home country personnel in interacting with task agents—customers, government agencies, employees, and the general public. This practice also minimizes the problem of cross-cultural adjustments for home country nationals and their families. Since their careers will be in their home country, nationals will provide stability and continuity in foreign subsidiaries. The firm can more closely identify itself with national aspirations when its affiliates are managed by nationals of that country. This is particularly true in developing countries, where economic progress and managerial skill development are important goals. In many countries, national laws require that a certain proportion of top managers, if not the chief executives, be nationals of that country.

The employment of host country nationals is not without its faults and problems. The education, experience, and cultural attributes they have developed in their home environment may create a communication gap with the parent company. They may also experience cross-cultural problems in utilizing management knowhow and technology largely developed in the parent company's home country. Additionally, many countries, both developed as well as developing, lack a large pool of qualified managers. Even in countries such as France, Belgium, The Netherlands, Italy, and Spain, business education has not kept abreast of the demands of the industry at the college level.

Third Country Nationals

The third country as a source of managerial personnel is quite limited at this stage. Some companies with fairly extensive multinational operations transfer managers from other overseas affiliates when they are unable to identify and attract competent local personnel. For example, several American firms have utilized Cuban nationals very effectively in managerial positions throughout Latin America; other American firms use British citizens in Asian countries. European-based multinational firms have often employed third country nationals as a matter of course.

Some of the advantages and disadvantages related to home country nationals also apply to third country nationals. However, there are two major differences. First, the cost of employing the third country national may be lower than that for the American national. Second, the third country national may be more knowledgeable about the host country than the home country national. The major disadvantage again is the desire of host countries to have their own nationals employed. On the whole, most companies operating abroad prefer personnel from the parent company country when qualified local nationals are not available. There is as yet no well-formulated policy among multinational companies on the issue of employing third country nationals.

Changing Trends

In addition to these choices, there are various combinations of home country nationals or expatriates, foreigners from the country of operation, or third country nationals. More and more American companies try to employ nationals as much as possible whenever the needed skills are available in the country in which they have operations. American firms in Brazil, for example, are increasing the proportion of local nationals in high-level positions (see Table 7-1).[3] The trend is changing in the direction of more local (and third country) nationals and fewer

Americans. Watson, who conducted this research, cites the following three major factors influencing this trend:

1. More well-trained Brazilians. Companies reported that the availability of increasing numbers of qualified local nationals was the factor most responsible for the change. In turn, better education, industrial experience gained in U.S. subsidiaries, and company training appear to have contributed to this increased availability of better-qualified Brazilians.
2. Cost of sending an American abroad. The cost difference between Americans and Brazilians has also encouraged companies to hire more Brazilians. Companies reported that the cost of sending an American manager (with wife and two children) to Brazil for a three-year stay amounted to between $12,000 to $14,000, plus additional expenses including a trial visit, travel, moving expenses, auto purchase subsidy, local expenses, and yearly trips back to the United States for the manager and his family.
3. Relations with the host country. The companies feel that nationals, rather than Americans, should manage their subsidiaries in Brazil. One reason for this preference is the advantage of long-term commitment by the local nationals to the company. The companies studied felt that morale could be maintained at a higher level if Brazilians were not limited to the lower job levels. When the Brazilians saw that higher-level jobs were not reserved for Americans, they were more committed to the success of the company.

TABLE 7-1

Number and Percentage of Brazilian, American, and Third Country Nationals in Managerial Positions of American-Owned Subsidiaries in Brazil

Nationality of Manager	*1950 (18 firms)*		*1960 (51 firms)*		*1970 (69 firms)*	
	No.	*%*	*No.*	*%*	*No.*	*%*
Brazilian	29	46.0	94	40.8	288	64.2
American	32	50.8	120	52.3	112	24.8
Third country	2	3.2	16	6.9	50	11.0
Total	63	100.0%	230	100.0%	450	100.0%

Source: Charles E. Watson, "The Brazilianization of U.S. Subsidiaries," *Personnel,* July-August 1972, p. 57. Reprinted by permission of the publisher. © 1972 by the American Management Association, Inc.

This and other studies show that in recent years there has been an increasing trend toward the employment of foreign nationals in managerial positions. Other reasons have also prompted this change. The laws of some countries limit the total number of nonnationals who may be employed. The governments of these countries see the foreign firms as not taking interest in contributing to the national economy if they are not required to train nationals and give them opportunities. Public opinion may be against the practice of hiring only nonnationals for key positions. The trend toward localization of management personnel is also based on the costs involved. The direct cost of moving an American family abroad usually amounts to a sizable sum ($30,000 for Brazil, $15,000 for Mexico). In addition, there are costs related to orientation and development of language skills, not to mention higher salaries and a host of allowances. According to some estimates, the direct costs of employing Americans in high-level posts abroad are approximately three to four times the average costs of employing nationals for the same positions.[4] In return, the expectation generally is that the company gets the services of a skilled manager who is an American. However, cultural differences may reduce the managerial effectiveness of American personnel in terms of dealing with people and becoming knowledgeable about local conditions.

Generally speaking, the current trend in most multinational firms is to follow a policy of favoring the recruitment of local nationals for their subsidiaries and home country nationals for headquarters management. A large number of companies initially staff the newly created foreign operations with home country personnel and then replace them with local personnel. Home country nationals are sent overseas to establish operations and to fill in until local talent can be found or developed. This practice has certain inherent advantages. The staff from the parent company can do the initial job of setting up the operation and providing useful guidance for potential local managers during the formative years of the affiliate company. They can effectively transfer the technological strength of the parent company to the subsidiary and be available for the required frequent contact in the initial period. Other companies send their home country personnel on a short-term basis to implement technological advances or introduce new products. On the whole, the proportion of local nationals as managers of American subsidiaries increases markedly with the age of operation.

Long-Run Strategy

The most appropriate strategy for a multinational company would seem to be one of staffing operations at all levels in the organization with truly multinational managers. That is, recruitment should transcend nationality considerations and the location of the job in question. This approach has a positive effect on the selection process; it increases the number of candidates available for selection and enhances the chances of finding qualified personnel. It also adds to the company's capacity to mobilize and shift management personnel from country to country and to one of the major economies contributing to the success of any large-scale enterprise. Such a strategy will also be consistent with the esprit de corps of a multinational company.

There have been, however, only limited beginnings by a relatively few multinational companies, such as Unilever, Royal Dutch-Shell, and Nestlé, toward developing a truly multinational managerial cadre. One can find Belgians in Unilever's office in Austria, Austrians in Greece, Spaniards in Germany, Germans in Portugal, Frenchmen in Italy, Italians in France, and so on. Royal Dutch-Shell has the policy of choosing the best man for the job regardless of nationality. Top management positions of various affiliates of the company are held by nationals of the country or executives who have been transferred from other countries. About one-third of the headquarters executives at Nestlé are non-Swiss.

There are a number of plausible reasons why this mode of developing truly multinational managers is not widely prevalent in American-based MNCs. First, such a policy is expensive; it involves widespread recruitment, substantial training and development, and extensive transfers. Second, many countries feel strongly that foreign subsidiaries should be staffed by local nationals and often pressure companies or legally require them to follow this strategy. Lastly, many companies are in the early stage of becoming truly multinational. The practice of developing multinational managers may become more widespread as MNCs mature. The need to develop teams consisting of different nationalities in the management of multinational companies is now generally recognized.[5]

Given these choices and their consequences, how does a multinational firm decide on a strategy for staffing global operations? The choice depends on an analysis of a number of factors: First, constraints that it faces by way of national controls and policies favoring the hiring of local nationals; second, the supply of managerial personnel in the countries of operation; third, the cost of alternative policies, including the cost of remedying the deficiencies of the policies; and fourth, the difficulties and importance of cross-national communication, coordination, and supervision for the type of business activity in which the firm is engaged.[6] Irrespective of the policies pursued by the company, it needs to develop a long-range strategy of exposing its managerial personnel, particularly the higher echelons of its management, to some multinational experience. Developing managers with a multinational outlook and frame of mind is essential for the continued success of the enterprise.

RECRUITMENT AND SELECTION

The success of an effective recruitment program will depend on how well a multinational company locates and taps sources of managerial manpower. The potential varies from one country to another.[7] Candidates for overseas assignments from the home country emanate both from within the organization and from outside. The vast majority of American managers overseas have generally come from within the organization. More important, the key positions in subsidiaries generally go to insiders. When outside people are utilized, they are generally from other companies. Colleges and universities are, of course, the major source for recruiting candidates for company operations at home and abroad. Similar practices are followed by Japanese- and European-based multinational firms. Although college recruitment is common in the United States, it is much less prevalent in less developed countries, where newspaper advertising, employment exchanges, and word-of-mouth are more popular for attracting new workers. Private employment agencies are common in European countries, and a number of American management recruiting and consulting firms have also established offices in major European cities to help multinational firms in their recruiting endeavors. In Japan, establishing close contact with higher educational institutions and making requirements known to authorities is an acceptable practice.

One source many American and European multinational firms have tapped is that of foreign nationals in their countries temporarily as students and trainees. This source may provide well-qualified applicants for future managerial positions in a firm's international operations. There is a large number of foreign students in the United States, a good proportion of whom are pursuing advanced studies in science, engineering, and business. These candidates have the proper combination of an understanding of the host country environment and an exposure to American management processes and behavior.

Generally speaking, various combinations of interviews and tests are utilized to judge the potential of candidates. Selecting a current employee for an overseas assignment, provided his or her abilities and skills match the requirements of the job, is much simpler than hiring someone from outside. The experiences of multinational firms show that certain qualifications are regarded as essential for an executive's success abroad.[8] Job competence and expertise should be one of the major criteria in screening a candidate for overseas assignment. As Francis J. McCabe, chief of personnel at International Telephone and Telegraph, put it, "Ability at his job is the sine qua non abroad, as it is here." In addition, a potential multinational manager should possess all the basic management qualifications; he should be able to plan, organize, communicate, and control the operations of the company. Here, broad knowledge of business and a multinational orientation are considered extremely useful. The personal qualities of the individual in terms of character, sincerity, integrity, and so forth play a more important role than in the domestic situation. One of the most important factors in the selection process is the ability and willingness of the individual and his family to adjust to working and living conditions abroad.

Cross-cultural Adaptation

Cross-cultural transfers involve the hardships of physical separation from home. In addition to this, the expatriate and his family must adapt to an unfamiliar cultural environment that may frequently be at odds with their own. Further, intercultural competence implies not only a facility in language, but a certain degree of sensitivity to local people and their ways of doing things. The problem of cross-cultural adjustment has come up again and again in the experiences of companies and in research studies. For example, during the early 1960s approximately 80 percent of American executives in Japan were transferred back to their bases in the United States because of their inability to adjust to the Japanese way of doing business.

Research shows that managers in charge of the selection for overseas assignment often discount the significance of the candidate's ability to live and work successfully in a foreign environment.[9] Technical and managerial skills have been considered of primary importance. Kapoor and McKay's study of training for multinational marketing management also shows that technical knowledge and past performance are primary considerations for overseas assignment.[10]

Another study, by Ivancevich, was designed to ascertain the opinion of selectors of overseas American managers and of the overseas managers themselves regarding the weight to be placed on various personal factors in screening candidates.[11] Respondents from the United States (that is, American executives in charge of selection) rated three factors as highly important: (1) the manager's independence and ability to achieve results with limited resources, (2) sincerity, and (3) technical knowledge of the job for which he was being considered. A person's previous overseas experience and his youthfulness were rated as least important. In contrast, the respondents from abroad (that is, American managers currently working abroad) chose the following three as being more important than others: (1) the wife's opinion about undertaking a foreign assignment, (2) sincerity, and (3) attitude and adaptability. What this means is that American executives responsible for selecting and assigning Americans overseas have a different set of expectations. For them, such factors as adaptability, interest in foreign culture, language ability, and so forth rank relatively low. The responses of those living and working abroad for some time, however, emphasize pragmatic considerations such as the wife's opinion and the manager's own attitudes and adaptability.

The following example of the failure of foreign subsidiary managers to adapt to a new environment in a culturally distant country is not uncommon:

> The Japanese parent company set up a subsidiary in Shannon to manufacture and assemble electronic products such as transistorized radios. Two men were placed in charge of the Shannon operations, both of them Japanese and, unfortunately, not very fluent in the English language, let alone the Gaelic.
>
> Because of the language difficulty, these two managers appeared to have relied too heavily upon the Irish and British subordinate managers for

> organizing and coordinating the day-to-day operations. These subordinate managers, for one reason or another, did not live up to the expectations of their Japanese managers, and internal problems became excessive.
>
> Externally speaking, the relations or interactions with other foreign managers (American, British and others) was little or none. Whether the Japanese managers shied away from other foreign managers, or whether the American, British, and French managers gave a cold shoulder to the Japanese is hard to discern. Possibly, both happened. In any event, the Japanese managers got little help from their colleagues in the industrial estate.
>
> Thus, the Japanese managers were confronted both by internal problems which were operational in nature and by external problems which were adaptational in nature. In short, the parent company decided to fold its operations in Shannon.[12]

This example and other research studies suggest that the selection practices of multinational firms in filling overseas positions are frequently unsystematic and occasionally chaotic.[13] They point to the need to pay increased attention, at the time of selection, to personal and family-related factors.

A major part of the human resources for foreign operations comes from the country in which the company operates. The success of those operations will depend greatly on the quality of local nationals employed. Thus recruiting and selecting the best available local talent is the crux of the problem. The methods employed to assess applicants and to select the most suitable vary considerably according to a country's cultural background and traditions, degree of industrialization, and the state of the labor market. Many multinational firms operate in both developed and less developed countries. Available manpower differs significantly from country to country, especially between developed and less developed countries.[14] Most of the less developed countries are characterized by serious shortages of many of the skills needed by modern industry and by a great surplus of people with little or no skills, training, or education. The development of adequate managerial resources has been one of the key problems of economic growth in the developing countries of Asia, Latin America, and Africa.

Once the sources of supply of talented and qualified candidates are identified, selection tools such as tests and interviews need to be carefully designed so that they are applicable to foreign nationals. Tests developed in the United States and in other industrialized nations need to be adapted to meet local conditions. Standard Oil of New Jersey (now Exxon) has developed its own tests of general ability and aptitude for use in the selection of foreign nationals in Belgium, Brazil, Iran, Lybia, Venezuela, and other countries.

TRAINING AND DEVELOPMENT

Orientation and training for multinational operations is the next important step in the staffing process. An orientation program covering the country, its people, and its culture will facilitate the adjustment of a home country national to the foreign environment, for experience shows that living in a foreign country without adequate orientation leads to ''culture shock.'' In order to overcome this problem, companies provide training in language skills, along with a basic knowledge of the host country, its people, and its culture. Because of the limited international perspective, orientation, and experience of most Americans, management development efforts aimed at United States nationals are likely to take on a more cultural orientation and be geared toward understanding the business and social environment, as well as gaining a good command of the language of the foreign country.

Frederick A. Teague, an international management consultant with Booz, Allen, and Hamilton, suggests the following training program for the American manager about to be sent overseas:

1. Ensure capability in the language of the country to which he will be sent. If at all possible, this ought to be accomplished before he leaves his country, both to reduce start-up time in the new job and to add an important element of confidence for the first few months.
2. Give him a basic understanding of business practices, competitive conditions, and market opportunities in the foreign country.
3. Extend this basic understanding to include more about the country—its geography, economy, and social structure.[15]

Multinational companies use various methods to train managers for their overseas operations. For example, Goodyear each year hires junior executives with an interest and some educational background in multinational business. These men and women are then given a year or two of training in the company's operating divisions and sent out to acquire practical experience with one of the thirty Goodyear subsidiaries. Having completed their on-the-job training, they are moved upward within the same subsidiary or within another company in another country, depending upon their success. National Cash Register too has established a training course for overseas managers at its headquarters office in Dayton, Ohio.

Companies also use outside facilities to train executives for multinational assignments. A number of universities and institutions in the United States have training programs for multinational managers, among them Columbia University's Graduate School of Business, the Institute for International Management at Northwestern University, the School of International Service at American Univeristy, the American Management Association, and the Thunderbird Graduate School of International Management. Their programs are aimed at developing understanding of the business and social environment and the language of the foreign country.

Similar practices are followed by European-based multinationals. The first stage of a training program in European multinational companies is preparation for the first overseas assignment. Some companies conduct in-company training programs in which candidates are exposed to veterans who have returned from abroad to the home office. Others send people out as junior managers and let them demonstrate on-the-job capabilities. Still others use programs developed by universities and institutions to train their candidates for overseas assignment. Such programs include management techniques, study of the foreign business environment, and foreign languages. A few institutions also provide a multinational faculty to give a global point of view. These are mostly limited to continental Europe—the European Institute of Business Administration (INSEAD) at Fontainebleu, France; the Center for Education in International Management in Geneva; and IMEDE in Lausanne, Switzerland.[16]

For the developing countries of Africa, Asia, and Latin America, the potential contribution of multinational firms is not only capital but also skill development in technical as well as managerial areas. Most such countries encourage the foreign investor, but with an understanding (or hope) that he will in some way guarantee employment and training of local nationals for managerial positions. Many multinationals have realized that their continued presence in these countries will depend to a great extent on their success in developing and training competent nationals. American multinationals overseas typically have extensive training programs for nationals.

When they establish themselves, particularly in developing countries, the foreign units have not only to follow their parent company policies in the area of training and development but also to overcome deficiencies in the training and education of their employees. A variety of programs are the major means for upgrading nationals in many firms—company training programs; training in outside educational and vocational institutions; development through self-improvement, private study, job rotation, and delegation of authority. According to various studies conducted by the National Planning Association on American business performance abroad, these training and educational programs are of several kinds, each designed to fit the needs of a particular country, industry, or group of employees.

For the most part, a foreign unit must expect to do most of the training within its own organization, because outside facilities are usually rather limited.[17] However, a number of countries have started institutionalizing management training programs modeled on American business schools; the American Management Association now has centers in Latin America and Europe, and several American universities conduct summer programs on other continents. As part of managerial development, some American multinational firms follow the practice of bringing foreigners who are in their employ elsewhere to the United States for training. For example, First National City Bank of New York has an elaborate training program for its multinational managers that involves visits to the United States and training at the main office. The experiences of companies show that such practices enhance the abilities as well as the loyalty of foreign employees. The development of an adequate managerial force has been one of the key problems of economic growth in a number of developing countries such as Argentina, Brazil, Chile, Egypt, and India.[18] One of the important contributions American multinational companies can make to these countries is the upgrading of skills through training and development programs.

In sum, multinational firms should have a well-planned strategy for training and developing managers for overseas operations. Such a strategy should specify clearly the types of training and development experiences, formal educational programs, on-the-job training, and so on available for managers at all levels. The strategy should be flexible so that it can be adapted to significant environmental differences among countries.[19] It should lay a sound foundation for the worldwide development of global executive personnel.

MULTINATIONAL COMPENSATION SYSTEMS

A multinational compensation system should effectively support the broad human resources objective of the company. To a large degree, the quality of multinational corporate management will depend upon how well the company administers its compensation system. Hence, a compensation system must be designed to attract, retain, and motivate the kind of managers desired in the multinational environment.

A vast majority of multinationals, particularly United States firms, developed compensation systems for expatriate employees with the following three components:

1. A base salary tied in with salary ranges of comparable domestic assignments
2. Premiums and inducements to encourage mobility and to compensate for the hardship of living in unfamiliar locations
3. Allowances to permit continuation of their style of living. Most common allowances are cost of living, housing, education, and tax protection[20]

The rates of base pay must of course be responsive to American labor market conditions and be equivalent to the pay for a similar job in domestic operations—in other words, the same base salary is paid all Americans whether at home or abroad. Such a system minimizes the difficulty of transfers, maintains common worldwide standards, and is easily justifiable.

Overseas employment involves working in a different environment, often with some disadvantages compared with working in a domestic environment. An American manager may have to work with a language barrier; may be separated from home, family, friends, and business associates; and may have greater responsibility in terms of overseeing operations with less assistance from the parent company. Finally, since he represents the company and home country in a foreign land, he has an added public relations responsibility. All these factors inherent in many foreign assignments seem to justify not only an attractive base pay, but also some form of premium to compensate the expatriate manager.

Most multinational companies pay their American managers abroad a premium in one form or another—usually a proportion of the domestic base pay. A few companies have established special overseas pay scales that are generally higher than the domestic base pay scales and thus incorporate a premium for overseas service into the total payment. The basic idea behind the premium is that it is a reward for moving away from one's home environment and living in an unfamiliar foreign environment. For example, Hewlett-Packard pays a "family hardship" premium for service in Moscow, Taiwan, Tokyo, and Singapore because of cultural differences.[21]

There are two types of premiums: (1) a uniform amount, which is given to people regardless of where they are located and determined on the basis of either a percentage or a fixed amount, and (2) a variable amount depending on where the personnel are assigned. The uniform amount has the advantage of simplicity and consistency, and it eliminates the administrative problem of measuring and justifying differences, particularly if a company faces moving its American managers from one country to another. The variable formula is used by few companies.

The following two factors peculiar to foreign assignments are considered in determining overseas premiums: (1) job-related factors—handling different government and personnel relations, training activities dealing with foreign nationals and language problems, ingenuity in solving technical problems without constant help from the home office, isolation from professional resources or contacts; and (2) social and cultural factors—separation from relatives and friends, language problems, social adjustments, climate, food and health standards, cultural shock and adjustments, limited and different recreational environment, a new political and legal environment, fears of living in a politically unstable area. Some firms quantify this as the location environmental factor index and show it as a percentage of base salaries. In recent past one MNC used the index shown in Table 7-2.

The compensation policies pursued by companies are not uniform by any means. Some pay base salary plus premium and allowances; others use alternative practices. For example, the European-based Nestlé provides a gross currency salary without defining its composition. But there is a general pattern of pay plus fringe benefits for expatriate employees. It is common practice for American and British multinational firms to pay a base salary determined according to the domestic salary structure and position evaluation plans, plus a salary premium.[22] Salary premiums are usually expressed as percentages of salary, and generally range from 10 to 30 percent of base salaries, depending on the area involved.

TABLE 7-2

Location Environmental Factor Index

Location	*Index**	*Location*	*Index**
Europe		*America*	
Austria		Argentina	
Wels	15%	Buenos Aires	15%
		Mendoza	20
Belgium			
Brussels	10	Brazil	
		Sao Paulo	15
Denmark		Mogi Gaucu	20
Copenhagen	10		
		Chile	
France		Santiago	15
Clamart (Paris)	10	Llay Llay	30
Herqueville	20	*USA*	
West Germany		New York	10
Hamburg	10	*Asia*	
Wittingen	20	India	
Ireland		Bombay	25
Dublin	10	Pakistan	
Italy		Lyallpur	30
Milan	10	Thailand	
Treviso	20	Bangkok	20

*Percentage of base salary.
Source: A recent international personnel policy administrative guide of a well-known MNC.

In order to reimburse employees for excessively higher costs of living abroad, companies usually pay a cost-of-living allowance wherever applicable. The most popular method of calculating this allowance is to base it on the U.S. State Department's local index. This regularly constructed index covers the major cities of the world and measures the difference between cost of living in Washington, D.C.,, and other major foreign cities. It has the advantages of convenience, ease of accessibility and application, and an air of authoritativeness. Other methods of calculating cost-of-living differentials include using the foreign government's index, calculating a company index, or using some other company's index. The index calculated by foreign governments may not be very reliable and may be difficult to compare. Constructing a company index for a multitude of countries is expensive, and its upgrading and maintenance may not be justified unless the company has a large number of expatriate employees. Using other companies' indexes may be the second-best method if there is mutual cooperation.

Most companies operating overseas pay this allowance to employees assigned to locations where living costs are higher than in the United States.

Payments are either in flat dollar amounts or percentages of spendable income. In certain cases, educational expenses are also granted to provide adequate schooling facilities for the employee's children whenever such facilities are not available. Among other extras are the housing allowance, personal adjustment payments (such as for language training), moving allowance, and income tax equalization allowance. The income tax allowance is intended to equalize the burden in terms of reimbursing the employee for any tax paid in excess of his normal U.S. tax or deducting the savings gained by foreign residence. Furthermore, rapidly changing exchange rates suggest a critical review of compensation policies of MNCs.

In recent years, the cost of these extras has risen dramatically. Many companies are said to be taking some hard looks at their policies for compensating foreign-based managers. MNCs are showing a marked trend toward cutting back on the proportion of Americans working for them overseas and toward making far greater use of the nationals of the countries in which they operate primarily because of the high cost of living abroad. Most companies tend to use the supplements not to compensate absolutely for rising costs but rather to make up cost differentials between what the manager would spend, say, for a house in the United States and what he might spend for a comparable house in a foreign location. As housing costs rise in the United States the differential narrows, and as a result companies have tended to revise housing supplements downward.

TABLE 7-3

Cost of Living Indexes

Location	*Index*	*Exchange Rate*
Europe		
Brussels	119%	49.5 BF
London	117	0.357
Milan	118	
Paris	127	4.9 NF
Zurich	118	4.35 Fr
Japan	130	
South America		
Buenos Aires	105	235 P
Caracas	130	4.4 B
Santiago	105	4.2 E
São Paulo	95	2,200 Cr

Source: A recent international personnel policy administrative guide of a well-known MNC.

In the area of compensating third country nationals, the problems faced by companies at this stage of development are many: First, there are few statistical data available that are applicable to various combinations of countries of origin and other country assignment locations. Second, there is no common industry practice to use as a guide. Some American companies treat third country nationals exactly like Americans as far as base salaries and allowances are concerned. Other companies handle the compensation of third country nationals on a case-by-case basis, and still others pay them as if they were local national employees. Third, there are some unique complications in establishing compensation for third country nationals. In the case of the American employee abroad, it is assumed that he will remain an American, but this is not necessarily true for the third country national.

The essential objectives in developing a compensation system for the third country national should be to relate base salary to what is prevailing in his home country with certain allowances to enable him to maintain his accustomed standard of living. Up to this point, the problem of designing a compensation program for third country nationals has not become serious because these people are few in number and can be treated on an individual basis. But when the numbers grow in terms of number of countries from which personnel are drawn and number of countries to which personnel are assigned, designing, operating, and maintaining a compensation program will present enormous problems.[23]

Compensation policies for host country personnel have serious implications for the quality of personnel a firm can attract and retain. As discussed earlier, the companies usually pay a higher basic salary to an expatriate employee than to a national doing a comparable job. The differential, according to companies, should reflect a premium for overseas service, which entails working in a different economic and social environment; salary and wage levels for local nationals are guided by the prevailing rates. In a number of countries, the compensation system is quite complicated. The extra allowances, multitudinous in nature, greatly outweigh in value the basic pay of the individual. For example, in Japan, salaries are traditionally computed on a monthly basis with numerous components, including a minimum rate, basic rate, family allowance, seasonal bonus, cost-of-living adjustment, regional allowance, transportation and housing allowance, and the like. Age and sex differentials further complicate the various wage items. In other cases it is much less complex. In India, the salary payment for managerial personnel consists of three main components—the minimum basic wages, a dearness allowance (an element related to cost of living), and a bonus (an element related to increase in productivity); in Egypt, compensation consists of the basic wage or salary, the cost-of-living allowance, and a special allowance wherever applicable.

When instituting compensation plans for host country personnel, it is essential for multinational firms to recognize that they may not be able to adopt plans and schemes that might have been workable in the home country. They must also recognize that the systems prevalent in Japan or West Germany have their own merits.

SUMMARY

With the growing emphasis on multinational business, the management of human resources becomes increasingly important. The human resource function entails the activities essential to attract, retain, and motivate the qualified personnel required by the company. In this chapter, the human resource question was examined from the point of view of multinational companies as it relates to employing home country, host country, or third country personnel for overseas managerial jobs. The discussion here centered around the pros and cons of filling managerial positions abroad with these different sources of personnel and the significant aspects of recruitment, selection, training, and compensation. Although the benefits from the use of expatriate personnel may be considerable and, on occasion, indispensable, the cost of using them is becoming higher. The human resource policy of a multinational firm should tie in with and reflect other broad policies of the company.

Beyond cost considerations, most multinational firms are concerned with the political environment and the image of the company. As a result, more and more companies are employing and training nationals for managerial positions. The most appropriate strategy for a multinational corporation would seem to be one of recruiting personnel for all levels without regard to nationality and location of employment. The indications are that such a practice will not grow easily because of the many constraints imposed by the host country as well as the high cost of recruiting, training, and transferring personnel around the globe. However, the need to combine multiple nationalities in the management of multinational firms is recognized.

Multinational firms provide various types of on- and off-the-job training programs for their expatriate managers. In order to overcome the problem of cross-cultural adjustment, companies provide training in language skills and in knowledge of the people and culture of the foreign country before managers are assigned abroad. The training and development programs of American multinational firms for their local employees are of several kinds, each designed to fit the needs of the particular country and the particular group of employees. In order to develop managerial skills among its local managers, a multinational company is expected to do most of the training within its own organization, because outside facilities are generally limited in many countries.

A large number of multinational firms develop compensation systems for their expatriate employees with three components: (1) a base salary comparable to domestic assignments, (2) premiums to compensate for the hardship of living abroad, and (3) allowances to permit continuation of their style of living abroad. Of course, as economic and social conditions change around the world, MNCs are modifying their compensation guidelines.

Notes

[1]Frederick A. Teague, "International Management Selection and Development," *California Management Review*, spring 1970, p. 2; Edwin Miller, "The International Selection Decision: A Study of Managerial Behavior in the Selection Decision Process," *Academy of Management Journal*, June 1973, p. 241; Leon C. Megginson, *Personnel: A Behavioral Approach* (Homewood, Ill.: Irwin, 1967), p. 1.

[2]Donald N. Leich, *Transnational Executive Development in the Royal Dutch-Shell Group of Companies* (New York: National Foreign Trade Council, February 1970), p. 4-A. Mimeo.

[3]Charles E. Watson,"The 'Brazilianization' of U.S. Subsidiaries," *Personnel*, July-August 1972, pp. 53-60.

[4]Richard D. Robinson, *International Management* (New York: Holt, Rinehart and Winston, 1967), p. 76.

[5]Peter Kuin, "The Magic of Multinational Management," *Harvard Business Review*, November-December 1972, pp. 89-97.

[6]Stefan H. Robock and Kenneth Simmonds, *International Business and Multinational Enterprise* (Homewood, Ill.: Irwin, 1973), p. 519.

[7]John C. Shearer, "The External and Internal Manpower Resources of MNCs," *Columbia Journal of World Business*, summer 1974, pp. 9-17.

[8]Cecil G. Howard, "Model for the Design of a Selection Program for Multinational Executives," *Public Personnel Management*, March-April 1974, pp. 138-45; Dimitris N. Chorafas, *Developing the International Executive* (New York: American Management Association, 1967).

[9]Miller, *op. cit.*

[10]Ashok Kapoor and Robert J. McKay, *Managing International Markets: A Survey of Training Practices and Emerging Trends* (Princeton, N.J.: Darwin Press, 1971).

[11]John M. Ivancevich, "Selection of American Managers for Overseas Assignment," *Personnel Journal*, March 1969, pp. 189-93.

[12]S. B. Prasad, *Enterprise in Ireland* (Milwaukee: Stein, 1969), pp. 50-51.

[13]James C. Baker and John M. Ivancevich, "The Assignment of American Executives Abroad: Systematic, Haphazard or Chaotic?" *California Management Review*, spring 1971, pp. 39-44; David A. Heenan, "The Corporate Expatriate: Assignment to Ambiguity," *Columbia Journal of World Business*, May-June 1970, pp. 49-54.

[14]Teague, *op. cit.*, pp. 4-5.

[15]Chorafas, *op. cit.,* pp. 17-18.

[16]Thomas Aitken, *The Multinational Man: The Role of the Manager Abroad* (New York: Wiley, 1973), pp. 140-41.

[17]Barry M. Richman and Melvyn R. Copen, *International Management and Economic Development* (New York: McGraw-Hill, 1972), pp. 508-10.

[18]For an analysis of the problems of management development in developing nations, see Y. K. Shetty, "Ownership, Size, Technology and Management Development: A Comparative Study," *Academy of Management Journal*, December 1971, pp. 439-49; also James Lee, "Developing Managers in Developing Countries," *Harvard Business Review*, November-December 1968, pp. 55-65.

[19]William A. Dymsza, *Multinational Business Strategy* (New York: McGraw-Hill, 1972), p. 150.

[20]Calvin Reynolds, "Career Paths and Compensation in the MNCs," *Columbia Journal of World Business*, November-December 1972, pp. 78-79; Hans Schollhammer, "The Compensation of International Executives," *MSU Business Topics*, winter 1969, pp. 19-31.

[21]*Business Week*, January 20, 1975, p. 66.

[22]For a discussion of the compensation practices of multinational corporations operating in Europe, see Jeremiah J. Reen, "Executive Compensation: The Trend Is Up in Europe," *Columbia Journal of World Business*, November-December 1969, pp. 55-61.

[23]David Young, "Fair Compensation for Expatriates," *Harvard Business Review*, July-August 1973, pp. 117-26.

8

Multinational Production

Direct private investment literally means direct participation in manufacturing and marketing. Manufacturing or production can usefully be considered as a subsystem function of a larger business system. Depending on the definition, this larger business system can be a parent firm or one of its subsidiaries. Since our interest is in the latter, we might keep in mind what the frame of reference for this chapter will be. From an analytical point of view, the production subsystem can be viewed as a transformation system, that is, a system that transforms certain inputs into defined outputs. These inputs may be classified as physical, human, and financial; the outputs may be classified as components, parts, and products. The transformation process itself can also be broken down into assembling, manufacturing, processing, and so forth.

What makes the managing of such production subsystems in various parts of the world a challenge are the significant differences in the realm of production subsystem elements. Overseas production takes place in a different economic, social, and political environment that has implications for system inputs, outputs, and the transformation process. The input variables differ in terms of scarcity, quality, cost mix, and procurement. Output-related factors, such as demand, price, product specifications, quality, and customer usage differ significantly from those of the home environment. These differences in input-output variables directly affect the transformation process through the choice of technology, scale of operations, equipment, maintenance, and manufacturing processes and techniques.

Multinational production management is confronted with three broad but basic areas of differences compared with domestic production in addition to product design: the market and supply environment, social and cultural differences, and technical factors.

MARKET FACTORS AND SUPPLY CONDITIONS

Production environments in less developed countries are characterized by small-scale production units throughout the economy and a limited range of demand. Market demand may not be sufficient to warrant the establishment of large plants, especially those using specialized machinery. Hence the utilization of less specialized machinery and processes becomes a necessity. The combined effects of beginning industrialization, limited market size, and the inevitable diseconomies of small-scale production lead to high unit costs. Less specialized techniques raise direct labor inputs substantially, and the smaller-scale plants increase indirect overhead charges, including capital costs and/or inferior quality of a wide range of materials and parts throughout the economy. Hence a cost-profit squeeze often results from manufacturing and procurement difficulties, intensified by national trade and industrialization policies designed to force a high rate of use of domestic materials. High costs are often hidden in the inferior quality of output, since manufacturers may be forced to purchase domestic materials and parts regardless of their acceptability.

The concept of factor scarcity and the relative ease with which production factors can be procured with an acceptable cost-quality-delivery mix is fundamental to decision making in the design and management of a production system. Research into the experience of many international firms operating in developing countries reveals that *procurement is one of the most critical production problems in these countries.* Skinner, after thorough research into the experiences of forty-nine American manufacturing plants operating in developing countries (Vietnam, Turkey, Spain, South Africa, Pakistan, and India), concluded that procurement is an immediate and major source of difficulty in overseas production management: "In their efforts to manage overseas production operations, Americans . . . are wrestling with problems such as . . . how to deal with vendors who are habitually late in delivery . . . how to minimize investment inventory and yet prevent stockouts."[1]

In the face of current world scarcities and import restrictions, firms operating in less developed countries are forced to procure materials and parts that are of higher cost or inferior quality or both relative to the items available in developed countries. The import substitution and domestic content requirements imposed by a number of these countries have had a profound effect on the cost and quality of procurement and plant operations. Most local procurement has to be custom-ordered in small quantities, which means considerably high unit costs. This is true not only of basic materials, but also of other items such as nuts and bolts, new castings, and forgings.

The quality of the supplied materials and parts is a major problem. It is reported that in some countries rejection rates run anywhere from 10 to 50 percent or more. Indicative of what a foreign manufacturer may expect is the experience of Cummins Diesel Company, which discovered that cap screws manufactured in India had been surface treated, which in combination with the lower quality of the steel resulted in the screw snapping or distorting under tension.[2]

In Mexico, it is reported that the major deficiencies among local suppliers of automobile parts were (a) inadequate quality control, (b) low level of technical sophistication and engineering capabilities compared to American suppliers, and (c) an almost complete lack of research and development capabilities to adapt parts design or production techniques to local materials, skills, and available equipment. On the whole, quality standards on supplied materials and parts were found to be substantially lower in Mexico than in the United States.[3] Similarly, a pharmaceutical company's preliminary survey of conditions in Spain indicated many sources of glass bottles and apparently reliable vendors for packaging supplies. But after production started, it found the vendors unreliable for quality and delivery. Standards were far below those expected by the company, and serious shortages and production line stoppages resulted.[4] In Turkey too, it is reported that foreign companies continuously face problems of quality, delivery, and pricing in their relations with local vendors. Of course, irregular transportation or lack of transportation may also make it difficult to provide an adequate supply of materials on time.

Costs, quality, and delivery are the three vital factors in supplier capability. In less developed countries, these variables pose serious problems for the design and efficient operation of the production system. As a result of inadequate procurement sources, considerable managerial talent has to be devoted to cultivating domestic suppliers and rendering technical and other assistance. Time and resources need to be expended to convey industrial techniques, develop quality control, and assist in equipment engineering. This is in marked contrast to industrially developed countries, where much of the technical knowhow comes from part suppliers who advise manufacturers on product design and production techniques. Often, companies are forced to shut down production for varying lengths of time because they are unable to obtain necessary materials.

SOCIAL AND CULTURAL FACTORS

The production system requires both human and material resources. Creating an efficient work force through systematic recruitment, selection, training, motivation, and supervision presents formidable problems in developing countries. Manufacturing plants have difficulty obtaining managerial and technical personnel to plan and carry out production programs that include effective controls, maintenance, and the efficient utilization of facilities.

Adapting attitudes and values to desired level of proficiency is one of the basic problems in the management of production systems in developing countries. The sources of this problem are numerous: lack of skills, education, an industrial tradition, and discipline; and certain cultural attitudes. Factory organization based on kinship and personal relation, rather than ability and productivity, can undermine labor force efficiency and the effectiveness of an entire system.

Workers, often recruited from traditional agricultural sectors in many developing nations, are only partly committed to industrial employment and seek personal relationships and individual recognition in their work environment. This partial commitment is a result of the new environment of the industrial setting, which is entirely different from the traditional environment. The socioeconomic

TABLE 8-1

Selected Cultural Factors Affecting Production Management

Factor	*Perceived as*	*Could Affect These Areas of Production Management*
Attitude		
toward the future	Luck or predestination	Planning and scheduling
toward life	"Here today"	Safety precautions, work schedule, deadlines
Personal belief of		
right and wrong	Ends justifying the means	Inventory control Supplies control
societal and management role	Providing for the individual	Labor and industrial relations
Source of authority	Absolute	Interpersonal and intragroup relationships
Status	Correlated with age and wisdom	Change and innovation in methods and procedures

Source: C. Wickham Skinner, "Management of International Production," *Harvard Business Review,* September-October 1964, pp. 125-26.

structure of an agrarian society—strong family ties and personal social relations—makes the worker seek a similar structure in his work situation. In many countries, individuals and groups accustomed to craft-oriented industry have had considerable difficulty adjusting to the techniques and organization associated with modern mechanized factories.

In a highly mechanized Indian textile mill, for example, efficiency of production and quality of output were lowered by social values oriented to small cohesive groups. Workers felt lost operating isolated machines in a huge factory building. On automatic machines, they no longer had to service their looms, refill shuttles, or stop equipment to prevent damage, making them feel they had been reduced from craftsmen to laborers.[5] An American manufacturer of diesel engines in northern Scotland encountered similar problems in adapting local labor to machine capabilities.

Manufacturing in diverse cultural environments brings a new dimension to many conventional decisions in production management. Effectiveness of the system, control procedures, and choice of equipment, for example, all depend on the values, habits, and attitudes of employees and supervisors. Table 8-1 suggests some of the impacts that cultural differences have on manufacturing operations.[6]

TECHNICAL FACTORS

The technical realm refers to differences relating to methods of production, which include choice of plant size, equipment, and processes; product design; and other technical aspects. To be effective and viable, a production system's ingredients must be congruent with those of the environment. It follows therefore that a successful production technology should be derived in part from a realistic assessment of the total environment in which it is to operate. As Farmer commented, "What is visible in a Western factory is the drama of machines in action. . . . What is not immediately seen, however, is the fact that when you take the machinery, you also take the organization that goes with it."[7]

Economists studying industrial development have devoted considerable effort to studying appropriate technological strategies for the less developed countries. Some argue that a labor-intensive technology is more appropriate for these countries because it means (a) increased employment; (b) lower capital requirements; (c) wider distribution of purchasing power; (d) lower skill requirements in maintenance, equipment operation, and management; and (e) shorter setup and breakdown times due to use of less complex equipment. This argument is based on the assumption that a developing country can utilize its resource endowments more effectively by economizing on scarce resources and making more extensive use of its abundant resources. Others recommend capital-intensive technology for the developing countries because it results in high efficiency and therefore greater production, higher national income, increased savings and investment, and hence a surplus for capital formation.

Even though labor rates are lower in the developing countries than in the United States and specialized machinery is available to multinational firms, this does not automatically mean that unit costs of production will necessarily be lower. In most of these countries, the market size for a large number of products is smaller because of lower purchasing power. This factor generally results in lower volume of production. Shorter production runs, lower labor rates, and lower skills mean that the cost of highly mechanized or automated machines cannot be justified. In choosing technology, more flexible thinking on equipment decisions to take into account the economic needs of the country, the skills and attitudes of employees, and short- and long-range cost considerations may be necessary. The choice need not be one or the other; many different combinations are possible depending upon the specific needs of the country and industry in question.

The experiences of multinational companies reveal that the standard machinery manufactured in the advanced countries has a much larger production capacity than that warranted by the prospective size of the domestic and foreign markets of most industrializing countries. Imbalance in the productive capacities of the equipment needed for carrying out a specific industrial operation may result in idle production periods and a rise in overhead costs. Technical experts consider it preferable to install, for certain essential operations, several small machines rather than a single large one, so that the entire factory will not have to shut down in case of a breakdown. There are also indications that the use of multipurpose machinery would permit more economic operation than single-purpose equipment. With multipurpose equipment, the size of the plant can be reduced and the production of small quantities may become economical.

Adaptations of the techniques of production, including the development of new technologies, may involve new combinations of machines, modifications in certain parts of the machinery, or the designing of new industrial apparatus. These changes are primarily made to achieve optimum utilization of capital, skilled labor, and other scarce resources. Speaking of the experiences of the Rockwell Manufacturing Company in West Germany, Bowman notes: "Shorter production runs and lower labor rates mean that highly mechanized machines cannot be justified. . . . The procedure to determine whether a certain machine or method will pay can be the same as in the U.S. . . . but the result frequently indicated that it pays to use more labor and a cheaper or less specialized machine."[8]

In practice, however, there is a wide gap between the theory of tailoring production processes to the environment and the actual, detailed plant design by the multinational company. Most companies, it is reported, tend to use basically the same processes and equipment abroad as currently or previously employed in the United States, for a number of reasons: the need for achieving quality and keeping maintenance to a minimum, the non-availability of alternative choices immediately, the length and complexity of the redesigning process, the considerable startup and "debugging" problems, and the advantage of familiarity with existing processes.[9] Actual design and construction of plants are often undertaken by American construction firms such as the Austin Company, Cunningham-Limp, and Bechtel.

PRODUCT DESIGN

The production system is also influenced by the nature of the parts or product design, the volume of demand, and local preferences. Even from the commercial point of view, there is often a need to modify product design and production techniques to meet the industrial capability of the developing nations. As Cateora and Hess remarked: "An ironic fact about U.S. companies is that on the domestic market they are very consumer-oriented . . . yet in their foreign marketing they are highly production-oriented."[10] Increased competition, say from a German or a Japanese subsidiary, may modify that orientation.

The production system encounters demands for changes in its configuration based on differences in economic conditions, physical and cultural environments, legal restrictions, and consumer preferences. For example, in the design of diesel engines for commercial trucks, such factors as horsepower, road speed, engine weight, longevity, reliability, and driver convenience have to be integrated to fit a particular market and customer usage. The Cummins Diesel Company's experience in countries such as Mexico, Japan, Germany, India, and Australia clearly demonstrates that the production system and the product must be designed according to the nature of the market and the production environment. The design of their diesel engine was largely influenced by physical environments, legal restrictions, customer habits, and economic usage.

Local Standards

The metric system is but one of the local standards to which a product manufactured for European markets must conform. The trend throughout Europe is toward more and more standardization. Good examples of the adoption of common standards are flange dimensions and face-to-face dimensions of valves. On the other hand, it will be a long time before all countries have common standards for everything, because of the history of development and individual market requirements in each country. For instance, electric power supplies vary. Some countries have 110 volts, others 220; most countries supply power at 50 cycles, but in some it is 25.

Availability of materials can affect product design and manufacturing methods abroad. Metal casting in Europe is generally not so advanced as in the United States. The reason is partly that foundries try to get too much yield from castings and partly that they often use somewhat less refined methods of temperature measurement. Composition of steels and stainless steels are generally slightly different from U.S. standards, but exact equivalents can be had on special order and at a higher price. Most special alloys are available in Europe, although some are still imported from the United States. Equivalents of Hastelloy, Monel, and Stellite are available from some European suppliers, but they generally do not equal the quality of the originals. Because of these variances, some parts must be redesigned to utilize locally available materials.

Safety standards in Europe are often more stringent than in the United States (OSHA has changed this). In West Germany, for example, they are governed primarily by three bodies whose areas and functions overlap to some extent. The PTB (Physical Technical Federal Bureau) is similar to the U.S. Bureau of Standards and concerns itself, among other things, with verification of weights and measures, effectiveness of explosion-proofing, and so on; the TUV (Technical Inspection Service) is interested mainly in the enforcement of specifications established for safety; and the Berufgenossenschaft (roughly, Government Safety Bureau) is a public association concerned with trial safety. This group sends inspectors into factories frequently and sees that industrial safety practices are complied with. One example of a special safety problem is that use of paints having a flash point normally considered safe in the United States would require a special installation in West Germany—sometimes even a completely separate building.

Generally speaking, safety standards applying to products are much more rigid in West Germany than in the United States—for instance, no electrical switches or outlets are allowed inside bathrooms. Severe safety and performance standards also apply to all measuring instruments that must be approved before sale. In connection with these approvals, it is important to know that when an instrument has been approved in West Germany (and it takes a long while), any basic or design defect discovered later is the responsibility of the government approval agency and not the manufacturer. In the United States, we like to have Underwriters' Laboratory approval, but if the product is not as it is advertised, the manufacturer takes the consequences. In West Germany, the government agency is responsible for such claims. This also applies to safety requirements on machine tools, presses, and other factory equipment.

Technical Coordination

Another problem in the case of managing overseas plants is the coordination between engineering support facilities in the parent company and the plants located overseas. Of course, part of the problem is the sheer quantity and complexity of the transfer process—the thousands of process steps and the hundreds of material standards and manufacturing specifications, in addition to the specific adaptations that have to be made in equipment and tooling to accommodate local supply conditions. The volume of technical interchange between the parent company and the foreign manufacturing unit is particularly high during the initial period of manufacturing operations, and in developing areas it may take several years before an acceptable arrangement is worked out.

THE ADJUSTMENT PROBLEM

Differences in overseas production management forces international firms to make a series of adjustments in the design of the production system and the product and in other aspects of the operation. Deficiencies in supplier capabilities, the dearth of qualified managers and technicians, the adjustment of production processes and techniques, and the adaptation of product design are some of the major obstacles to be overcome.

Developing Supplier Capability

The burden of developing a supplier industry falls heavily upon the manufacturers in many industries. The manufacturer-supplier relationship in developing economies is the exact reverse of what is typical of industrialized countries, where the manufacturer often relies upon supplier knowhow even to design required components and parts. In developing areas, it is the other way around; manufacturers have a heavy responsibility to help develop the supplier industry. Even in slightly more industrialized countries like Mexico and Brazil, suppliers typically lack the engineering capability to adapt production techniques and establish adequate quality control systems. Under these circumstances, manufacturers often have to assume the burden of providing suppliers with tooling and technical assistance.

One possible solution, found in the automotive industry, is to persuade suppliers to standardize major parts such as generators or transmissions and to combine manufacturing operations for different makes overseas. Also, as a consequence of weakness in supplier capability, many international firms have developed a high degree of vertical integration in operations in developing countries. Companies like Willys-Overland of Brazil and Industries Kaiser Argentina are completely integrated, with their own engine, axle, and transmission plants, foundry and forging facilities, and so on.

Irregular transportation, or lack of adequate transportation facilities, may make it difficult for companies to maintain economical production runs unless additional outlay is incurred for a larger stock of materials and parts. In the initial stages, companies may have to expend time and resources to make sure that the facilities are adequate, and/or develop them themselves. In the transition stage, therefore, it may be helpful to have both domestic and foreign sources of raw materials and parts, if the necessary import licences can be obtained.

Another avenue available to minimize procurement problems is to manufacture spare parts internally. Production of spare parts is occasionally carried out in the firm's own workshops in a few companies. In a less developed country, this is done with a twofold purpose: to save on foreign exchange and to reduce delays in obtaining the parts from abroad. Wherever possible, a well-equipped workshop makes it possible to reduce considerably the stock of parts to be carried —many of which may not, in fact, ever be needed. Emergency repairs can be carried out at once without waiting for the arrival of parts. These advantages outweigh in many cases the drawbacks of possibly higher costs for the parts; in the long run, the cost situation is likely to improve. A good arrangement seems to be to order a set of parts when equipment is purchased. These parts can then be studied and reproduced in the workshop as needed.

Overcoming Design Problems

The process of designing the production system in environments of the type described above is one of adjustment, adaptation, and compromise. To design the production systems also means to overcome the basic problems of scale. Obstacles and deficiencies may be best overcome through a combination of economic and technological adjustments. The adjustment of a technology to fit an economy's resources and capabilities is one of the major contributions that multinational corporations can make to developing economies.

Production issues in developing countries are blurred. Small-scale size is fostered in a market environment in which domestic demand is limited. One alternative is to promote export which may result in larger volume. The higher level of output can be maintained if the size of the market in which the firm's product can be sold is large. This focus, however, treats market size as the strategic variable affecting plant size and efficiency of production. The increase in market size would increase output through larger scale of production, specialization of capital, and standardized products and parts. Economies of size and specialization that cannot be achieved within small markets can be obtained by combining markets through exports. But this alternative often is not open because domestic products are not competitive in world markets. Wherever such use of export is feasible, it will simultaneously serve two purposes. First, it will help enlarge the size of the market and thereby achieve the benefits of economies of scale. Second, it will help the developing country to increase its export capability and earnings and thereby enlarge the domestic market in the long run.

Another alternative available to companies is to standardize parts and subassemblies so that they can assemble the end product in a few locations and then ship the finished product to various marketing areas. This allows firms to minimize the total cost of supplying finished goods to world markets. Massey-

Ferguson has used this strategy very effectively for its international production. Its product line is standardized throughout the world, except for small differences caused by local needs. Massey-Ferguson's vice-president of manufacturing explained this approach as follows:

> The optimum location of manufacturing facilities depends entirely on the product. With tractors, for example, the economies of mass production are such that it would be economically most desirable to produce all the world's requirements in one plant and then ship them to the various markets. Politically, it is not possible to do this and even if it were, we'd probably want at least two locations in order to have some flexibility if, for any reason, one plant were shut down. On some other products, however, it would be economically more desirable to produce in every major market area because transportation costs would be so high relative to manufacturing costs.
>
> The manufacturing strategy that has evolved to meet the many economic and political constraints we face is complex. First, we try to design our products in order to achieve the greatest possible interchangeability of parts and of major subassemblies. This allows us to mass produce all these parts and subassemblies in one or two locations. Then we try to set up two or three assembly plants for each major product, if it is economically desirable to have a few plants, and export the finished product to the rest of the world. We try to satisfy political concerns by locating a different product assembly plant in each country. For example, we manufacture most of our tractors for the European market in Beauvais, France. However, we manufacture our self-propelled harvesting equipment in Eschwege, Germany. For each product there we get the benefit of mass production and yet we also satisfy political considerations.
>
> With many of the developing countries, it is necessary for us to manufacture locally if we wish to compete in the market. If we deem the market potential good enough, we will usually set up local tractor assembly operations. We are thus able to compete but still enjoy mass-production of parts and subassemblies, which we export to those countries. Generally, we have to increase local content, but we try to point out the economic disadvantage of this to the country whenever possible.[11]

In a less developed country, a more efficient utilization of production facilities and effective adaptation of products calls for gearing down in design to the lower volume in demand, to the dearth of technical skills, and to lower supplier capability. Adjusting to local supply capabilities may mean selection of products and techniques in a less exacting range of materials, standards, and manufacturing specifications. Engineers familiar with local supply conditions can help make these adjustments.

For example, several international firms have designed cars and light trucks to minimize tooling costs and simplify manufacturing procedures on low-volume production runs. This has been done by using straight-line bodies, thereby avoiding expensive investment in contoured dies, and developing a family of models using interchangeable body elements. Much less expensive press bends and hammer forms are used to shape angular-edge fenders, hoods, and side panels. Examples of straight-line design include the British Land Rover, the Toyota Land Cruiser, the Ford Bronco, the Kaiser-Willys Jeep, and the Chrysler XLV truck designed for manufacture in Turkey.[12]

Such changes, whether in the area of product design and/or production system, to more nearly match the industrial environment of the country will help minimize the problem of critical resources.

Personnel

The design of the control system in a less developed country is aimed at overcoming certain environmental differences discussed earlier. Basic to this is the need to develop proper skills and attitudes among personnel involved in implementing planning and control functions. The experiences of successful companies show that substantial improvement is possible in this area if class consciousness is not deep-rooted. Based on experience with U.S. manufacturing subsidiaries in developing countries Biggs has noted that some have compared very favorably with successful operations in the States in their planning, procedures, personnel and performance.[13] The practices of these companies in the production area provide an excellent example of what can be accomplished in developing countries with little exposure to scientific management techniques. Many of the shortcomings can be overcome, of course, by systematic training of personnel within the firm as well as by taking advantage of courses offered by outside educational institutions. In a country such as Britain, where class consciousness is very much alive, workers would hold the view that militant union action is the only way to get better wages or working conditions. Rearranging factory work flows for greater efficiency is almost automatically opposed, as it would only mean more profits to "them"—the management.[14]

CONTROL SYSTEMS

The manufacturing operation, whether in a foreign or domestic environment, necessitates an effective system of control. However, control problems in a foreign manufacturing operation are unique because of many significant environmental differences. What needs to be controlled in a manufacturing system is more or less the same anywhere: output, quality, and cost. However, controlling a production system in a developing country is a formidable task. Let us briefly examine some of the reasons.

Production Control

The dearth of technical personnel and the social factors prevailing in the less developed country have serious implications for production management. Once the system is set up, it has to be maintained for efficient performance by production planning and control, quality control, inventory control, maintenance, and other activities. The adequacy of managerial and technical capabilities often determines the efficiency of the operation. The skills needed are those necessary to maintain budget controls (planning and executing production plans), production standards (formulating equipment requirements and scheduling production controls over the flow of materials and output), and quality control (ensuring minimum standards in purchased materials and parts and programed performance of end products).

It is reported by many that in the developing countries, overall scheduling and coordination of production are the most deficient aspects of production management. The difficulty may be traced back to some of the basic problems identified earlier. There is the lack of skilled workers who can read blueprints, set up tools, and in other ways substitute human skills for machine capabilities. Apart from the skill aspect, there is also the problem of adjusting and adapting personnel from craft industries to a factory system. In the developing countries much time and effort are required to introduce the concept and use of production standards, materials control, and other control procedures. When adapted, techniques are rarely applied in a systematic and comprehensive way, and the results are invariably bottlenecks, shortages, and idle capacity.

To a large extent, the problem is also one of acceptance. For example, managerial acceptance of control systems and followup on technical coordination were found to be thorough and complete in the case of Japan and lacking in the case of Turkey, Pakistan, and India. Internal problems in maintaining production schedules are compounded by the inevitable delays and uncertainties in dealing with local suppliers and differences in the quality of procurement.

Quality Control

Quality control is another major problem faced by production managers abroad. Major differences in local materials and parts specifications is a basic problem. Apart from this, personnel attitudes are another difficulty. In Japan, it is reported that quality control has become an industrial ritual, and much of the success of Japan's postwar industrial effort is in large part traceable to programs designed to instill reliability. In many less developed countries, however, this is a serious problem. Workers and supervisors in many of these countries are not exposed to the meticulous technical precision and industrial planning that is an integral part of industrial proficiency in developed nations.

One of the reasons often cited for poor performance of control and maintenance functions in production units is inadequate technical support at the plant level. One cause of this may be the lack of sufficient technical personnel in the plant. The other, and probably more important, reason is that severe shortages of many products cause production personnel to concentrate their efforts on quantity to the detriment of quality.

Maintenance and Repair

Many UN experts assisting developing nations have stressed the neglect of maintenance as an important cause of chronic underutilization of equipment and low quality of output. Many instances of equipment being allowed to deteriorate beyond repair and having to be replaced have been cited. In a typical case, a technical assistance expert who was visiting a recently established large-scale chemical enterprise noted that defective maintenance had been the main cause of declining output.

There are many reasons for the neglect of maintenance and repair. UN experts have noted instances of new factories furnished with improved equipment being set up without a single spare part in stock. There were long delays in delivery of parts, particularly since importers were often reluctant to maintain large inventories; on the other hand, very limited stocks of parts were kept by the plants themselves. In many countries, the spare parts situation was adversely affected by shortages of foreign exchange and by lengthy delays arising from inefficient and cumbersome administration of import controls. Management is often not aware of the necessity of carrying adequate inventories of parts; the difficulties are often compounded when exchange authorities, because of their lack of appreciation of the spare parts problem, are reluctant to allow adequate imports.

United Nations experts have also reported on a number of occasions that, because of neglect, valuable equipment operated at only a fraction of capacity, was out of production for prolonged periods of time, and in some cases, had been damaged beyond repair. Lack of skilled operators as well as inadequate care are generally the main causes. In many cases, however, lack of attention to maintenance is due to indifference on the part of management. The seriousness of this factor may be illustrated by the dilemma of an expert in an Asian country who found it difficult to issue maintenance instructions because the local language did not even have a word for the concept! There is often reluctance to incur expenses that may not yield immediate returns; a maintenance department is considered an unnecessary burden.

Developing Control Systems

Several steps must be taken to develop an acceptable system of controls within the firm, the first of which is the development of personnel skills and attitudes. One way is to train workers in the plant, using foremen and other skilled workers as teachers. Unfortunately, the latter are not always effective transmitters of their own knowledge. There is also the training-within-industry (TWI) job instruction program—a device limited in scope but yielding fairly quick results. Large-scale TWI programs have been carried out by International Labour Organization (ILO) experts in Burma, Pakistan, India, Israel, and other countries. Along with such a program, companies should emphasize methods and techniques of production control, quality control, and improved utilization of equipment.

An example of a short- to medium-run problem is the question of what firms must do to substantially increase the effectiveness of control systems. In the short run, the training program can be supplemented by a number of management actions. For example, in the area of production control, management should emphasize the function of production planning and control and generate an internal environment conducive to developing positive attitudes toward this function. In the area of quality control, sound procedures for inspecting and sampling should be set up to ensure that finished parts meet standards and specifications. In the area of maintenance and repair, financial and fiscal incentives may be provided to increase cooperation.

In many developing countries, technical support staff has often been at relatively low level, so that operational and facilities standards are seldom complete or adequate. Management should endeavor to provide and train a technical staff sufficient to maintain acceptable levels of control.

A FRAMEWORK FOR PRODUCTION MANAGEMENT

Although this brief exploration of manufacturing abroad has only catalogued some of the most prevalent problems and important considerations, it should suffice to alert American manufacturers to the difficulties—many of them totally unexpected and unforeseeable—they will confront in establishing overseas plants. The examples given here are typical of what to expect throughout the developing world and in some developed areas as well.

In the case of the less developed countries, our own experiences suggest that there is yet another significant difference between a production system in the United States and one in a developing area. In the case of the United States, it seems to us that the critical variable is the human factor—in the sense that it is the source of constant interruptions to the smooth working of the production system. The typical plant manager is likely to point to labor problems as the crucial variable that affects his job and responsibilities and subsequently the total effectiveness of the production system for which he is accountable.

In a survey of production managers in India (nationals and foreign-born), we found that inadequate supplies of materials and proper plant maintenance were the crucial issues.[15] The business literature also points to a similar difference in critical variables. In order to recognize the implications of these crucial differences as they affect managing production abroad, operational managers might benefit from a theoretical framework within which they can view specific problems. The framework presented here is focused on developing nations, but it can be refined and expanded by managers to encompass all the overseas situations they may encounter.

As noted at the beginning of this chapter, the manufacturing unit can be considered as a production system, that is, as an input-transformation-output system. A salient feature of this system in a developing nation, in contrast to a similar system in the United States, is that the physical inputs and transformation processes are more critical than the human or financial inputs. The factors that determine the exact nature of production systems are, of course, the scale of operations and the specific technology relevant to the output. In a foreign country, this model of a transformation system becomes workable once decisions about location, layout, scale of operations, production methods and processes, and a system of controls are made. On top of these, in developing countries, cultural differences need to be accommodated.

Among the various cultural factors that influence production management in developing countries, the following are important enough to be recognized and adequately accommodated: perception of time, philosophy of life, perception of job, class or sect consciousness, view of the employer, and loyalty to family. Then one might ask: Is it not sufficient to design the system with some consideration for cultural factors? The answer cannot be a definite yes. As important as this dimension of the system are its overall goals and the role of the manager who controls it. *Why are these factors so important?*

First, in the developing nations, manufacturing and assembly-type operations are recognized as being more significant for the nation's economic goals in the long run than such endeavors as advertising, banking, and construction. Second, nationals in developing countries (workers, managers, public administrators, legislators, business people) are likely to be more immediately concerned with policy issues than with the specific ways in which a foreign-affiliated production unit resolves its operational problems. Third, managers of production systems, whether they be foreign-born or nationals, are likely to better discern, identify, and examine operational problems if they themselves are clear about their roles and the goals of the system.[16]

This mail questionnaire survey consisted of ten internally consistent phrases that led respondents to express their agreement or disagreement on a 5 point scale with this statement: "The main purpose of private and public sector firms should be to increase productivity even if this means foregoing high profits." An overwhelming majority of the 212 respondents preferred productivity as a goal rather than profitability. Another aspect of the questionnaire dealt with the role of managers of industrial concerns. Respondents were asked to rank ten role descriptions of managers or executives. Among the ten roles, those descriptive of a leader, educator, and output optimizer had higher mean ranks than other role descriptions. The manager's role as output optimizer is consistent with the goal preference for productivity. The other two equally important roles—leader and educator—suggest that the multifunction rather than single-function role is an important expectation in developing countries.

In essence, these results suggest that the framework for production management should include accommodation not only to cultural variables but also to productivity-oriented goals and leadership/education-oriented managerial roles. This framework, of course, will not solve the problems. But it may reorient the thinking of foreign production managers enough that they will begin to view the problems from the perspective of the country and its people rather than from the perspective of what James Lee calls the "self-reference criterion."[17]

SUMMARY

American direct private investment has meant direct participation in the management and control of manufacturing and marketing in foreign countries. Although manufacturing as a transformation process is a concept relevant to all nations, there are differences in the technical, human, and regulatory aspects of production systems from one country to another. Manufacturing firms going international do experience a number of problems in their efforts to develop an operational production system, particularly in developing countries. Considerable time and resources must be expended to develop supply capability. Adaptation of production techniques and control mechanisms to local conditions is another issue.

To highlight some of these differences, we discussed some of the issues with significant comparisons to the American context. Then, focusing on developing countries, we pointed out that operational problems can best be solved within a clear organizational framework that takes into account such elements as accommodation to cultural factors as well as the goal and role expectations of the people of the country. In conclusion, we tend to think that although technical issues pose problems in the short run, an MNC faces greater human relations problems in the long run. Two other general problems of great concern to multinationals are multinational unionism and codetermination, which are treated in Appendixes 8-A and 8-B following this chapter.

Notes

[1]C. Wickham Skinner, *American Industry in Developing Economies* (New York: Wiley, 1968); also "A Test Case in Turkey," *California Management Review*, spring 1964, pp. 53-66.

[2]Jack Baranson, *Manufacturing Problems in India: The Cummins Experience in India* (Syracuse, N.Y.: Syracuse University Press, pp. 70-73.

[3]Guillermo S. Edelberg, "The Procurement Practices of the Mexican Affiliates of Selected United States Automobile Firms" (Unpublished Doctoral thesis, Harvard University, June 1963), pp. 8-24.

[4]Skinner, *op. cit.,* p. 19.

[5]A. K. Rice, *Productivity and Social Organization* (London: Tavistock, 1958), pp. 225, 250.

[6]C. Wickham Skinner, "Management of International Production," *Harvard Business Review,* September-October 1964, pp. 125-26.

[7]Richard N. Farmer, "Organizational Transfer and Class Structure," *Academy of Management Journal,* September 1966, pp. 204-16.

[8]Gilbert T. Bowman, "Production Problems in Doing Business Abroad," *Financial Executive,* February 1963, pp. 26-31.

[9]Jan Tinbergen, "Choice of Technology and Industrial Planning," *Industrialization and Productivity,* April 1958, pp. 24-33.

[10]Philip R. Cateora and J. M. Hess, *International Marketing* (Homewood, Ill.: Irwin, 1975), pp. 366-67.

[11]Edmund P. Learned, et al., *Business Policy* (Homewood, Ill.: Irwin, 1969), pp. 264-65.

[12]Harry G. Biggs, "What the U.S. Manufacturer Faces When He Goes Overseas," *Management Review,* February 1969, pp. 72-76.

[13]Ibid.

[14]*The Wall Street Journal,* June 9, 1975, p. 1.

[15]S. B. Prasad, "Managing Production Systems Abroad: A Note on Organizational Framework," *Academy of Management Journal,* December 1970, pp. 457-59.

[16]Ibid.

[17]James A. Lee; "Cultural Analysis in Overseas Operations," *Harvard Business Review,* March-April 1966.

Suggested Readings

BUFFA, ELWOOD S., *Basic Production Management.* New York: Wiley, 1975, pp. 254-61.

ULMAN, LLOYD, "Multinational Unionism: Incentives, Barriers, and Alternatives," *Industrial Relations,* February 1975, pp. 1-31.

VANEK, JAROSLAV, *Self-Management.* Baltimore, Md.: Penguin Press, 1975.

APPENDIX 8-A: A Note on Multinational Unionism

In recent years, the trade union movement has been increasingly concerned about the potential impact of, and the problems resulting from, the multinationalization of corporate entities. Although labor unions realize that MNCs can play an important role in the diffusion of technology and in giving impetus to economic and social progress, they are seriously concerned about their impact on the interests of workers.

The power of multinational corporations to shift production from one country to another is seen as overwhelming. The existence of multiple facilities in several countries does allow the multinational firm to shift production in a way that ensures continuous production. Consequently, the threat of transfer of production can seriously weaken the union position in collective bargaining.

Another aspect of the problem relates to company financial practices and the availability of financial data. Unions claim that the size and extensive operations of the MNCs can make it difficult for the national trade union in a given country to obtain relevant and complete financial information for the purpose of collective bargaining. Transfer pricing is generally used for tax purposes. However, unions claim this technique can be used to weaken the union's collective bargaining position. Transfer pricing, when used for tax liability purposes, can give a misleading picture of profitability that can be used by the subsidiary against local wage demands.

Unions also claim that MNCs establish global industrial relations policies at their headquarters without giving due consideration to local issues and problems. As a result, trade union negotiators will have no opportunity to personally present their case to those who ultimately decide. It is exceptionally difficult for a trade union, which is confined to one country, to exert effective influence on a management that is located in another and that oversees operations in a number of countries.

Although these claims may be true in some cases, their universality cannot be substantiated. There are limits to these purported practices. For example, in the case of temporary transfer of production during a strike, there would have to be readily available additional plant facilities capable of producing the same product. In the case of a shutdown of a whole production facility, the multinational firm must certainly take into account other costs such as severance pay, labor costs in the new location, raw material supply conditions, trade barriers, political stability, possibility of capital repatriation, and so on.

Trade unions have been stressing the need to coordinate their actions as a counterforce to the multinational corporations. Essentially these activities are aimed at building the strength and the abilities of the unions in their confrontations with multinational management, and they include collection and dissemination of information, international consultation, and coordination of union policies and tactics with respect to specific multinational firms.

The International Trade Secretariats (ICFTU) are playing a major role in coordinating trade union activities in this regard. The International Metal Workers' Federation (IMF) and the International Federation of Chemical and General Workers Union (ICF) have taken steps to establish permanent world councils that meet regularly to exchange information and agree on bargaining tactics. This structural innovation has so far mainly served the purpose of information exchange.

Coordinated bargaining is also sought by many unions. It involves simultaneous bargaining with all or most subsidiaries of a multinational corporation, either throughout the world or in a given region. Such an arrangement would be facilitated if trade unions were to work for common termination dates of existing and future collective bargaining agreements in the subsidiaries concerned. Unions feel that such an arrangement would result in direct access to the locus of decision making in the multinational corporation. Multinational collective bargaining would give the unions greater influence over decisions concerning employee relations.

APPENDIX 8-B: A Note on Codetermination

The concept of "codetermination" or *Mitbestimmung* (literally, "having a voice in") is the process whereby employers and employees are represented on the supervisory boards of management in industry. This trend toward greater worker influence in corporate management, which has spread through much of Western Europe, was implemented in West Germany shortly after World War II, when steel and coal unions were given 50 percent representation on industry boards. The idea has grown so that now all limited companies with over 500 employees have to give one-third of the seats on the supervisory board to worker representatives. Apart from giving workers more say in company decisions and keeping each side in touch with what the other thinks, the system does seem to have improved industrial relations in West Germany.

In Britain there is still no consensus about what worker participation actually means and how far it should supplement or supersede collective bargaining. Many union leaders feel that codetermination is a last resort to reduce the number of industrial disputes so that Britain can regain competitiveness in world markets. Those with management interests feel that the unions want more than a voice in how companies are run; they want dominance. Most European unions are strongly in favor of worker-directors, but the Italians and French are not. The big Communist unions in both countries regard worker-directors as an undesirable form of collaboration with capitalism. They prefer confrontation by strike rather than cooperation and negotiation by codetermination to settle their disputes.

American corporations will not soon face codetermination demands within the United States, but companies that operate in Europe are already affected, and soon may be more so. The American unions feel that board representation creates a conflict of interest and compromises the union. A top union official has stated: "There is no major perceptible demand by American workers today for participation in the decision-making process. You must be on one side or the other to maximize your effectiveness."

Employers throughout Europe tend to be hostile to the idea of workers-directors, believing that they interfere with the profitable and efficient operation of business. One of the more common arguments is that there is an irreconcilable gulf between the interests of those who seek to maximize profits and those who seek to protect the interests of the workers. However, worker participation is expected to go on rising in Europe even as recession continues. Six nations in Europe now have laws requiring labor representation on the boards of major companies. Some feel that there is a "revolution" toward "industrial democracy" taking place, a process vaguely defined as workers sharing in management, gaining control over their jobs, and tearing down authoritarian boss-worker relationships, of which codetermination may turn out to be an important first step.

9

Multinational Marketing

Marketing is a managerial activity undertaken by the firm in order to coordinate its production operations with its markets to make a profit. A marketing orientation, as opposed to a production orientation, is required of firms not only in the free enterprise economies but also in centrally planned ones such as those of the USSR and the block of Eastern European countries known as Comecon. The major marketing activities are generally marketing research and intelligence, product development, distribution, promotion and advertising, and pricing.

The evolution of the multinational corporation has also meant the evolution of a multinational marketing strategy. Multinational marketing is a *micro* concept that refers to the marketing activities of an MNC in places other than its own domestic market. For an American-based MNC, marketing in Japan would be multinational marketing. Similarly, for a Japan-based MNC, marketing in the United States would be part of its multinational marketing.

Multinational marketing is different from both world trade and international trade. World trade is a *macro* concept that refers to the sum of all nations' imports and exports in a given period of time. The value of world trade (expressed in U.S. dollars) was about $415 billion in 1972, $570 billion in 1973, and a little over $800 billion in 1974. How the value and the volume of world trade have changed since 1965 are shown in Table 9-1.

International trade, also a macroconcept, refers to the value and volume of the flow of goods from one country to another. Importing and exporting are performed mostly by firms within a framework set not only by the government of the country in question, but also by supranational agencies such as GATT (General Agreement on Tariffs and Trade). International trade accounting gives the performance measure of a country's international trade in terms of a balance, and balance of trade trends then indicate the debtor or creditor position of the country. How much a nation participates in international trade depends on a variety of circumstances:

1. The degree of economic and industrial development of the country. The United States and Japan are highly industrialized countries; they also participate in and depend, more than other countries, on world trade.
2. Endowment of natural resources. Consider, for example, Japan and Kuwait. Japan, poorly endowed, relies heavily on imports of materials and exports of manufactured goods. Kuwait, richly endowed in mineral resources (crude oil) but not industralized, relies heavily on exporting oil and importing manufactured goods.
3. Human resource endowment. Many nations have had a tradition of excellence in one or another special skill, such as watchmaking in Switzerland

TABLE 9-1

Growth in the Value of World Trade*

Year	*Percentage Change in Value*
1960-1970	9.0
1965	8.0
1966	9.0
1967	5.5
1968	11.5
1969	14.5
1970	14.2
1971	12.0
1972	19.0
1973	38.0
1974	48.0
1975**	30.0

*Growth measured in terms of approximate percentage changes of the value of exports expressed in U.S. dollars. Based on world exports excluding the USSR, China, and other nonreporting countries.

**Authors' estimate.

Source: United Nations, *International Financial Statistics*.

and wine making in France. In these days of MNCs, perhaps it is more appropriate to refer to possession of technology—engineering, management, and marketing—as a part of this endowment.

All these factors, singly and in combination, point to the "theory of comparative cost advantage," the concept commonly used to account for the flow of goods from one country to another. (See Chapter 2.)

Common trade problems have, in the past, brought into existence various market groups which afford greater opportunities as well as challenges to the international market. Among these, two European groups, EEC and Comecon, are prominent and viable. The European Economic Community (EEC), or the Common Market, which began with the Treaty of Rome in 1957, consisted originally of six member nations: Belgium, France, West Germany, Italy, Luxembourg and The Netherlands. In 1973, membership was expanded to include Britain, Denmark, and Ireland. Two key aims of this multinational market group are (a) the abolition of tariffs among member nations, and (b) the institution of uniform tariffs on imports from nonmembers. The Council of Mutual Economic Assistance (Comecon) is a much older multinational market group made up of Eastern European countries. Its chief architect was the Soviet Union, and its members are Albania, Bulgaria, Czechoslovakia, Poland, and the Soviet Union. If we examine the data, we find that there is more international trade among Communist countries than between Communist and non-Communist countries.

Our concern in this chapter is primarily with the marketing activities of MNCs. Although there is ample literature on large U.S.-based MNCs such as Coca-Cola, Gillette, IBM, and International Harvester, some smaller companies have also entered the multinational arena and done well. For this reason, we have included material on the National Insurance Company in addition to that for Gillette and Heinz in the appendixes to this chapter.

APPRAISING MARKET OPPORTUNITIES ABROAD

A company's decision to enter a new market abroad usually involves a major commitment. Although it was once possible to enter export markets on a short-term, in-and-out basis, it is very difficult now in the face of current world regulatory and competitive trends. Management, basing its decision on sound reasoning and comprehensive analysis, must have a solid basis for committing the company's funds and manpower.

Analyzing market opportunities essentially means attempting to predict the likely levels of sales, market shares, and profits on the basis of a study of the market potential. The job of appraising these possibilities abroad is usually considered much more difficult than doing so in the firm's own domestic market. In a general way, we can point to differences in consumer behavior, in regulations, and in marketing infrastructure as the reasons for much of the difficulty involved in marketing in foreign countries. Let us examine these one by one before inquiring how a company might proceed to formulate a multinational marketing strategy.

Consumer Behavior

Crossing national boundaries for purposes of marketing means stepping into a different social and cultural environment. The problems faced by a firm that does business in one language and one culture are much less complex than those faced in dealing with two or possibly three languages and cultures at the same time. *What does culture mean and how does it act as a constraint on multinational marketing?*

The American anthropologist Edward T. Hall has written a classic essay called "The Silent Language in Overseas Business" that contains a number of perceptive observations on how to understand foreign cultures. According to Hall, communication entails not just written and spoken languages; far more important are the unwritten and unspoken ones—the silent languages. These are the perceptions of time, space, things, and friendship, and they determine the behavior of consumers in different cultural groups.[1]

Although there are many definitions of culture, here we mean the entire set of social norms and responses that condition the behavior of a group of people. Anthropological studies have provided marketers with a set of elements with which they can grasp various cultural patterns. Some of these elements, called "cultural universals," are given in Table 9-2. Note that they cover a wide spectrum from "age grading" to "weather control." Cultural universals are to be found in all societies; it is the perception of them that differs among social groups and shapes consumer behavior. The international marketing manager in charge of razors and razor blades, for example, can benefit by being aware of the fact that he must take into account the puberty customs of different cultures if he is going to embark on a marketing campaign in Africa. Furthermore, he can see that other cultural elements such as gift giving, courtship, and family patterns may also enter his matrix.

Cultural differences that can affect multinational marketing operations arise in all aspects of marketing. Marketing managers need not become expert anthropologists and social psychologists, but they should become generally familiar with those cultural elements that affect their products and services. This is especially true of consumer goods—food, clothing, cosmetics, personal hygiene products. Cultural influence is of much less significance in the case of durables such as appliances, equipment, and machinery.

In examining cultural patterns, perhaps it is desirable to start off with a small number of broad questions:

What are the assumptions and attitudes prevalent in a defined market?

What are the motives?

How are such facts as work, authority, family responsibility, and choice behavior perceived?

What is happening to the social structure? That is, in what ways are interclass mobility, status positions, and patterns of education changing?

What may come out of an analysis of questions like these is an understanding of a *modal pattern* of consumer behavior. Experienced MNCs, especially those in the consumer goods industry, have sought to work within the boundaries of the accepted behavior patterns and customary consumer goals of the particular society.

TABLE 9-2

Some Cultural Universals

Age grading	Inheritance rules
Athletic sports	Joking
Bodily adornment	Language
Cleanliness training	Law
Cooking	Luck and superstition
Courtship	Marriage
Decorative arts	Medicine
Division of labor	Music
Dream interpretation	Mythology
Education	Personal names
Ethics	Population policy
Family	Postnatal care
Feasting	Property rights
Folklore	Puberty customs
Food taboos	Religious rituals
Games	Sexual mores
Gestures	Soul concepts
Gift giving	Status differentiation
Greetings	Tool making
Hospitality	Trade
Housing	Weaning
Hygiene	Weather control
Incest taboos	

Source: George P. Murdock, "The Common Denominator of Cultures," in *The Science of Man in the World Crises,* ed. Ralph Linton (New York: Columbia University Press, 1945), pp. 123-42.

Marketing Infrastructure

We regard distribution channels as an important part of the marketing infrastructure. Considerable differences exist among countries, so that each channel must be evaluated on an individual basis. The basic question is this: Should the company set up its own channels of distribution or employ local firms? The answer rests on a number of factors, such as the existence of effective local channels, product and customer requirements, potential volume of business, desired control over distribution channels, and legal restrictions.[2]

The choice is affected by the existing channels of distribution within a given country, their effectiveness, and their availability to the multinational marketer. These channels tend to reflect the different socioeconomic characteristics of each country. For example, areas with low per capita income and few customers for a product cannot support high-volume, and low-margin distribution outlets. They have to be served by low-volume institutions. In many developing countries, therefore, the distribution channels are fragmented and small in scale. This is also true of many advanced countries. For example, in 1967 Belgium had 1.9 employees per retail outlet; The Netherlands had 3.4; Sweden had 5.5; and the United States had 6.4. The average number of consumers per retail outlet in 1967 was approximately 54 in Belgium and Italy, 75 in France and The Netherlands, 135 in Finland, and 196 in the United States. In Japan, a few large trading companies, which have extensive and well-developed networks, are responsible for marketing the bulk of Japanese goods. They virtually control distribution at all levels.[3]

Trading companies can be quite helpful to multinational firms in increasing the effectiveness of their distribution and their other marketing programs. For example, Nestlé, in Japan, needed to secure an effective distribution network as quickly as possible. Instead of attempting to bypass the trading companies, Nestlé reportedly employed its powerful brand name and the promise of solid promotional support to persuade four trading companies to act as its primary distributors. Only at a later date did it form its own distribution setup. In general, wholesalers and retailers perform fewer functions and have a less aggressive approach to marketing in other countries than do their counterparts in the United States. And the less developed countries usually have much smaller distribution outlets than those found in Western Europe and the United States.

The nature of the product and customer requirements significantly influence the selection of a distribution channel. Product characteristics—technical complexity, perishability, weight and bulk—vary from product to product. For example, the complexity of a product may be such that it needs technical advice and service before and after the sale. In many of the less developed countries, the marketing outlets may not be in a position to handle such services because of lack of resources and/or training. A perishable product needs short channels of distribution. If potential buyers are widely dispersed geographically and buy the product frequently, then the product must be available in retail outlets throughout the area. This situation might necessitate the use of wholesalers, since direct sales to many widely scattered small retailers may not be economically feasible.

One major determinant of channel is the existing volume of sales. Where the volume is large and the company possesses adequate technical and financial resources, it can develop its own distribution system. The choice of channel must also be evaluated against the long-range goals of the company. If the company is planning to expand, it may be worthwhile starting its own distribution system. Channel selection is also influenced by the desire for control. Through the use of direct distribution, the company can closely control selling, advertising, and servicing.

Many American firms accept indirect distribution as the only feasible choice because most foreign markets are smaller and less concentrated, and there are fewer large-scale buyers. For example, Procter & Gamble uses an indirect channel—selling agent to wholesaler to retailer—in some of the European countries and emphasizes advertising to promote its products. On the other hand, some firms such as Singer have developed or are developing more direct distribution as the best way to attain a strong market position.

The choice of available channels may be influenced as well by legal restrictions in the country of operation. In some countries, laws restrict certain channels and encourage others. Other variables that influence the selection of distribution channels may also be found, but the point for the multinational company is that those critical to its operation should be sorted out and examined before the selection is made. Specific criteria should be developed and used to analyze the situation within the particular country.[4]

MARKETING STRATEGY IN A MULTINATIONAL CONTEXT

Marketing strategy is concerned with the choice of goals as well as with major policies and programs utilizing company resources for achieving these goals. The aim of a multinational marketing strategy is to optimize company resources on a worldwide basis. The components of marketing strategy specify the role and emphasis of product planning, pricing, distribution, and promotional efforts for the company as a whole as well as for its affiliates abroad.

Standardization vs. Differentiation

To what extent can a multinational company adopt a standardized marketing strategy throughout the world? This is, of course, not a clear-cut issue. Multinational standardization, in a literal sense, would mean the deployment of an identical marketing mix in every market. On the other hand, complete differentiation or a localized marketing strategy would theoretically contain no common elements. But neither strategy is realistic. From a manager's viewpoint, the important question is *What elements of the market mix can or should be standardized, and to what degree?*

The experiences of a number of multinational companies suggest that there are real benefits to be gained from standardizing some elements of marketing strategies in different areas of the globe. Significant cost savings can result from having standardized products, packaging, brand names, advertising, and service approaches. For example, Italian appliance companies have made substantial sales of refrigerators in Western Europe by standardizing the product in automated plants in which they have achieved considerable economies of scale. Such standardization also achieves consistency in dealing with customers, which in turn ensures and probably increases sales. Savings also result from standardized advertising. With more widespread communications, internationalization of media and publications, and worldwide travel, multinationals such as Nestlé and Unilever have moved to uniform advertising. Similarly, IBM has standardized the services provided to its customers, its sales approaches, and even its organization on a worldwide basis in order to provide a consistent level of service to major customers such as international banks. Standardization in marketing also leads to more improved planning and control. For example, Philips, one of the world's largest producers of electrical products, prevented its subsidiary from competing aggressively on price with its other affiliates by price standardization. Finally, standardization also helps companies to explore ideas on a global scale. Esso (now Exxon), for example, has used its "Put a tiger in your tank" advertising campaign with minor changes in art and wording in many countries. Avis Rent-A-Car has used its theme "We Try Harder" with minor variations in Europe as well as in the United States.

The strength of the argument that marketing strategies should be tailored to various country or national markets because of unique national, cultural, and institutional differences is also quite strong. Complete multinational standardization of marketing strategy is not realistic because of wide variations among nations. However, the degree of adaptation required may be different for different products. Some products are environmentally insensitive and do not require adaptation to differences in the socioeconomic environments of markets around the globe. A computer line is a good example of a relatively environmentally insensitive product. As Holton has said, "The world of advanced technology is more nearly a single world than the world of consumer goods."[5] Other products may be highly sensitive to environmental variations in markets. Convenience foods are an example of a relatively sensitive product. In other words, *the range of adaptation would depend upon the nature of the product in question.* Likewise, markets also show similarities and differences. The greater the similarities in markets, the more room there is for standardization. Though each environment is unique, it also contains elements of similarity. Multinational marketing-mix strategies should take into account both similarities and differences. In order to determine which components can be standardized and which have to be uniquely designed for different markets, clustering techniques may be used.

Product Development

MNCs face enormous challenges in the field of product design, packaging, and branding. Often, products successful in the United States must be adapted to suit the needs, tastes, and preferences of a particular foreign environment. A thorough analysis of the characteristics of the foreign country indicates the necessary degree of adaptation. The company can examine several product characteristics as possible areas for modification, as shown in Table 9-3. Because production costs increase quickly as the initial adaptive measures are taken, it is necessary to consider the economics of adaptation. This problem should be resolved by management's examining the incremental cost and the revenue obtained from adapting the product. If costs are prohibitive, an entirely new product may be in order.

Packaging must be adapted to factors such as climate, availability of refrigeration, income levels, warehousing facilities and the like. Labels must be changed to identify quantity. Colors have different meanings in foreign countries; for example, red is popular in China, but not in some African and Asian countries; white indicates mourning in China and Korea. Therefore, choices must be based on careful consumer analysis.

Branding is also important in foreign marketing. The purpose of branding is

TABLE 9-3

Product Characteristics

Key Factor	*Design Change*
Level of technical skill	Product simplification
Level of labor costs	Automation or manualization of product
Level of literacy	Remaking and simplification of product
Level of income	Quality and price change
Level of interest rates	Quality and price change (investment in high quality might not be financially desirable)
Level of maintenance	Change in tolerances
Climatic differences	Product adaptation
Isolation (heavy repair difficult and expensive)	Product simplification and reliability improvement
Differences in standards	Recalibration of product and resizing
Availability of other products	Greater or lesser product integration
Availability of materials	Change in product structure and fuel
Power availability	Resizing of product
Special conditions	Product redesign or invention

Source: Richard Robinson, *International Business Policy* (New York: Holt, Rinehart, and Winston, 1964), pp. 179-180.

to facilitate identification of the product. Brands often serve as a source of information, aid in differentiating products and help promote them. Where consumer literacy is low, the brand symbol and the trade name may be the only parts of the product consumers can recognize. There are two conflicting views on branding. Should the company maintain an existing trademark (a symbol of quality) or should the trademark be tailored to the specific country? The brand policy a company follows depends on the image it wants to project. Coca-Cola has created a multinational image of the trademarks "Coke" and "Coca-Cola." Often consumer preference for American or foreign products overcomes nationalistic feelings, and companies can use the same brands used in the domestic market.

One American firm located in Mexico, for example, picked a Spanish name for its product and built around it a snappy Spanish slogan, assuming that nationalistic Mexicans would prefer a product identified with the country. But sales did not increase, while those of a competitor that had stuck to its American name and packaging design soared. It soon became apparent that nationalistic feelings were much less important in the store than the desire for the class and quality associated with American-made goods. In other cases, products using a foreign image may not be easily accepted. Under these circumstances, it is advisable to use separate brand names, preferably taken from a local source, so that the product may be identified as locally produced.

Strategic Alternatives in Product Planning

Keegan provides an excellent analysis of some strategic alternatives available for international product planning. He identifies five alternatives and provides some guidelines as to which a company should adopt.[6]

Strategy 1: One Product, One Message, Worldwide. The first strategy involves the straight extension of the product into the foreign market in the same form the company uses in the home market. In other words, the same product is marketed throughout the world using the same message. This strategy has been successfully used by Pepsi Cola to introduce its soft drinks worldwide. It has, however, failed for other products such as Philip Morris cigarettes in the Canadian market and Campbell soup in the British market. As it turned out, the Canadians prefer a straight to a blended tobacco and the British like their soup with a more bitter taste. The product extension strategy has great appeal to many multinational marketers because it results in substantial cost savings. It involves no additional expenditures on research and development, retooling for manufacturing, and preparing marketing communications.

Strategy 2: Product Extension, Communication Adaptation. The second strategy involves the introduction of the same product but modification of communication. Perhaps the product serves a different need, though the conditions of use are similar. For example, Americans use bicycles mainly for recreation, but this may be a basic mode of transportation in other countries. One American farm machinery firm decided to market its lawn and garden power equipment as agricultural implements in the less developed countries where it was ideally suited to farming needs and could be sold at a reasonable price. This strategy generally results in substantial savings in research and development, manufacturing, and inventory. Its only cost arises from identifying different product functions and changing marketing communications (advertising and sales promotion) to fit the newly identified functions.

Strategy 3: Product Adaptation, Communication Extension. Strategy 3 is to adapt the product to meet local conditions or preferences and extend the basic communications strategy without change. Exxon for example, adapted the physical characteristics of its gasoline to different climatic conditions while it continued to advertise "Put a Tiger in Your Tank." Many multinational companies in foods, fertilizers, clothing, and appliances have adjusted their products to meet local conditions. Soap and detergent firms have adjusted product characteristics to meet local water conditions and the nature of local washing machines. This strategy involves additional engineering and production efforts to make the product appealing and functional in different countries.

Strategy 4: Dual Adaptation. The fourth strategy is to adapt both the product and the communications in order to increase the product's acceptability. In a sense, this is a combination of strategy 2—communication adaptation—and strategy 3—product adaptation. The National Cash Register Company took an innovative step backward by developing a crank-operated cash register that could sell at half the price of a modern cash register and emphasized its low price in advertising. The product became popular in the Orient, Latin America, and Spain. American greeting card firms have faced this problem in Europe, where the function of a greeting card is to provide space for the sender to write his own message, in contrast to the American situation, where cards contain prepared messages.

Strategy 5: Product Invention. The last strategy is that of product invention. This approach is effective when potential customers cannot afford a product. In this situation, an opportunity exists to invent or design an entirely new product that satisfies the need at a price the consumer can afford to pay. For example, there are more than 600 million women in the world who still wash their clothes by hand. The multinational soap and detergent firms have served them for decades. Until recently, however, not one of these companies had attempted to develop an inexpensive manual washing machine. But a newly invented inexpensive, all-plastic, hand-powered washer that has the tumbling action of a modern automatic machine has been given an enthusiastic response in a Mexican test market. There is an enormous need in the less developed countries for low-cost, high-protein food products. Food companies such as Swift, Pillsbury, and Quaker Oats are attempting to analyze the food needs of these countries, develop new foods, and formulate messages to promote the new products.

The Choice of a Product Strategy

Is there a best product strategy for a company? The appropriate strategy depends upon the specific product-market-company mix.[7] Some products demand adaptation, others lend themselves to adaptation, and still others are better left unchanged. Similarly, some markets are similar to American markets and hence require little adaptation. Other markets are moderately different and lend themselves to adaptation, and still others are so different as to require drastic adaptation. Likewise, companies differ in their cost structure and in their ability to identify and produce profitable products. In order to develop the best multinational product strategy, a company needs to analyze three important elements: product, market, and the company resources in question. Define the product in terms of the functions or needs it serves; analyze the market, the conditions under which the product is utilized, the preferences of potential buyers, and the ability of customers to buy the product; and evaluate the cost-benefit analysis of the product and communication adaptation. This analysis of product-market-company mix can help multinational managers to choose the most profitable and viable strategy.

PRICING POLICY

Pricing policies in foreign markets follow basically the same pattern as those used in domestic markets except for variations in environmental conditions. In making a pricing decision it is important to consider the following crucial variables: the marketing strategy of the firm, market conditions, cost factors, and legal implications.

As one element of the marketing mix, prices are intended to contribute to achieving the sales and profit goals of the company. In terms of objectives, pricing is essentially a promotional instrument designed to influence sales and profits. The basic marketing strategies available to a company are just about the same in international as in domestic markets. For example, a company might set a high initial price coupled with large promotional expenditures and lower prices at a later stage to tap other market segments. This is known as a ''skimming'' policy. Or it might set a low initial price to reach the mass market quickly—''penetration'' pricing. Because of widely varying market and competitive conditions, this marketing strategy decision will be more complex for the company that operates in multinational markets than for the domestic company, for the appropriateness of the strategies may vary from country to country and from time to time.

Market conditions, the needs of the market, and the competition are the major determinants of pricing. Demand conditions set the range of prices the product can fetch. Research must be conducted and forecasts prepared on market potential on a country by country basis. The demand forecast is based on factors such as number of potential customers, their income or ability to pay, customs and traditions, customer acceptance, impact of competing substitutes, and so on, whether the forecast is for a domestic or a foreign market. But there are two important differences in the case of a foreign market. First, the degree of forecasting error is likely to be much higher because of lack of pertinent data and practical problems involved in doing research. Second, the nature of the demand function as expressed in terms of price and income elasticity may vary from market to market. Income distribution, consumption habits, differences in the cost of borrowing, geographic and demographic diversity, to mention a few factors, create wide differences in the willingness and ability of the consumer to pay a given price.

Competition is another variable affecting pricing policy. Many American firms abroad generally do not try to undercut the competition, but prefer to compete on a nonprice basis. For example, when Singer faced strong price competition in sewing machines from local businessmen and Japanese manufacturers in a Far Eastern market, it emphasized product quality, credit terms, and consumer education programs in order to attempt to maintain its market position although its prices were higher than those of its competitors.

Pricing decisions in multinational markets also have legal implications. Many nations have antitrust laws similar to those in the United States restricting certain business practices. Government agencies often set prices. In addition, pricing policies must be consistent with a number of constraints such as dumping legislation, tax policies, and resale price-maintenance legislation. Legal factors act primarily to restrict the freedom of the firm to set prices strictly on the basis of economic considerations.

PROMOTION AND ADVERTISING

Though promotion involves many activities, such as personal selling, publicity, and so on, advertising is perhaps its major component. The advertising task is essentially the same at home and abroad—namely, to communicate information and persuasive appeal as effectively as possible. The specific differences involved concern attitudes toward advertising, media selection, and translating advertisements. Multinational advertising programs must be conceived and implemented according to the characteristics of foreign markets.

Attitudes toward Advertising

Generally speaking, there is a negative attitude toward advertising in many countries. Some foreign consumers feel that a product is of dubious value if it has to be advertised. In some countries, custom dictates only the most dignified of appeals. The typical appeal to the consumer in the United States often fails in other countries. Pseudoscientific, hard-sell techniques and sexual appeals often create negative attitudes toward the product in question. The basic point is that promotional appeals must be tailored specifically to the cultural and social values of particular countries.

The government's attitude is also important. In some countries, certain classes of media are government-controlled, the most regulated being radio and television. In other countries, newspapers are government-controlled or owned. Many countries have stringent laws regulating advertising copy and media; various kinds of appeals and methods may be expressly banned. For example, in Mexico and Italy, spot TV commercials cannot exceed 20 seconds and must be visual only; in Venezuela, sound tracks are permitted, but only if the announcer is a native of that country.

Comparison of brands in advertising is prohibited in some countries. For example, in West Germany it is against the law to use comparative terminology or even to imply that another product is inferior. France also bans many comparative claims. Some countries require both good and bad aspects of the product to be communicated. Other types of legal restrictions range from limiting the sums that may be spent on advertising, taxes on various types of advertising, specifying the way in which price may be indicated, and prohibiting the advertising of certain products. For example, strict limitations exist on advertising drugs in most European countries. Advertisements of whiskey are prohibited in France. As a general guideline, advertising must be factual, employ dignified selling appeals, and be based on the local environment and attitudes. In addition, United States companies such as Procter & Gamble, General Foods, and Colgate-Palmolive have experienced a host of problems and restrictions in using promotional techniques like contests, sampling, and couponing in most European countries. In Belgium, premiums must tie in with the product and must be small. In Greece, Colgate was sued when it gave away razor blades as premiums with its shaving cream.[8]

Media

The media available and the nature of the consumer restrict the choice of advertising. One major problem in foreign countries is the lack of reliable media information. For example, the number of radio listeners in Africa, Asia, and Latin America cannot be accurately determined from the estimated number of radios because loudspeakers have been installed in public squares, markets, cafés, hotels, and amusement parks. Even in developed Western European countries, the media available vary considerably. Television, for example, is not freely available in a number of countries that have government-operated networks. Because advertising is often banned on government-regulated or controlled radio stations, a company may decide to use newspapers and magazines. But circulation figures are hard to come by in many countries. This creates problems for managers who must make decisions in terms of spread and effectiveness.

For companies interested in printed media, magazines such as *Time, Newsweek, Reader's Digest, Paris-Match, Der Spiegel,* and a number of technical and professional publications are circulated abroad in foreign countries or, in a few cases, published in foreign languages. Except for some emulation effect, the possibility of any international popular magazine reaching the middle and lower class markets is relatively negligible. In most cases, mass circulation can only be achieved by a large number of small advertisements in many local publications.

Outdoor advertising (billboards, electric or illuminated signs, and posters) is quite popular in less developed as well as developed countries. One can often see signs for Coca-Cola, Ever-Ready, Raleigh, Philips, Colgate, Firestone, and other internationally known products in many parts of the world. Billboards are most commonly used along major roadways and seem to be quite effective, since a large segment of the population moves in and out of metropolitan areas and trading centers. Different types of posters—metal, paper, hardboard—are also widely used in public places, such as in retail outlets, trains, buses, railway stations, and on walls. Motion picture advertising is very popular in less developed countries, and many companies, such as Vicks in India, claim they have had great success with this medium. Distributing samples is also becoming popular. In order to reach the greatest number, particularly in less developed countries where many people have no access to modern communications media, companies use various other techniques. These include sending salesmen to rural marketing centers on bazaar days to distribute samples and handbills and demonstrate products in bazaars and village fairs. It is interesting to note, for example, that in order to reach Africans who cannot read advertisements or see them on TV, Coca-Cola passes out free dresses on which images of Coke bottles are colorfully printed in indelible ink.

National variations in literacy, cultural and political factors, government control, and available media influence total advertising expenditure as well as the proportion of total advertising devoted to a particular medium. Generally speaking, it is necessary to utilize a broader approach to advertising in foreign countries.

The paucity of advertising media is of greater concern for consumer products than for industrial products. Industrial markets can be reached through catalogs, direct mail, trade centers, and trade fairs. Many governments sponsor international trade fairs within their own countries that are open to producers in foreign countries. They also maintain trade centers in other countries to promote foreign trade. Most industrial marketers also use trade and technical journals to advertise their products. The greater homogeneity of requirements among industrial buyers permits greater standardization of advertising.

Translating Advertisements

Advertising in foreign countries is more difficult than in the United States because the motives and desires of consumers are different. Copy should be specifically designed for the particular country to avoid misinterpretation and possible embarrassment. In preparing copy, the manager must keep in mind the technical limits of local printers.

Most of the problems, however, involve translating the advertising message properly. In mapping advertising campaigns, foreign companies have tried to translate directly into a foreign language, with the result that the ad has become a local joke. A few American promotions, of course, move easily into any language—most notably Exxon's "Put a Tiger in Your Tank." Others lose in translation. In West Germany, 3M's "Scotch" tape becomes "Scotch schmick." In Japan, 3M's slogan "Sticks like Crazy" comes out "Sticks Foolishly" and General Motors' "Body by Fisher" emerges as "Corpse by Fisher." In Brazil, one U.S. airline that proudly advertised the swank "rendezvous lounges" on its jets learned belatedly that "rendezvous" in Portuguese means a room hired for assignations. Translation is made difficult by the fact that there are variations in language from one country to another as well as in different parts of the same country. Foreign consumers may attach different meanings to symbols and colors. English spellings and phonetics differ in Commonwealth countries, where British influence is great. The advertiser must be aware of the different interpretations given to colors and the different meanings attached to symbols. For example, Japanese revere the crane as being very lucky, for it is said to live a thousand years, whereas the use of the number four should be avoided, since the word for four, *shi,* is also the word for death in Japanese.[9] To convert a message from one language into another, it must be interpreted rather than translated; the objective is to convert the idea rather than the meaning of the words as such.

A major advertising issue deals with the extent to which a multinational advertising program can be standardized throughout the world.[10] A number of multinational enterprises—for example, Unilever, Nestlé, and Procter & Gamble—use fairly standardized advertising approaches in Western Europe. Coca-Cola, Pepsi Cola, and Schweppes have used similar themes throughout the world with some adaptations. Manufacturers of industrial products use similar approaches in advertising in technical and trade journals. This uniformity is aimed at achieving economies of scale, utilizing good ideas, and developing a uniform worldwide company image. Generally speaking, multinational companies in both consumer and industrial products are striving to standardize advertising and other promotional efforts as much as possible. Frequently, however, a promotional strategy must be adapted to sociocultural, legal, and institutional differences. This is reflected in a more sophisticated approach being tried by a number of companies in recent years—the two-tier system of international advertising. The first tier is strategic, similar-looking advertisements emphasizing familiarity and using international magazines. To support this, additional advertising is done in the top local newspapers and magazines and in outdoor sites in urban centers. The second level of attack is in local mass media; the advertising looks familiar to the visitor from abroad, but it speaks the local language to the native customer. The primary emphasis in the international familiarity approach is on the visual elements such as package design, point of sale material, and billboards with minimum copy.

SUMMARY

Multinational marketing differs significantly from domestic marketing. In order to understand the foreign market and effectively penetrate it, it is necessary to understand different crucial aspects, such as income levels, attitudes toward selling and promotional efforts, education and culture, and legal restrictions. People throughout the world differ in their values and respond differently to promotion and selling strategies. So, diversity is a salient characteristic of international marketing. Multinational marketing managers should take into account the differences in various markets and adapt their product, price, and promotion strategies to fit local needs. The requirements of the consumer depend on his consumption parameters, both technical and psychological. Foreign markets must be treated as separate target markets. Product development must be adapted to suit the economic and cultural aspects of a particular foreign environment. Promotional appeals must be tailored to the cultural and social values of the specific country and cannot be applied across the board. Failure in multinational marketing does not occur because marketing management principles do not apply, but rather because the principles have not been adapted to foreign market parameters. The development of a successful strategy for global marketing depends, to a large extent, upon a company's ability to classify and segment its world markets in such a way that a set of marketing decisions can be applied to either a group of countries or to a particular type of consumer in different countries.

Notes

[1]Edward T. Hall, "The Silent Language in Overseas Business," *Harvard Business Review,* May-June 1960.

[2]Edward M. Mazze, *International Marketing Administration* (San Francisco: Chandler, 1967), pp. 67-68.

[3]Sueyuki Wakasugi, "The Mighty Japanese Trading Companies," *Business Horizons,* winter 1964, pp. 5-19; and S. B. Prasad, "The Marketing Role of Japanese Trading Companies," *Management International,* 1, 1970, pp. 79-82.

[4]For a detailed analysis of foreign retailing, see Michael Yoshino, "International Opportunities for American Retailers," *Journal of Retailing,* fall 1966, pp. 95-96.

[5]Richard H. Holton, "Marketing Policies in Multinational Corporations," *Journal of International Business Studies,* summer 1971, p. 18.

[6]This section is based largely on Warren Keegan, "Multinational Product Planning: Strategic Alternatives," *Journal of Marketing,* January, 1969, pp. 58-62. Our gratitude to Professor Keegan is acknowledged here.

[7]Stefan H. Robock and Kenneth Simmonds, *International Business and Multinational Enterprise* (Homewood, Ill.: Irwin, 1973), p. 457.

[8]S. Watson Dunn, "The Changing Legal Climate for Marketing and Advertising in Europe." *Columbia Journal of World Business,* summer 1974, pp. 95-96.

[9]"Key to Asia: Respect for Differences," *Printers Ink,* February 21, 1964, pp. 47-48; also Philip R. Cateora and John M. Hess, *International Marketing* (Homewood, Ill.: Irwin, 1971), p. 118.

[10]Erik Ellinder, "How International Can European Advertising Be?" *Journal of Marketing,* April 1965, pp. 7-11; Gordon E. Miracle, "International Advertising Principles and Strategies," *MSU Business Topics,* autumn 1968, pp. 29-36.

Suggested Readings

GENERAL

Business Week, "Why a Global Market Doesn't Exist," December 19, 1970.

FREMONT FELIX, *World Markets of Tomorrow.* New York: Harper & Row, 1972.

LEE, JAMES H., "Cultural Analysis in Overseas Operations," *Harvard Business Review,* March-April 1966.

PRICING

ARPAN, JEFFREY S., "Multinational Firm Pricing in International Markets," *Sloan Management Review,* winter 1972-1973.

BAKER, JAMES C., AND JOHN K. RYANS, JR., "Some Aspects of International Pricing: A Neglected Area of Management Policy," *Management Decisions,* summer 1973, pp. 177-82.

Business Week, "A Drug Giant's Pricing under International Attack," June 16, 1975.

PROMOTION AND ADVERTISING

DONNELLY, JAMES, AND JOHN K. RYANS JR., "Agency Selection in International Advertising," *European Journal of Marketing,* spring 1972.

MIRACLE, GORDON E., "International Advertising Principles and Strategies," *MSU Business Topics,* autumn 1968.

RYANS, JOHN K., JR., "Is It Too Soon to Put a Tiger in Your Tank?" *Columbia Journal of World Business,* March 1969.

THEORY

HOLTON, RICHARD B., "Marketing Policies in Multinational Corporations," *California Management Review,* XIII, 4, summer 1971, pp. 57-67.

SETHI, S. PRAKASH, AND D. CURRY, "Variable and Object Clustering of Cross-Cultural Data," in S.P. Sethi and J. Sheth, eds., *Multinational Business Operations: Marketing Management.* Pacific Palisades, Calif.: Goodyear, 1973.

APPENDIX 9-A: National Insurance Company

National Insurance is an Athens, Georgia, based insurance firm. Compared to the giants in the field, such as Prudential Life, it is small—its total sales in 1974 were in the neighborhood of $75 million. John M. Dexter, who founded the company after a successful career as an insurance sales representative and a regional accounts executive for several large insurance companies in the southern part of the United States, has been an innovative and market-oriented businessman.

The major line of business National writes is cancer insurance. In looking around for new markets for his product, Mr. Dexter came across Japan, a burgeoning nation of about 120 million people who were moving up the socioeconomic ladder by world standards. He found that entry into Japan would be difficult, if not impossible; and that after passing that hurdle he would encounter stiff competition from twenty or so companies, both domestic and American-based. An associate who happened to visit Japan in 1971 pointed out to him that during his visit he found the word "cancer" virtually taboo in Japan. There were recent medical journal reports, however, underscoring the growing awareness of cancer risks, and cancer checks and treatment had begun to make the disease less terrifying.

Mr. Dexter wants some sound ideas to come up with a tentative marketing strategy. Search the relevant literature, and sketch out a marketing strategy for Mr. Dexter. Be sure to add your comments on the probable success or failure of such a strategy.

APPENDIX 9-B: Gillette International—Success in the Seventies

Gillette International is one of the three organizational units (the other two are Gillette North America and Diversified) of The Gillette Company of Boston,

FIGURE 1

Officers and Staff
The Gillette Company:

Chairman of the Board and Chief Executive Officer
Vincent C. Ziegler

Vice Chairman of the Board, Technical Operations
George O. Cutter

President and Chief Operating Officer
Colman M. Mockler, Jr.

President, Gillette North America
William G. Salatich

President, Gillette International
Stephen J. Griffin

Executive Vice President, Diversified Companies
Thomas E. Singer

Senior Vice Presidents
Walter Hunnewell,
Deputy General Manager—Operations,
Gillette International
Edward G. Melaugh, Finance
Charles F. Woodard, Legal

Vice Presidents
William F. Brackman, Investor Relations
Robert W. Britton, Operations Services
Thomas W. Casey, Business Development
Marcel C. Durot, President, Personal Care Division
Clifton H. Eaton, Group Vice President,
Gillette North America
Paul N. Fruitt, Corporate Planning
Robert P. Giovacchini, Corporate Product Integrity
James A. Hebbeler, Corporate Research
and Development
Robert W. Hinman, President's Office
Edward P. Kellar, Control and Management Services
William J. McMorrow, Administration
Sam T. Papps, Corporate Trade Relations
George H. J. Robinson, Gillette Industries Ltd. (U.K.)

Treasurer
Milton L. Glass

Controller
Thomas F. Skelly

Source: Annual Report, 1974, p. 39.

Massachusetts. Gillette International has its own president and its own marketing director (see Figure 1). It comprises the Australian group, the Continental group, Gillette Industries Ltd. (U.K.), and the Latin American group. Gillette first began manufacturing abroad in 1909.

MARKET PERFORMANCE OF GILLETTE INTERNATIONAL

Sales of Gillette International in 1974 were sharply above those of 1973. Profits also moved well ahead to set a record for the ninth consecutive year. The first quarter 1975 results were ahead of the 1974 first quarter. Worldwide inflation and energy problems have had an unfavorable impact on manufacturing costs. Further gains in sales and profits of blades and razors, the largest and by far the most profitable product line of Gillette International, were realized in 1974. The importance of the G II shaving system, the name for Trac II in international markets, was a major factor. Manufacturing facilities for G II were expanded in West Berlin, Spain, and Brazil, and new moderate-sized factories began production in Morocco and Kenya in 1974.

Combined financial data for both Gillette International and the foreign-based diversified companies were as follows for the years 1972-1974:

Net Sales (000):	*1972*	*1973*	*1974*
U.S. and Canada	$489,014	$544,551	$617,289
Foreign*	381,518	$519,876	629,133
Net Income (000):			
U.S. and Canada	$ 36,513	$ 33,614	$ 38,026
Foreign*	38,505	53,051	49,713

*Gillette International and diversified companies.

TOP-NOTCH MARKETER

Although the Gillette Company has been known to be a top-notch marketing company, in the early 1960s the introduction of the stainless steel blade by Britain's Wilkinson marred this image a bit. In addition, Gillette's profit margin on sales declined from 16.5 percent in 1960 to 12.6 percent in 1964, and its return on shareholder's equity was 41 percent in 1960, 30 percent in 1964. What happened in the early 1960s was that Gillette ran into a marketing environment in the United States that was far more competitive than anything it had ever faced before. After 1965, the company seemed to pick up again, as the following figures show:

	1960	*1962*	*1964*	*1970*	*1972*	*1974*
Net income ($ million)	$ 37.1	45.3	37.6	66.1	75.0	87.7
Sales ($ million)	224.7	276.0	290.0	673.0	870.0	1,246.0
ROR on SE (%)	41.0	41.0	30.0	25.0	24.0	21.0
Net margin (%)	16.5	16.4	12.6	10.0	8.6	7.0

In 1974, razors and blades accounted for 30 percent of net sales and contributed 73 percent to profits. Toiletries and grooming aids accounted for 31 percent of net sales and 18 percent of contributions to profits. Since 1971, Gillette has been earning over half its income from its operations abroad. But according to *Forbes*,

> Gillette's skill has always been not innovation, but in its ability to exploit new products introduced first by others. In a market environment where the competition that introduces a new product is more likely to be as big and tough as you are, it will be ever harder for Gillette to make off with the big share of the profits by dint of sheer marketing muscle. In fact, unless it develops a new knack for coming up with important new products, it could well need all its marketing strength just to stay where it is.*

In 1962 the company's share of the United States razor and blade market was 70 percent. Since then, the company has deepened its involvement in several other areas, although razors and blades are still Gillette's chief business. The approximate percentage of consolidated net sales and contributions to profits during the years 1970 to 1974 for the four major lines of business are as follows (other activities accounted for 12 percent of net sales and 3 percent of contributions to profits in 1974):

Year	*Blades and razors*		*Toiletries and grooming aids*		*Writing instruments*		*Braun products*	
	NS	CP	NS	CP	NS	CP	NS	CP
1970	39	70	38	23	7	5	15	4
1971	37	68	37	26	7	4	17	2
1972	33	62	35	28	7	4	18	5
1973	31	66	32	21	7	5	22	7
1974	30	73	31	18	7	6	20	—

NS=net sales; CP=contribution to profits.

Some of the other fields into which the company has diversified have become separate divisions in the United States. The following table shows five of the major divisions of Gillette North America and the stage at which each is.

**Forbes,* July 15, 1971, p. 29.

Division	Newborn	Vigorous	Mature	Declining
Safety razors	Twinjector Adjustable Trac II Daisy Shaver	Trac II Cricket Lighter	Platinum Plus Stainless blades Techmatic	Carbon blades
Toiletries	Trac II Shave Cream Handler Shampoo Soft & Dri Roll-On Right Guard Roll-On	Dry Look Hair Groom Foot Guard Soft & Dri Right Guard A-P	Foamy Right Guard Deodorant	Brushless, Lather Cream Heads Up
Personal care	Firm & Free Earth Born Conditioner	Tame Earth Born Shampoo	Adorn White Rain Shampoo Deep Magic	Home Perms Dippity-do
Appliances	Pro Max Super Curl Steam Styler	Super Max		
Paper Mate	Hardhead Flair Fi Fo Fum	Flair Write Bros. (commercial)	Paper Mate Pens El Marko	Write Bros. (retail)

Coming up with important new products may mean added imaginative R&D or successful diversification. Since Wilkinson Sword introduced its stainless steel blade, it has become apparent to Gillette that overdependence on any one product line can be dangerous. The company now markets well over 850 products in two hundred countries and territories around the world.

NEW PRODUCTS FOR THE DOMESTIC MARKET

Cricket, the disposable lighter ($1.49 in the United States), first introduced by the S. T. Dupont Company of France in the early 1960s, is now one of the fastest growing products for Gillette. Cricket is marketed in the United States by the Safety Razor Division. According to *Fortune,* "S. T. Dupont, formerly photographers to Napoleon III, is a French company well known for its elegant and expensive writing instruments and lacquered lighters. Dupont was the first firm to introduce a disposable lighter that is called Cricket; but Cricket became a success beyond expectations for a small French company which had neither the capital funds for expansion nor the marketing clout."† Gillette came in at just the

†*Fortune,* November 1974, pp. 172-73.

right time and negotiated a deal to buy 48 percent of Dupont. In 1973 the S. T. Dupont group showed good gains in sales and earnings. Gillette purchased an additional 32 percent interest in Dupont, bringing its total ownership to 80 percent (the purchase was accomplished with the approval of the French government). The company began importing Cricket into the United States—a market S. T. Dupont had barely touched—and now the item is also manufactured in Brazil, Mexico, Puerto Rico, and Spain. When Gillette acquired a minority interest in S. T. Dupont in 1971, Dupont was selling about 7 million Crickets yearly; this number swelled to 41 million in 1973 and 65 million in 1974.

What was the environment that led Gillette to seek out a product like Cricket? The introduction of the stainless steel blade by Britain's Wilkinson in 1962, declining profit margins between 1960 and 1970, discontinuation of Eve of Rome cosmetics products in 1971, legal problems connected with the acquisition in 1967 of Braun A. G. (makers of small appliances and electric razors), and a declining share of the domestic market in razors and blades all had made Gillette look like a company that was losing its competitive advantage. Under these pressures Gillette turned to new markets abroad for its razors and blades as well as new products for its domestic market.

NEW MARKETS FOR OLD PRODUCTS

When Gillette turned to foreign markets for products other than razor blades, it discovered all sorts of opportunities. The company believes that "there is no *international* market—there are many individual ones."* In most foreign countries, Gillette's share of the blade market exceeds 50 percent. (The consolidated net sales of blades and razors both in the United States and abroad contributed to one-third of the company's total sales and two-thirds of company profits in 1972, 1973, and 1974.)

The Gillette name is well established in most nations, and according to *Fortune,* Gillette "has probably sold more blades, from *blue blades* to *platinum plus,* abroad than in the U.S. ever since World War II."** Gillette's modified marketing policy, framed with a view to better penetration of markets abroad, allows its subsidiaries to develop and sell products on their own. As noted in the *Financial Times* (April 25, 1975), over the post-Wilkinson period, Gillette has completely revolutionized its attitude to overseas business. Net sales of The Gillette Company in 1974 were well above those of 1973; however, net income was about the same as in the previous year. Better results from Gillette North America and Gillette International, in sales, were offset by a decline in earnings of the Braun group of companies. Yet, it should be noted that Gillette North

---

*Remarks by W. F. Brackman, vice-president Investor Relations, November 8, 1973.

***Fortune,* November 1974, pp. 172-73.

America and Gillette International, responsible for the Company's traditional consumer products businesses, each achieved record levels of sales and profits in 1974. These and other financial data are highlighted in Figure 2.

FIGURE 2

The Gillette Company and Subsidiary Companies: Financial Highlights

(Thousands of Dollars)

	1974	**Percent**	1973	Percent	Percent Change
Net sales:					
U.S. and Canada	**$ 617,289**	**50**	$ 544,551	51	+ 13
Foreign	**629,133**	**50**	519,876	49	+ 21
Total	**$1,246,422**	**100**	$1,064,427	100	+ 17
Income before income taxes	**$ 149,339**		$ 149,965		—
Federal and foreign income taxes	**$ 61,600**		$ 63,300		− 3
Net income:					
U.S. and Canada	**$ 38,026**	**43**	$ 33,614	39	+ 13
Foreign	**49,713**	**57**	53,051	61	− 6
Total	**$ 87,739**	**100**	$ 86,665	100	+ 1
Per share	**$ 2.92**		$ 2.91		—
Dividends paid per share	**$ 1.50**		$ 1.47½		+ 2
Net additions to fixed assets	**$ 65,419**		$ 51,686		+ 27
Depreciation	**$ 31,676**		$ 25,382		+ 25
Current assets	**$ 666,671**		$ 523,129		+ 27
Current liabilities	**352,156**		251,742		+ 40
Working capital	**$ 314,515**		$ 271,387		+ 16
Net fixed assets	**$ 235,249**		$ 201,506		+ 17

Source: Annual Report, 1974, p. 1.

APPENDIX 9-C: H. J. Heinz Company— Its Marketing Task in the Multinational Context

Heinz is not just a catsup company; it is a diversified multinational firm. Famed for its 57 varieties, H. J. Heinz now turns out 1,250 products in forty factories in thirteen countries. It employs 30,000 people worldwide, and markets its products in 145 countries. By these measures, it has a formidable marketing task. Its total sales revenues exceed $1 billion (1973, $1.234 billion; 1974, $1.438 billion).

The management structure of this billion-dollar corporation looks like this: there is the chief executive under whom are five vice-presidents. Three are in charge of corporate finance, development, and services, respectively; the other two divide up the marketing responsibility for Heinz's worldwide activities. One looks after the North American market; the other, the European and the Latin American. From a modest beginning in Sharpsburg, Pennsylvania, as a farm-house-based bottling and pickling outfit started by H. J. Heinz in the late 1800s, the company has evolved into a giant multinational food processor.

The food processing business is aptly described by some as a "contest of invention and of marketing." Although product development in a company such as Heinz is a continuous *must,* success is not always easy to achieve. For instance, one in fifty embryonic ideas will reach the experimental marketing stage, and only one in three of the new products introduced will survive once they reach the retailer's shelf. Multinational operations for Heinz means a multiplicity of resources, severe competition (competition in the food processing business amounts to a battle to win and hold shelf space in stores and supermarkets), and varied consumer preferences.

See if you can answer a few of these questions:

1. Should R&D be decentralized; that is, should foreign subsidiaries do their own R&D? What are the pros and cons?
2. How much vertical integration should Heinz engage in? If it should, in any degree, what would be the advantages?
3. Suppose Heinz, or a firm like Heinz, wants to explore a market such as Japan. Which of the marketing activities (marketing intelligence, product development, pricing, distribution, promotion) might emerge as the major problem?

SUPPLEMENTAL READING

Fortune, "Heinz Battles for Space on a World Wide Shelf," October 1971.

Fortune, "The Long Reach of Tony O'Reilly," December 1973.

Sales Management, "Heinz is Changing Sloow Fast," August 5, 1974.

Part III: Some New Issues

10

East-West Business: Quo Vadis?

Realizing the need to rebuild their economies, East European countries after World War II stressed development of trade among themselves; trade with the rest of the world was considered supplementary. The situation changed in the 1960s, when it became increasingly clear that economic cooperation between the Communist bloc and the rest of the world could be mutually beneficial. The role of foreign trade in Eastern Europe took on a new dimension.

During the 1960s foreign trade became a part of domestic growth efforts, and its renewed importance reinforced links between East European economies and the rest of the world. East-West trade expanded, and East European countries came to rely more and more on imports of manufactured goods from the non-Communist developed countries. To finance these imports, East European countries sought to increase their exports to Western countries and cooperated with Western firms, especially in the development of natural resources and the creation of industrial infrastructures. Although the East European countries accounted for about one-third of total industrial output (East and West) in 1970, they accounted for only one-tenth of total trade of the Eastern and Western countries. The seventies ushered in a new awareness that there was room for increased trade with the West.

Contrasting political systems account for the main differences in the foreign trade characteristics of Eastern and Western countries. For example, a major determinant of trade flows in Western countries is relative prices, which in turn reflect relative costs between countries. Within a Western economy, demand and supply are the most important factors determining prices. In East European countries, however, five-year plans and planning requirements determine trade flows; pricing policy does not necessarily reflect market conditions. In an East European country, trade is conducted by state trading organizations, whereas in Western countries trade is predominantly a matter for the private sector. East European exports to developed countries consist mainly of raw materials. Since East European countries are seeking to industrialize their economies rapidly, their demand for imports from developed countries is consistent and high. There is also a major difference in the role of services in East-West trade, particularly managerial services. Although management is often ignored in discussions of East-West trade, reform-minded East European countries have long been interested in importing managerial as well as technical skills. Relatively less developed managerial skill is probably one of the most important comparative disadvantages of Eastern countries compared with Western countries.

EVOLUTION OF EAST-WEST TRADE

East-West trade is of far greater importance to the East European countries, representing some 30 percent of their total trade, than to Western countries, where it represents only about 3.5 percent of total trade. However, the relative importance of East-West trade differs markedly among individual countries. In 1972 the share of exports of East European countries to the West ranged from 23 percent to 45 percent.

In 1972, the value of imports by the East European countries from all Western countries totaled US $9.5 billion, and the corresponding export total was US $8.0 billion. The East European countries' imports from developed countries were US $8.0 billion, and their exports amounted to US $6.8 billion; the corresponding figures for the less developed countries were US $1.9 billion for imports and US $1.5 billion for exports. The most active trading country has been East Germany.

Two-thirds of total world trade, including trade between East European countries, is in manufactured goods and one-third is in raw materials. The pattern of the total trade of East European countries, including trade among themselves, is divided in almost exactly the same proportions. But in their trade with the West, East European countries are much more dependent on raw materials, which account for 45 percent of exports and 39 percent of imports.

During the 1960s, imports by East European countries flowing from developed countries not only grew faster than East European industrial production but also faster than the area's imports from all Western countries. Between 1960 and 1969, East European countries' exports to the developed countries increased at an average annual rate of 10 percent. In 1970, there was an acceleration of imports from developed countries, particularly in the first half of the year, as import allocations that had not been filled earlier were utilized while they were still available. Romania, Poland, and Bulgaria achieved the fastest rates of export growth to developed countries in 1970, with increases of more than 20 percent. The exports of other East European countries to the West rose by between 12 and 15 percent.

During the Cold War period, most Western nations were in general agreement on imposing severe restrictions on East-West trade. The United States maintained strict controls over exports to the Eastern bloc. The Export Control Act of 1949, amended in subsequent years, imposed restrictions on some 1,300 product categories. Such products could not be exported to Eastern bloc countries without the permission of U.S. Department of Commerce. The purpose of the law was to prevent Communist countries from acquiring goods and technologies that would strengthen their capabilities. By the 1960s, however, most such products and their technologies had become available to Eastern bloc countries from other industrialized nations of the West.

The major moves by the United States to liberalize export controls began with the passage of the Export Administration Act of 1969. This act liberalized U.S. trade policies by decreasing the number of product categories restricted for export and brought the United States closer to the export control policies of Western European countries and Japan. The 1970s saw further trade liberalization. The United States lifted its embargo on trade with China in 1971, and in 1972 the list of restricted items was made the same as that for the Soviet Union. The United States entered into negotiations to work out a comprehensive trade agreement with the Soviet Union including most favored nation (MFN) treatment for Soviet exports to the United States. Furthermore, these negotiations involved business facilities for American companies in the Soviet Union; the handling of commercial arbitration; granting of trade credits to the USSR; joint venture projects; treatment of patents, copyrights, and licenses; and settlement of the Soviet Union's World War II Lend-Lease debt.

The Trade Act of 1974 opened up market opportunities for United States firms in the Eastern bloc economies. Under the act the President is authorized to extend most favored nation treatment, grant Export-Import Bank credit facilities, provide guarantees for credit and investment, and conclude commercial agreements with a nonmarket economy country if that country does not deny its citizens the right to emigrate, impose more than a nominal tax on emigration or on documents required for emigration, or impose material taxes, fines, or other charges on a citizen as a consequence of his desire to emigrate.

Nonmarket economies that had been receiving MFN treatment before the passage of the act—Poland and Yugoslavia—will continue to receive that treatment. MFN treatment will be given and will remain in effect as part of a bilateral agreement. The International Trade Commission is responsible for investigating if exports from a Communist country are suspected of causing market disruption. Finally, an East-West Foreign Trade Board was established to coordinate and oversee the orderly development of trade with nonmarket economy countries. The high hopes of developing a new commercial era in East-West trade as a result of this legislation, however, may have experienced a temporary setback. The Soviet Union, annoyed by the terms of the new legislation, particularly the controversy concerning free emigration of Soviet Jews, recently withdrew from its trade pact with the United States.

The small volume of trade between the United States and the East has up to now been due in large part to the strict U.S. government regulations. With the removal of the restrictions, the growth of trade will be determined more by economic and commercial considerations, such as the export potential of Eastern countries. Most Communist countries, as suggested earlier, are only in a position to supply the United States with raw materials and low-technology goods such as semifinished products, shoes, ceramics, and some industrial equipment. The need in the United States for such products is rather low. Furthermore, the available credit facilities will also influence the demand for American products in Eastern bloc countries. Additional barriers to U.S. trade with Communist countries can also be attributed to competition from other Western countries and Japan, which impose fewer restrictions on their trade with the Eastern bloc.

As far as American exports are concerned, U.S. firms are in a favorable position to supply certain types of heavy machinery and advanced technology that the Communist countries need. In addition, the Soviet Union and China may want to buy American agricultural products such as wheat, corn, oilseeds, and other products. Consumer goods, on the other hand, are not likely to find active markets in the Communist nations at the present time. Given their level of economic advancement, these countries prefer to use scarce foreign exchange earnings to buy the industrial goods needed for rapid industrialization.

Nevertheless, normalization of trade with the Soviet Union would give the United States a more important supplier position in competition with other Western nations. This would help increase sales over existing levels, at which the United States, the world's largest trading nation, supplied only about 1 percent of Soviet Union imports and took only 1 percent of Soviet exports. Recently, however, trade developments between the United States and the Soviet Union have shown encouraging signs. For example, American exports increased from $353 million in 1970 to $1,190 million in 1973, with estimates that U.S.-USSR trade will be worth $3 billion in 1976. The potential for U.S.-USSR trade is high because of certain structural dissimilarities in their respective economies. For example, the United States needs increasing quantities of raw materials, while the USSR requires substantial capital and technology. The USSR has an abundance of such unexploited raw materials as natural gas, petroleum, nonferrous minerals, and forest products. The fact that each country requires different goods for their development strategy suggests good trade potential.

The pattern and structure of East-West trade are complex and changing. They depend in part upon the economies of the various countries and in part upon political attitudes. Moreover, the situation of individual countries within each of the two broad groupings differs significantly. The evidence of the 1960s was that both Eastern and Western countries have become increasingly aware that a growing volume of trade can be mutually beneficial. The events of the mid-1970s, however, could put a damper on that zeal.

TRADE WITH CHINA

China possesses vast human resources but it is presently a small market for imported products and can be expected to remain so for some time to come. One writer aptly described China as a mini market with a maxi potential. Imports at present consist mainly of capital goods and equipment for industry, as well as raw materials and semifinished goods. Demand for products such as electric locomotives, equipment for railroad electrification, aircraft, cargo vessels, and commercial vehicles will grow as China modernizes her communication and transportation systems. Hence China's foreign trade is expected to increase in the future. The American share of the trade should increase more rapidly than general foreign trade because of the low base from which the U.S.-China trade starts and China's interest in products where the United States has particular advantage.

China frequently refers to the lack of MFN treatment as the impediment to trade with the United States. The Trade Act of 1974 should clear the way for such treatment in the near future. Other problems in U.S.-China trade are lack of patent and trademark protection and American labeling requirements for imported goods and other regulations on the import of Chinese products. The Trade Act of 1974 should also help minimize these obstacles.

After President Nixon's visit to China, the possibilities of American trade with Peking opened up. Given a modest beginning, the volume of exports and imports amounted to about $940 million in 1974, but was expected to reach only $400 million in 1975. Declining Chinese needs for food imports might account for much of the downturn; China's cancellation of $200 million of wheat purchases from the United States in 1975 is one specific indicator. However, trade fairs play a key role in China. Foreign business transacted at the fall 1974 Canton trade fair also showed a decline, yet trade in producers' goods seems to hold some promise. It is too soon to tell what will be the impact on trade, if any, of President Ford's visit to China in December 1975.

TRADE WITH RUSSIA

The 1972 trade agreement with the Soviet Union called for increased flow of goods and technical knowhow. The United States agreed to grant the Soviet Union most favored nation treatment, which meant that Soviet exports to the United States would not be subject to tariff discrimination. It also offered Export-Import Bank low-rate financing for trade. The Russians promised to pay off their World War II Lend-Lease debt. This agreement led to a relaxation of American trade restrictions on export of technical knowhow to Russia, and an increase in contacts between American firms and Soviet trading enterprises. With a modest start of less than $200 million, the volume of American exports reached a peak in 1973 of nearly $1.2 billion, including massive grain sales. However, American exports in 1974 dropped to around $500 million. Imports from the Soviet Union were valued at $350 million and consisted mainly of nonferrous metals and platinum.

Early in 1973, a U.S.-USSR Trade and Economic Council was set up to further the trade initiative. Of the twenty-six members, some were well known: David Rockefeller of Chase Manhattan, Gerstenberg of GM, and Jones of GE. Their Soviet counterparts were mostly trade ministry deputies and heads of trading and manufacturing enterprises.

The three-year agreement which the United States entered into with the Russians in 1972 promoted trade. However, due perhaps to the terms of the U.S. Trade Reform Act of 1974, the Russians canceled the 1972 agreement and left many American firms in doubt about the future. The Russians charged that the requirements vis-à-vis Russian emigration policies violated the 1972 agreement. But the setback to trade does not appear to mean an end to moves toward detente in other areas. One Russian official had expressed hope of a trade volume of $10 billion annually. Although the volume could easily reach $1 billion, it would have to be shared by the fourteen American firms already there and the other ten who are negotiating to get into Russia. One American firm awarded an export license in 1971 was the Swindell-Dressler division of the Pullman Corporation, which is aiding the Russians to build a truck and diesel engine plant that could change the shape of the Soviet industry. The Kama plant is being designed to produce 150,000 heavy-duty trucks and 250,000 diesel engines annually to help modernize the Soviet Union's transportation system. The value of this project to Pullman was said to be $10 million. Further, up to 1974, the Russians had signed some 100 contracts with forty American firms for more than $500 million worth of Kama equipment and machinery.

EMERGING EAST-WEST BUSINESS VENTURES

Along with the improved trade relations between East and West, opportunities for other types of business ventures have developed during the past decade. Consequently, an increasing number of multinational firms, both American- and foreign-based, have been active in developing business ventures with Eastern bloc countries. Such ventures include licensing arrangements, sales of processes and knowhow, sales of complete plants and technology, turnkey arrangements, and some types of joint production arrangements.

Under licensing arrangements, a Western firm sells the Eastern enterprise a license to use its technology that includes the sale of the technology along with whatever training is required to utilize it. For example, La Precision Industrielle, a French manufacturer of highly specialized machine-tool equipment, has signed a licensing agreement with Hungary's Licencia for the production of hydraulic trucks. Occidental Petroleum Corporation of the United States and the Soviet Union entered into an agreement for a series of management, technical assistance, and long-term purchase agreements in industries such as natural gas, chemicals, metal treating and plating, and hotels. Kaiser Industries has signed an agreement with Bulgaria to develop that country's oil shale and aluminium industries.

Sales of franchises are similar in that the Western partner makes available technical and management assistance, training of personnel, and equipment. Land, labor, construction material, engineering, and technical services are provided by the Eastern partner. Some Western enterprises, for example, have entered into such agreements for the construction of Intercontinental Hotels in Prague, Budapest, Bucharest, and Zagreb. Hilton International Hotels has also made similar agreements.

Investment and Joint Production

Trade must be distinguished from direct business investment, since trade does not carry with it collaboration in production, marketing, management, and a share in enterprise profits. Over the years, there has been some movement toward direct business investment through arrangements for joint production or joint ventures. Under joint production arrangements, the Western side supplies a mix of capital equipment, technology, and components while the Eastern enterprise builds the plant and undertakes production. This concept, of course, covers a wide range of arrangements. At one end, the participants maintain their separate organizations and the details of the relationship are specified in contracts. At the other end, the partners create true joint ventures in which a new organizational entity performs the business operations. Joint ventures go beyond trade and involve risk capital. Payments are generally made in the form of earnings in hard currencies, products derived from the project for marketing elsewhere, or possible long-term capital gains.

Such arrangements have been developed by the Simmons Machine Tool Corporation of the United States with Skoda of Czechoslovakia. A similar contract has been entered into by Krupp of West Germany with the Csepel Machine Tool Factory in Hungary. Yet another example of such a venture is the United

States-based Control Data's joint venture in Romania. The new company, ROM CONTROL DATA SRL, is 45 percent owned by Control Data Corporation and 55 percent owned by a state enterprise of the government of Romania.

There appear to be several reasons for this shift from trade to joint venture arrangements. For Eastern bloc countries, such arrangements mean better access to Western technology and related production and management knowhow, and help attract Western capital. The use of a Western partner to assist in the production and marketing of products destined for Western markets improves the hard currency earnings of the Eastern partner. Furthermore, the Eastern partners feel that if risk capital is committed, the Western partner will be more actively concerned with the success of the enterprise. Such concern might encourage the Western enterprise to transfer the latest technology, provide better financial support, and take more interest in the management of the venture. Joint venture arrangements also minimize the obligations of the Eastern partner because payments to the Western partner are contingent upon the earnings of the joint enterprise.

For the Western partner, joint ventures can provide some advantages over the straight licensing agreement. Studies have shown that earnings from licensing agreements are lower compared to those from joint venture arrangements, especially during the rapid growth stage of the product life cycle. In other words, joint ventures have the special advantage of giving the Western partner a continuing interest in the efficiency, profitability, and success of the operation. For the Western partner, such arrangements provide opportunities to expand markets, sell prepaid technology, and gain access to cheap labor and raw materials.

On the other hand, joint ventures are not without difficulties. Compared to other types of business ventures such as licensing, sales of process and knowhow, and turnkey arrangements, joint ventures involve problems of mixed management, risk of investment capital, operating conflicts, and so on. Nonetheless, Western companies seem to welcome joint ventures as a means to have greater participation in company affairs and a greater share of the profits of the enterprise.

Joint ventures vary from country to country in the Eastern bloc. Yugoslavia was the first Communist country to invite Western firms to invest capital in local enterprises. Romania and Hungary have passed joint venture legislation, and Poland is moving in this direction. So far there is no evidence that China is considering joint production arrangements. The Yugoslavian joint venture legislation provides for pooling of resources in terms of sharing control, income, and proceeds from liquidation. According to the Yugoslavian law, the foreign company is entitled

> To share operational management through representation on a joint business board.

To transfer its share of profits after taxes. According to the formula, a firm may remit up to 53 percent of the joint venture's foreign currency earnings (20 percent retention quota—in some fields more—plus 33⅓ percent of the foreign currency earnings of the joint venture) on a cumulative basis in the specific currency earned. However, exceptions are possible when deemed in the country's interest.

To repatriate "invested" property and the monetary value of other tangible and intangible assets less depreciation as and when specified in the contract. The amount repatriated, however, is also limited to 33⅓ percent of the enterprise's annual foreign currency earnings, and the 20 percent retention allowance as in the transfer of profits, plus 10 percent of the annual depreciation allowance, 5 percent of which is payable in convertible currency and 5 percent in the currency of a country with which Yugoslavia has a commercial clearing agreement.

To repossess tangible property contributed to the joint venture, when specified in the contract.

To transfer interest and rights in the joint venture to a third party, subject to an option which must by law be granted to the Yugoslav partner.

To share in the proceeds from the disposal of joint venture assets.[1]

NEW TRENDS

Recent developments in the East-West business arena point to important new directions. Multinational firms are increasingly participating in new types of business ventures. The experiences of many multinational firms also show that opportunities for profitable business exist in Eastern bloc countries. The easing of export controls and international tensions would certainly improve business activities. However, there are still many obstacles. Three that are especially relevant to future progress are relaxation of the political climate, creation of a favorable legal atmosphere, and business initiatives to develop opportunities for profitable ventures.

East-West business, a relatively new dimension of the American scene, is not going to be free from current international problems. The hostilities in the Middle East, the energy crisis, the arms race, and the basic conflict between different political and economic systems prevalent within the two blocs are the major forces that can mean setbacks for East-West relations and hence for East-West trade. Relations still are afflicted by political mistrust and tension. Smooth development of business between East and West is not going to be easy because the distrust and suspicion of decades will not disappear quickly. However, in the current time frame, the prospects for improvement are good.

For more than two decades the United States has adhered to a liberal policy for trade with non-Communist countries and a restrictive one for trade with Communist countries. Recent changes have certainly raised the hope of future improvement in East-West trade. Liberalized trade relations and considering the granting of MFN treatment to nonmarket economies in spite of current uncertainties are positive signs.

Because of long-standing government restrictions on East-West business, American multinational firms have much less experience in trading with Eastern bloc countries than have multinational firms based in Europe and Japan. To activate business with Eastern bloc nations, American companies should take the initiative and try to understand the economic and political systems of these countries. Methods of negotiation, procurement procedures, attitudes toward foreign business, and roles of government in Eastern bloc countries differ from those of the United States and Western Europe. American multinational firms must build upon the experience of government agencies and other companies to avoid costly errors. Firms should develop and maintain contacts with officials of foreign trade organizations and industrial enterprises in Eastern bloc countries.

For example, before trying to market a product in Communist countries, a multinational firm should predetermine that the need for its product is not being met adequately by internal sources. The product, capital equipment, or knowhow offered for sale should be superior in price and technology to the products of competitors. The purchasing decision in an Eastern bloc country such as the Soviet Union will depend upon (1) Soviet end-users perceiving a high-priority need for the product, (2) the product being unavailable within the country in the necessary quantity and quality, and (3) the product being competitive in price and quality with similar products available domestically or from other foreign competitors.[2]

Trade and investment negotiations with Eastern bloc countries are extremely difficult and demanding, so it is important that managers be trained in how to work with a centrally planned economy, protect contracts, and consummate financial and technical arrangements. The capacity to enter into protracted and detailed contract negotiations with the parties concerned is important to developing business opportunities. Flexibility with respect to types of ventures, financing, and other provisions is essential in business negotiations with Eastern bloc countries. At the company level, then, the development of an effective and profitable business venture in an Eastern bloc economy requires three basic considerations: First, an analysis of the relevant country's potential and constraints; second, an analysis of the company's own products, resources, and desires with regard to the market potential in that country; third, considerable emphasis on developing an effective strategy that matches opportunities with the resources and desires of the company.

WHAT ABOUT THE FUTURE?

The United States assumes that the Soviet Union wants to keep expanding trade for both economic and political reasons. Two of the main stipulations of the trade reform bill signed by President Ford on January 3, 1975, pertained to Soviet emigration policy and the Export-Import credit limit. Two weeks later, Secretary of State Kissinger announced that the Soviet Union had abrogated the 1972 trade pact with the United States. The 1972 agreement had placed some prominent executives of American multinational corporations, including banks, in the position of serving as instruments of foreign policy as well as representatives of business enterprises.

The Russians still want American knowhow and goods. Since they are dealing with American multinational firms, they may choose to buy more items from subsidiaries—for example, from France-based subsidiaries of MNCs. France was planning to extend a $3 billion line of credit at 7¼ percent to cover 85 percent of the cost of exports to the Soviet Union. GE and Amtel, Inc., were said to be working out major deals through their foreign subsidiaries.

The Russians have made the point that they can always do business with European and Japanese companies. Yet, Moscow needs American technology and capital to develop its vast Siberian resources to supply its growing domestic economy. The steadily increasing number of high-technology deals between American firms and the Soviet Union has, however, stirred up a serious policy dispute; there is concern now about Soviet acquisition of technological knowhow that may have important military applications. The areas involved in the recent sales range from computers and communications to shipbuilding and aircraft.[3]

There has been no indication so far that the Russians will close any American corporate offices or refuse to accredit new applicants. But it is going to take long and delicate diplomacy before U.S.-Soviet trade regains its momentum.

SUMMARY

Foreign business in Eastern and Western countries differs significantly because of differing economic and political systems. Trade in Eastern bloc countries is conducted by state-owned enterprises operating under government control. Trade in Western nations is predominantly conducted by private enterprises. The volume of trade between the East and the West has been and remains modest. Because of government export controls, American business firms and their subsidiaries have been deprived of export opportunities in Eastern bloc countries over the years. Now, with more liberalized trade relationships, United States firms will have an opportunity to develop exports to Eastern bloc nations.

Along with the improved trade relations between East and West, opportunities for other types of business ventures such as licensing, sales of processes and knowhow, sales of complete plants, turnkey arrangements, and joint venture arrangements have also developed.

Notes

[1]John Holt, "New Roles for Western Multinationals in Eastern Europe," *Columbia Journal of World Business,* fall 1973, p. 138.

[2]John Huhs, "Developing Trade with the Soviet Union," *Columbia Journal of World Business,* fall 1973, p. 129.

[3]*Business Week,* "Detente: A Trade Giveaway?" January 12, 1974, pp. 64-66.

Suggested Readings

Economist, "Rush to Russia," February 22, 1975, p. 92.

GOLDMAN, MARSHALL S., "Who Profits More from U.S.-Soviet Trade?" *Harvard Business Review,* November-December 1973.

HAMBLETON, GEORGE B., "Company Presence in the U.S.S.R.," *Columbia Journal of World Business,* winter 1973.

HERTZFELD, JEFFREY M., "Setting Up Shop in Moscow," *Harvard Business Review,* September-October 1974.

LAUTER, GEZA P., and P. M. DICKIE, *Multinational Corporations and East European Socialist Economies* (New York: Praeger, 1975).

RAMSEY, JAMES A., "The People's Republic of China: A Mini-Market with Maxi Potential," *Columbia Journal of World Business,* September-October, 1971.

Time, "A Serious But Not Fatal Blow to Detente," January 27, 1975, p. 34.

11

The Political Ethics of Multinational Business

When one examines the legal and political environment in which MNCs operate, one finds it far from clear. Even taking into account the different laws and political systems of nations around the world, there are still many gray areas. When issues do arise, unfortunately, there is no international law or court where they can be resolved.

The legal environment of the host country, for the most part, guides and regulates the behavior of the MNC's subsidiaries. The parent firm is, of course, bound by the laws of its home country. National laws, at least on paper, clearly spell out the overt behavior of the foreign unit. In most nations, the general framework is provided by foreign investment laws. Covert behavior, on the other hand, is more a matter of political ethics than of legality. We will focus on the latter dimension here, but first a few words about national laws, with particular reference to Indonesia as an illustration. In the final section, we will discuss how Polaroid met its corporate social responsibilities in South Africa.

NATIONAL LAWS

Each nation-state (there are about 170 in the world) has its own laws pertaining to investment from abroad. Details of foreign investment, incorporation, industrial relations, plant management, utilization of domestic materials and manpower, and even expropriation are generally spelled out. The Foreign Investment Law (Law No. 1 of 1967) of Indonesia contains, among other things, the following stipulations:

> Approved investment will enjoy exemptions of import duty on machinery, equipment, raw materials, spare parts, tools, etc.
>
> Provision is made for carry forward of losses, investment allowance, improved land rights, freedom to manage, and compensation in the event of nationalization.
>
> Foreign investors will have to organize a limited liability company under Indonesian law. These companies are called PTs (Perseroan Terbatas), comparable to the Dutch NV. To organize a PT, it is necessary to work through an Indonesian Notary Public. Such a PT may not organize a wholly owned subsidiary of its own, although the foreign parent may organize more than one wholly owned (or controlled) PT for Indonesian business activities.

Similar legal frameworks exist in every country. Yet, the legal environment for multinational business operations is a maze of overlapping national legal systems. Perhaps treaties and conventions such as the Treaty of Rome, which laid the foundation for the Common Market, will in the future lead to multinational corporate laws to govern the overt behavior of MNCs. But multinational corporate laws will not necessarily mean a reduction in the political risk that confronts all subsidiaries abroad in different degrees. Political risk connotes the probability of mild financial hardship at one end of the spectrum and expropriation without compensation at the other.

The Expropriation Game

Political considerations are almost always present, but the degree to which they affect the business environment of a particular multinational firm varies from time to time and place to place. Even if there is a shift of power from a moderate leftist government to an extreme leftist one, it does not mean the same degree of risk for all foreign-owned assets. To constitute a political risk, political changes must be significantly detrimental to the economic goals of the MNC. The sources of political risks as well as the influences they exert on the MNC have been neatly put together by Robock (see Table 11-1).

Political risks may be classified as *macro* and *micro* risks. When politically induced environmental changes affect all foreign enterprises in a country, that is a macro political risk. It does not mean nationalization of all foreign assets; it may simply mean added regulation. Consider, for example, the proposed regulation of foreign banks in the United States. A draft bill (1975) by the chairman of the House Banking Subcommittee on International Trade, Investment, and

TABLE 11-1

Political Risk: A Conceptual Framework

Sources of Political Risk →	*Groups Through Which Political Risk Can Be Generated* →	*Political Risk Effects: Types of Influence on International Business Operations*
Competing political philosophies (nationalism, socialism, communism)	Government in power and its operating agencies	Confiscation: loss of assets without compensation
Social unrest and disorder	Parliamentary opposition groups	Expropriation with compensation: loss of freedom to operate
Vested interests of local business groups	Nonparliamentary opposition groups (Algerian FLN, guerrilla movements working from within or outside of country)	Operational restrictions: market shares, product characteristics, employment policies, locally shared ownership, etc.
Recent and impending political independence	Nonorganized common interest groups: students, workers, peasants, minorities, etc.	Loss of transfer freedom: financial (e.g., dividends, interest payments), goods, personnel or ownership rights
Armed conflicts and internal rebellions for political power	Foreign governments or intergovernmental agencies such as the EEC	Breaches or unilateral revisions in contracts and agreements
New international alliances	Foreign governments willing to enter into armed conflict or to support internal rebellion	Discrimination such as taxes, compulsory subcontracting
		Damage to property or personnel from riots, insurrections, revolutions and wars

Source: Stefan H. Robock, "Political Risk: Identification and Assessment," *Columbia Journal of World Business*,. July-August 1971, p. 7. Reprinted with permission. Copyright © 1971 by the Trustees of Columbia University in the City of New York.

Monetary Policy provides for (1) mandatory Federal Reserve membership of state-chartered subsidiaries, and Federal Reserve-determined reserve requirements for branches and agencies of foreign banks; (2) mandatory divestiture of interests held by foreign banks in firms that underwrite or deal in securities; (3) "grandfathering" of multistate branching operations of foreign banks licensed as of December 3, 1974, while requiring them to convert to federal license; and (4) limiting the deposits of American residents with branches of foreign banks to "credit balances."

When the impact of politically induced changes is more specific and dramatic, as in the case of mining and utility firms in Latin American countries, one might consider these micro risks. Expropriation of the properties of an MNC would be the extreme consequence of such a risk. Expropriations in Latin American countries have captured the headlines in recent years. In order to understand the implications of expropriation, one must consider the political changes in the country or region, what world opinion may be, and whether and to what extent it represents financial loss to the parent firm. We can merely touch upon these ramifications here.

Some of the larger countries in Latin America, such as Brazil and Mexico, have already reached the takeoff point of sustained economic growth, with annual increases in real national output ranging up to 11 percent. Current prosperity is based increasingly on the production/manufacturing capability in many of the Latin American countries; some, like Ecuador, Mexico, and Venezuela, are also enjoying an oil boom. Politically, Latin American nations are evolving their own diverse forms of government. There is a single-party regime in Mexico; Venezuela has a multiparty system. While the military junta in Peru is characterized as left-wing, it is right-wing in Chile. There was a time when the United States regarded Latin America as its own province. Although the United States is still the biggest single customer and supplier, its economic and political influence appear to be waning. More and more, economic and political alignments manifesting the interplay of common interests and rivalries among Latin countries themselves appear to be building up strength within the hemisphere and relegating the United States to a lesser role.

Although expropriation of foreign business interests makes headlines, private firms, and the public at large, tend to accept it with relative calm. This is quite a contrast to the stir that was created when, for instance, American oil firms were expropriated in the 1930s in Mexico, Bolivia expropriated American interests in tin and petroleum in the early 1950s, and Brazil expropriated utility companies in the late 1950s. The main reason is that expropriation, as an act by a national government, has achieved a better standing in world public opinion, provided the foreign owners are compensated. American private investment abroad is partially insured against such political risks as expropriation by the Overseas Private Investment Corporation, a government agency. Thus, from the point of view of the MNC, when its subsidiary is expropriated or nationalized, the financial loss is seldom total. Uncompensated losses can be treated as business losses. More often than not, partial compensation follows after a year or two. A subsidiary of H. J. Heinz which was engaged in fish-meal production in Peru was nationalized in 1973; over the next two years, the parent company received compensation from the Peruvian government.

The controversy surrounding expropriation of American firms, we tend to think, is not likely to be hot in the future. Such prime targets as mining and utility companies have already been taken over. MNCs are also increasingly moving toward joint ventures with local investors, and this approach is likely to reduce the risk of exposure of foreign assets even in the so-called politically volatile nations. However, what is a hot issue is the covert behavior of some American MNCs in their transactions with nationals of other countries. Let us briefly examine this political-ethical issue.

MULTINATIONAL BUSINESS AND BAKSHEESH

Call it "influence peddling," "dash," "grease," or "baksheesh," one aspect of the covert behavior of American MNCs in foreign lands boils down to a basic ethical question: Are payoffs necessary to succeed abroad? The answer is not simple.

What have come to the fore recently are a small number of isolated instances in which American firms have made payoffs. Of course, the firms contend that payoffs are necessary. The moralists say that MNCs should not give in to pressure from foreign influence peddlers. The fact of the matter is that there exists an institutionalized web of payoffs in one form or another all over the world. One should not automatically include the less developed countries and exclude the United States or Japan. For instance, in the Mideast baksheesh, or gratuity for services rendered, is a way of life and involves everything from getting a telephone installed to signing a multimillion-dollar contract. In Southeast Asia, gifts from cameras to cars are said to be commonplace to butter up bureaucrats. In Japan, political donations (and bribes) are often treated as necessary business expenses and the payoffs disguised as part of a sales contract. Outright money bribes are rarely used in northwestern Europe and in North America, but payoffs often take the form of expensive gifts or other favors, including reciprocity.

As a result of recent Security and Exchange Commission inquiries and the Senate subcommittee investigations, a number of payoff incidents have come into the open, of which three have been given much publicity.

1. Gulf Oil Company disbursed more than $4 million overseas, most of it reportedly to a single unidentified country (presumed to be South Korea) in two successive cash "contributions" in order to stay in business there. The chairman of Gulf did not disclose the recipients of these payments on the grounds that he would jeopardize company investments to the tune of $700 million. On another occasion, according to Gulf's chairman, the company was *required* to pay $200,000 or so as "the only way" of obtaining the permits necessary to start operating a foreign oil installation in which the company had invested $150 million.

2. The revelation that Northrup Corporation paid or committed $30 million in sales commission and expenses to foreign sales agents from 1971 through 1973 touched off a Defense Department investigation. The U.S. Defense Department authorizes defense contractors to pay "reasonable" fees for agents as a part of their "costs of sales." This is usually limited to a standard agent's fee of 4

to 6 percent of the selling price. Mr. Richard Miller, chairman of Northrup's executive committee, disclosed that the company earmarked, through an agent (presumably Mr. Adnan Khashogi of Saudi Arabia), $450,000 in bribes for two Saudi Arabian generals in 1972 and 1974.

3. In April 1975, United Brands admitted that it made a $1.2 million payment to an official of Honduras to reduce the country's export tax on bananas. This disclosure provoked Honduran labor and student groups to demand that the food company's assets be nationalized. United Brands also admitted that between 1969 and 1974 it made payments totaling $750,000 to officials of a European country (believed to be Italy). As a result of public disclosure of these payoffs, United Brands is awash in stockholder suits and has come under scrutiny by the U.S. Attorney-General's office and by the Senate subcommittee on multinationals. Shortly before the company's overseas bribes became known publicly, Eli M. Black, chief executive of United Brands, committed suicide. The ensuing scandal also resulted in the overthrow of the chief of state of Honduras, General Oswaldo Lopez Arellano.

In these three instances, American firms, for different business purposes, paid bribes to foreign nationals. Attacks have naturally come from all quarters —from stockholders, federal agencies, congressional committees, and even foreign governments and nationals. In the midst of the imbroglio, MNCs maintain that they cannot operate successfully in some foreign countries without making payoffs. Here are three examples of this stance. Mr. John R. Hunt, a former Northrup executive, reportedly said that "the role of the agent is primarily that of influence peddling; that is, he knows who to talk to and whose pockets to line in a particular country to get the job done."[1] The head of an American oil company subsidiary in Rome pointed out: "If you don't [make a political contribution], you get on a black list, and then you have trouble getting government permission to expand your refinery or a license to build a gas station on the Autostrada."[2] A banker observed: "Without grease, you can't do business in countries like Taiwan, South Korea, Thailand, the Philippines and especially in Indonesia."[3]

In the world of multinational business, there is skepticism that the institution of bribes and payoffs can be dismantled even with tough American as well as foreign legislation. In other words, it is doubtful if the political ethics of multinational business can be legislated. However, what Ronald Muller, co-author of *Global Reach,* says is worthy of note. He insists that the system of bribes and donations has hurt economic stability worldwide and disturbed market prices, and he calls for making donations illegal in all countries.[4]

We feel that, first of all, it is of paramount importance to distinguish between minor payoffs such as one for having a telephone installed in a foreign land and a major million-dollar payoff, deftly arranged through a circumlocutory channel, with serious political and economic implications. Second, we tend to subscribe to the view that the most immoral position for an MNC is to allow payoffs to continue but deliberately look the other way.[5] As *Business Week* put it, "It is time for the top management of U.S. companies to establish a single standard of ethical behavior for their executives, at home and abroad."[6]

MULTINATIONAL CORPORATE RESPONSIBILITY

The topic of corporate social responsibility came to the fore at the end of the 1960s in the United States. Corporations are now expected to be socially responsible, although different people give this dictum different interpretations.

While no one would dispute the idea that American firms, especially the large ones, should behave in a manner far more responsive than in earlier times, in the United States only small segments such as church and minority groups vocalize their concern about an MNC's responsibility in foreign lands. One example of the responsible behavior of a well-known American firm in South Africa is provided below, based on the contents of a working paper by Alan Booth.[7]

Polaroid, in many ways, was the least likely candidate to lead an anti-Apartheid campaign because it did not have direct investment in South Africa. It has been marketing its products since 1938 through a South African distributing firm, Frank & Hirsch. However, Polaroid's history of corporate liberalism in the United States impelled it to opt for the "experiment" rather than choose any other alternative. Dr. Edwin Land, founder and chief executive of Polaroid, once wrote: "This is no ordinary company . . . it is the proud pioneer that set out to teach the world how people should work together."[8]

Despite its small investment in South Africa and the small number of African employees of Frank & Hirsch involved, Polaroid was still potentially open to attack. The one individual, according to Booth's analysis, who was instrumental in forcing the company to launch its "experiment" in South Africa was Kenneth Williams, a black employee of Polaroid in Cambridge, Massachusetts.

Williams organized the Polaroid Revolutionary Workers Movement (PRWM) in 1970, and brought up the issue of the company's involvement in South Africa before its management and before the public. Capitalizing on its initial success, PRWM delivered three demands: the company should (1) completely disengage from South Africa, (2) make a public statement condemning Apartheid, and (3) turn over some of its "ill-gotten profits" to liberation movements in South Africa.

The company refused to meet or negotiate these demands. However, it set up a fourteen-member multiracial committee to inquire into Polaroid's involvement in Apartheid, and the optional courses of action open to it. Based on this committee's recommendations, Polaroid launched its "experiment" in January 1971. The salient features of the program were these:

1. Polaroid would remain in South Africa for a one-year trial period, at the end of which it would reevaluate the situation. (It did not make withdrawal an explicit option at year's end.)
2. Its affiliate, Frank & Hirsch, was to improve dramatically the salaries and other benefits of its nonwhite employees. (It did not commit itself to the maxim of "equal pay for equal work.")
3. Parts of the profits stemming from its South African business activities would be committed to further African education.

These and other details of the Polaroid program were given simultaneous wide publicity through full-page ads in seven major dailies and twenty black newspapers in the United States. The announcement, however, met with a wide spectrum of reactions, ranging from endorsement to militant skepticism. PRWM labeled it a "deliberate fraud" and "an insult."

While the merits and faults of the experiment were being hotly debated, Polaroid found itself in another sort of dialog with a large number of other American subsidiaries in South Africa. An appreciable number inquired about the experiment, but few displayed any penchant to follow Polaroid's example. (The Norton Company subsidiary, however, reportedly took steps toward designing a Polaroid-type program.) At any rate, the Polaroid experiment, according to statements of the Institute of Race Relations, "caused more publicity and press attention to be focused on black wage levels, working conditions, and employment practices."[9]

Polaroid proceeded with its program launching and there were practical achievements in the salaries, benefits, and educational aid for the African workers employed by Frank & Hirsch. In conclusion, says Booth, whatever its motives—undoubtedly an attempt to blunt the PRWM more than anything else—Polaroid managed to raise the question of corporate responsibility for its African workers in such a manner as to prevent its suppression. That contribution was not an insignificant one. Polaroid forced the issue of withdrawal vs. constructive engagement to the forefront of the dialog over what could be done about Apartheid in South Africa by a multinational corporation.

SUMMARY

The legal environment of the host country guides and regulates the overt behavior of foreign subsidiaries. The foreign investment law of a country provides the general framework. Yet, the legal environment for multinational business operations is a maze, for there is no such thing as a body of international law that regulates MNCs.

The political risks entailed in multinational operations connote economic hardship and loss. Although expropriation or the threat of expropriation is the most serious risk, we tend to think that the controversy surrounding expropriation will not be a serious one in the future. MNCs' own modes of investment, particularly joint ventures, are likely to minimize this risk.

SEC and congressional hearings have brought to public attention several instances in which large hearings have brought to public attention several instances in which large American-based MNCs made payoffs, contributions, or bribes to foreign nationals. Although it is easy to condone such practices on the grounds that payoffs are a necessary evil in doing business abroad, they do pose a political-ethical dilemma that MNCs must face squarely. As a recent article in *The Wall Street Journal* put it, "Disclosure of briber, 'slush funds' and political manipulation have badly damaged the public image of multinational firms."[10] Institutional image-building would continue to be an important dimension of MNCs strategy.

Notes

[1]*The Wall Street Journal,* June 10, 1975, p. 10.

[2]*The Wall Street Journal,* May 19, 1975, p. 2.

[3]*U.S. News & World Report,* June 2, 1975, p. 28.

[4]Richard Barnett and Ronald Muller, *The Global Reach* (New York: Simon and Schuster, 1975).

[5]*The Wall Street Journal,* June 2, 1975, pp. 6-7.

[6]*Business Week,* June 23, 1975, p. 56.

[7]Alan Booth, ''Polaroid's Experiment and the Withdrawal Debate,'' working paper (Ohio University, December 1974).

[8]Letter from Chairman Edwin Land to Polaroid employees, August 20, 1970.

[9]John Kane-Berman and Dudley Horner, ''Report on the Polaroid Experiment,'' Institute of Race Relations, November 1971, p. 1.

[10]*The Wall Street Journal*, December 3, 1975, p. 1.

Bibliography

AGUILAR, FRANCIS H., *Scanning the Business Environment*. New York: Macmillan, 1967.

AHARONI, YAIR, *The Foreign Investment Decision Process*. Cambridge, Mass.: Harvard Business School, 1966.

AITKEN, THOMAS, *The Multinational Man: Role of the Manager Abroad*. New York: Wiley, 1963.

AL-OTAIBA, MANA SAEED, *OPEC and the Petroleum Industry*. London: Croom Held, 1975.

ALSEGG, ROBERT J., *Control Relationships Between American Corporations and Their European Subsidiaries*. New York: American Management Association, 1971.

BARANSON, JACK, *Technology for Underdeveloped Areas*. New York: Pergamon, 1967.

———, *Industrial Technologies for Developing Economies*. New York: Praeger, 1969.

BARNETT, RICHARD, AND R. MULLER, *Global Reach*. New York: Simon & Schuster, 1975.

BARTELS, ROBERT, ed. *Comparative Marketing–Wholesaling in Fifteen Countries*. Homewood, Ill.: Irwin, 1963.

BIVENS, KAREN, AND E. B. LOVELL, *Joint Ventures with Foreign Partners*. New York: National Industrial Conference Board, 1966.

BLOUGH, ROY, *International Business: Environment and Adaptation*. New York: McGraw-Hill, 1966.

BODDEWYN, JEAN, *Comparative Management and Marketing*. Chicago: Scott, Foresman, 1969.

———, et al., *World Business Systems and Environments*. New York: Intext, 1972.

———, AND ASHOK KAPOOR, *International Business–Government Relationships*. New York: American Management Association, 1973.

BRANNEN, T. R., AND F. HODGSON, *Overseas Management*. New York: McGraw-Hill, 1965.

BROOKE, MICHAEL Z., AND H. L. REMMERS, *The Strategy of Multinational Enterprise*. New York: American Elsevier, 1970.

———, AND ———, eds., *The Multinational Company in Europe*. Ann Arbor: University of Michigan, 1974.

BROWN, COURTNEY, *World Business: Promise and Problems*. New York: Macmillan, 1970.

CARLSON, SUNE, *International Financial Decisions: A Study of the Theory of International Business Finance*. Amsterdam: North-Holland, 1969.

CARSON, DAVID, *International Marketing–A Comparative Systems Approach*. New York: Wiley, 1967.

CATEORA, PHILIP R., *International Marketing*. Homewood, Ill.: Irwin, 1975.

CHORAFAS, DIMITRIS N., *Developing the International Executive*. New York: American Management Association, 1967.

CHRUDEN, HERBERT, AND A. W. SHERMAN, *Personnel Practices of American Companies in Europe*. New York: American Management Association, 1967.

CHUDSON, WALTER A., AND L. T. WELLS, *The Acquisition of Technology from Multinational Corporations by Developing Countries*. United Nations, 1974.

CLEVELAND, HARLAN, et al., *The Overseas Americans*. New York: McGraw-Hill, 1960.

CULLMAN, ARTHUR W., AND H. KNUDSON, *Management Problems in International Environments*. Englewood Cliffs, N. J.: Prentice-Hall, 1972.

DONNER, FREDERICK G., *The Worldwide Industrial Enterprise: Its Challenge and Promise*. New York: McGraw-Hill, 1967.

DOWD, LAWRENCE P., *Principles of World Business*. Boston: Allyn & Bacon, 1965.

DYMSZA, WILLIAM A., *Multinational Business Strategy*. New York: McGraw-Hill, 1972.

EITEMAN, DAVID, AND A. I. STONEHILL, *Multinational Business Finance*. Reading, Mass.: Addison-Wesley, 1973.

FARMER, RICHARD N., AND B. M. RICHMAN, *Comparative Management and Economic Progress*. Homewood, Ill.: Irwin, 1966.

FAYERWEATHER, JOHN, *International Business Management*. New York: McGraw-Hill, 1969.

———, *International Marketing*. Englewood Cliffs, N.J.: Prentice-Hall, 1965.

———, *Management of International Operations*. New York: McGraw-Hill, 1960.

FOY, NANCY, *The Sun Never Sets on IBM*. New York: Morrow, 1975.

FRANK, ISAIAH, ed., *The Japanese Economy in International Perspective*. Baltimore: Johns Hopkins Press, 1975.

FRIEDMAN, WOLFGANG, AND G. KALMINOFF, eds., *Joint International Business Ventures*. New York: Columbia University Press, 1961.

GOLDMAN, MARSHALL T., *Detente and Dollars*. New York: Basic Books, 1975.

GRANICK, DAVID, *Managerial Comparisons of Four Developed Countries*. Cambridge, Mass.: M.I.T. Press, 1972.

HARBISON, FREDERICK, AND C. A. MYERS, *Management in the Industrial World*. New York: McGraw-Hill, 1959.

HAYS, RICHARD, C. M. KORTH, AND M. ROUDIANI, *International Business: An Introduction to the World of the Multinational Firm*. Englewood Cliffs, N.J.: Prentice-Hall, 1972.

HELLMANN, RAINER, *The Challenge to U.S. Dominance of the Multinational Corporation*. Port Washington, N.Y.: Dunellen, 1970.

INTERNATIONAL LABOUR ORGANIZATION, *Multinational Enterprises and Social Policy*. 1974.

JACKSON, RICHARD A., ed., *Multinational Corporations and Social Policy*. New York: Praeger, 1974.

JOHNSON, R. J., et al., *Business Environment in an Emerging Nation*. Evanston, Ill.: Northwestern University, 1969.

KAMIN, ALFRED, ed., *Western European Labor and the American Corporation*. Washington, D.C. Bureau of National Affairs, 1970.

KAPOOR, ASHOK, AND R. J. MCKAY, *Managing International Markets: A Survey of Training Practices and Emerging Trends*. Princeton, N.J.: Darwin, 1971.

KASSALOW, EVERETT M., *Trade Unions and Industrial Relations: An International Comparison*. New York: Random House, 1969.

KENEN, PETER B., *International Economics*. Englewood Cliffs, N.J.: Prentice-Hall, 1967.

KIDRON, MICHAEL, *Foreign Investment in India*. Cambridge, Eng.: Oxford University Press, 1965.

KINDLEBERGER, CHARLES P., *American Business Abroad*. New Haven: Yale University Press, 1969.

———, *International Economics*. Homewood, Ill.: Irwin, 1968.

KOLDE, ENDEL J., *International Business Enterprise*. Englewood Cliffs, N. J.: Prentice-Hall, 1972.

———, *The Multinational Company*. Reading, Mass.: Lexington, 1974.

KUJAWA, DUANE, *American Labor and the Multinational Corporation*. New York: Praeger, 1973.

LEIGHTON, DAVID, *International Marketing*. New York: McGraw-Hill, 1966.

LEVINSON, CHARLES, *Capital, Inflation and the Multinationals*. New York: Macmillan, 1971.

LITVAK, ISAIAH A., AND C. J. MAULE, *Foreign Investment: The Experience of Host Countries*. New York: Praeger, 1970.

LOVELL, ENID B., *Appraising Foreign Licensing Performance*. New York: National Industrial Conference Board, 1969.

———, *The Changing Role of the International Executive*. New York: National Industrial Conference Board, 1966.

MARTYN, HOWE, *International Business*. New York: Free Press, 1964.

MASON, R. HAL, R. MILLER, AND D. R. WEIGEL, *The Economics of International Business*. New York: Wiley, 1975.

NEGANDHI, ANANT R., AND S. B. PRASAD, *Comparative Management*. New York: Appleton-Century-Crofts, 1969.

———, AND ———, *The Frightening Angels*. Kent, Ohio: Kent State University, 1975.

NEHRT, LEE C., *International Finance for Multinational Business*. New York: Intext, 1971.

NEUFELD, EDWARD P., *Global Corporation: A History of the International Development of Massey-Ferguson Limited*. Toronto: University of Toronto Press, 1969.

PARK, YOON S., *The European Bond Market: Function and Structure*. New York: Praeger, 1974.

PENROSE, EDITH T., *The Large International Firm in Developing Countries: The International Petroleum Industry*. London: Allen & Unwin, 1968.

PHATAK, ARVIND V., *Managing Multinational Corporations*. New York: Praeger, 1974.

PRASAD, S. BENJAMIN, *Enterprise in Ireland*. Milwaukee: Stein, 1969.

———, ed., *Management in International Perspective*. New York: Appleton-Century-Crofts, 1967.

———, AND A. R. NEGANDHI, *Managerialism for Economic Development*. The Hague: Martinus Nijhoff, 1968.

RICHMAN, BARRY M., AND M. R. COPEN, *International Management and Economic Development*. New York: McGraw-Hill, 1972.

ROBBINS, SYDNEY, AND R. B. STOBAUGH, *Money in the Multinational Enterprise*. New York: Basic Books, 1973.

ROBINSON, RICHARD D., *International Business Policy*. New York: Holt, Rinehart, and Winston, 1964.

———, *International Management*. New York: Holt, Rinehart, and Winston, 1967.

ROBOCK, STEFAN, AND K. SIMMONDS, *International Business and Multinational Enterprises*. Homewood, Ill.: Irwin, 1973.

RODRIGUEZ, RITA M. AND E. EUGENE CARTER, *International Financial Management*. Englewood Cliffs, N.J.: Prentice-Hall, 1976.

RYANS, JOHN K., ed., *The Multinational Business World of the 1980's*. Kent, Ohio: Kent State University Press, 1974.

———, AND JAMES BAKER, *World Marketing: A Multinational Approach*. New York: Wiley, 1967.

SALERA, VIRGIL, *Multinational Business*. Boston: Houghton Mifflin, 1969.

SCHWENDIMAN, JOHN S., *Strategic and Long-Range Planning for the Multinational Corporations*. New York: Praeger, 1973.

STEINER, GEORGE, AND W. M. CANNON, eds., *Multinational Corporate Planning*. New York: Macmillan, 1966.

STEVENS, ROBERT W., *A Primer on the Dollar in the World Economy*. New York: Random House, 1972.

STOPFORD, JOHN, AND L. T. WELLS, *Managing the Multinational Enterprise*. New York: Basic Books, 1972.

SUMMERS, MONTROSE, AND J. B. KERNAN, eds., *Comparative Marketing Systems*. New York: Appleton-Century-Crofts, 1968.

TERPSTRA, VERN, *International Marketing*. New York: Holt, Rinehart, and Winston, 1972.

UNITED NATIONS, *The Impact of Multinational Corporations on Development and International Relations*. 1974.

VAUPEL, JAMES W., AND J. P. CURHAN, *The World's Multinational Enterprises*. Cambridge, Mass.: Harvard Business School, 1973.

VERNON, RAYMOND, *Sovereignty at Bay*. New York: Basic Books, 1971.

———, AND LOUIS T. WELLS, JR., *Manager in the International Economy*, 3rd ed. Englewood Cliffs, N.J.: Prentice-Hall, 1976.

WESTON, FRED, AND B. W. SORGE, *International Managerial Finance*. Homewood, Ill.: Irwin, 1972.

WILKINS, MIRA, *The Emergence of Multinational Enterprises*. Cambridge, Mass.: Harvard University Press, 1970.

———, *The Maturing of Multinational Enterprise*. Cambridge, Mass.: Harvard University Press, 1974.

ZENOFF, DAVID B., *International Business Management*. New York: Macmillan, 1971.

———, AND J. ZWICK, *International Financial Management*. Englewood Cliffs, N. J.: Prentice-Hall, 1969.

Index